Rick's Rules for Raising a Rottie

1. **The Personal Suitability Test.** This is the first thing you have to do before you even think about owning a Rottweiler.

2. **Choosing Your Rottie.** This is definitely not something to do on impulse. Do not buy a Rottie without making sure both parents have been temperament tested and you have a health guarantee.

3. **Shopping List.** Making sure you have all the supplies and diversionary safeguards you need before your Rottie pup arrives will save many headaches and reduce wear and tear on your home.

4. **Thought Process.** Dogs are not little people. They think and communicate differently. Understanding how your Rottie does both will assist you tremendously when it comes to teaching your dog.

5. **Rottie Kindergarten.** Basic training, starting in puppy-hood, is a Rottie must! "No," "come," "sit," "stay," "down" and "heel" are lessons that absolutely cannot be neglected.

6. **Proper HEN.** Not poultry, but Health, Exercise and Nutrition. A Rottie needs all three to grow up strong and healthy. Regular grooming keeps you ahead of health problems. Exercise keeps your pal in shape and helps use up some of that excess energy. Nutritious food in the correct amount is the bottom line for those growing boys (and girls)!

7. **Emergencies!** Set up your home E.R. before the pup even arrives and make sure the emergency kit is kept replenished at all times.

8. **Veterinarian.** Next to you, your local vet is your Rottie's best friend. Make sure the three of you get along well.

9. **Lifestyle.** Introduce your Rottie pup early on to the way you live and the things you like to do, so that the two of you can share all those pleasant experiences.

10. **Rottie Resources.** Your Rottie is not only capable of learning games and fun things, but the breed has a vast storehouse of capabilities that can help and protect not only you and your family, but others in need as well.

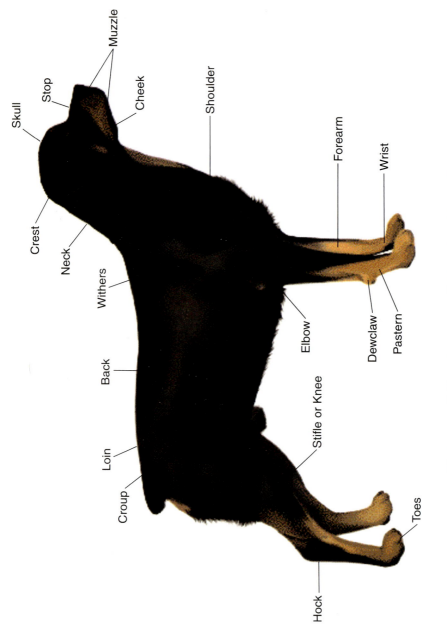

External Features of the Rottweiler

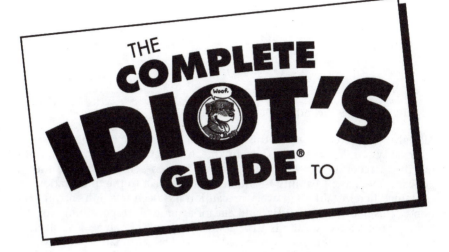

THE COMPLETE IDIOT'S GUIDE® TO

Rottweilers

By Richard G. Beauchamp

Howell Book House   Alpha Books
Divisions of Macmillan General Reference USA
A Pearson Education Macmillan Company
1633 Broadway, New York NY 10019-6785

THE COMPLETE IDIOT'S GUIDE TO & Design are registered trademarks of Macmillan, Inc.

Macmillan Publishing books may be purchased for business or sales promotional use. For information please write: Special Markets Department, Macmillan Publishing USA, 1633 Broadway, New York, NY 10019.

International Standard Book Number: 1-58245-041-2
Library of Congress Catalog Card Number: 99-62691

01   00   99   8   7   6   5   4   3   2   1

Interpretation of the printing code: The rightmost number of the first series of numbers is the year of the book's printing; the rightmost number of the second series of numbers is the number of the book's printing. For example, a printing code of 99-1 shows that the first printing occurred in 1999.

Printed in the United States of America

Alpha Development Team

Publisher
Kathy Nebenhaus

Editorial Director
Gary M. Krebs

Managing Editor
Bob Shuman

Marketing Brand Manager
Felice Primeau

Acquisitions Editor
Madelyn Larsen

Development Editors
Phil Kitchel
Amy Zavatto

Production Team

Development Editor
Beth Adelman

Production Editor
Christy Wagner

Copy Editor
Molly Schaller

Cover Designer
Mike Freeland

Photo Editor
Richard H. Fox

Illustrator
Bryan Hendrix

Designer
George McKeon

Indexer
Riofrancos & Co. Indexes

Layout/Proofreading
David Faust, Pete Lippincott

Contents at a Glance

Contents

Appendices

Foreword

When a long-time fancier of Rottweilers finds a book about his chosen breed, it is always met with a certain smugness and a bit of anxiety. This was certainly true of my reading of Mr. Beauchamp's book. After all, what could Mr. Beauchamp tell me about Rottweilers? Would he be able to capture the essence of the breed in a truthful manner?

The answer to both questions is a very big yes. Mr. Beauchamp has done a remarkable job of explaining the Rottweiler's character and what it takes to have an enjoyable life with him. This is a very easy read and complete accounting of what is a Rottweiler; if the Rottweiler is the breed for you; and how to raise a healthy, well-adjusted companion. It also may deter the reader from purchasing a Rottweiler. This can be a good thing, as a mismatched pet to owner leads to unhappy families and pets.

This book answers most of the frequently asked questions that breeders spend hours answering. The backyard breeder may not appreciate a client that has read this book. On the other hand, responsible Rottweiler breeders will be thrilled that their clients have taken the time to become as knowledgeable as possible. As a Rottweiler breeder, I may very well make reading this book a prerequisite for clients before making an appointment.

I hope you enjoy this book as much as I did, and welcome to the world of the Rottweiler.

Catherine M. Thompson

Introduction

As you read along in *The Complete Idiot's Guide to Rottweilers*, you will be introduced to all the good, the bad and the ugly that surrounds the breed. There are too many books that have been written about purebred dogs that do nothing but try to convince you that the breed at hand is faultless and suitable for every household in America (or anywhere else in the world, for that matter). I seldom find this to be true of any breed, and I certainly do not find this describes the Rottweiler by any stretch of the imagination.

So in this book, as I say, you will get the real skinny on what's good about the Rottie, what isn't so good and what is downright ugly. Let's start with the good.

A Rottweiler is one of the smartest, most trainable breeds I have ever known. Not only is the Rottie capable of learning just about everything any other breed can master, it also has the energy, the strength and the determination to carry it all off. A Rottie is smart, affectionate, protective and easy-going around those it loves.

So what's so bad about all those sterling qualities? Nothing at all. What's bad about the picture is that those same qualities have made the Rottweiler one of the most popular breeds in the entire world. The breed's popularity, as well as population, has soared over the past decade, and it looks like there is not going to be any sudden reversal of this trend. This puts the breed into the hands of people who are completely incapable of providing the training and care a Rottweiler needs.

This takes us right to the ugly. Ugly is the Rottweiler whose owner has neglected training and allowed the dog to become an unruly brute. A Rottweiler wants—make that needs—a leader in its life. If an owner doesn't provide that leadership, the Rottie assumes the role itself, and a Rottweiler acting on its own volition can be difficult—if not downright dangerous.

The information contained here will help you decide if you should even consider taking on the responsibility of Rottweiler ownership. If the answer is yes, there is plenty of valuable data that will assist both you and your Rottie along the road to a mutually delightful relationship.

Who Am I?

So, who died and made me Dog Tsar? In a word (well, two words), no one. Nothing in this book came by way of divine inspiration. Just about everything you will read herein has come by way of trial and error, or through the kind intervention of my many mentors through the years.

My interest in purebred dogs goes back as far as I can remember and has led me through practically every facet of dogs: breeding, exhibiting, professional handling, publishing, writing and judging. All that experience has also assisted me in presenting lectures to dog fanciers throughout the world.

For over 30 years I was fortunate to own and publish *Kennel Review Magazine*, and doing so associated me with some of the most learned dog men and women the world over. As a breeder-exhibitor, using the Beau Monde kennel prefix, I have bred nearly 100 American Kennel Club champions.

My judging assignments have taken me to practically every major dog showing country in the world, and this has given me the opportunity to judge Rottweilers in most every instance. I now judge for both the American Kennel Club and the United Kennel Club here in the United States.

Decoding the Text

Whenever I embark on a journey into the vast unknown (like the time I decided I couldn't exist another minute without breeding long-coated hamsters), I immediately head for the library or the nearest bookstore. I want to know everything and I want to know it immediately, so I look for a book that tells all. This is all fine until I suddenly realize the book I've obtained assumes I've been breeding hamsters, growing exotic orchids or what-have-you since the year one.

Now, if I knew how to do it all I wouldn't have gotten the book in the first place, right? So, when I sat down to write this *Complete Idiot's Guide*, I promised myself to keep it all as simple and straightforward as possible. You won't have to take a graduate course in canine anatomy or animal husbandry in order to understand what I've written. At least I hope it's all crystal clear. Whenever I've had the least bit of doubt about your not understanding a word or a term, I've included it in the Glossary that appears at the end of the book. Look there for clarification.

And Some Extras

Another thing that disturbs me in the how-to books I've read is having the author go off on a tangent that is only obliquely related to the subject at hand. By the time we get back to where we left off, I've totally lost the train of thought.

To avoid doing that to you, I have used a lot of little boxes throughout the text. You can stop your reading midstream and read the boxes, or you can wait until you've completed the text of the chapter and go back. Don't miss the boxes, however, because they contain information that can be quite useful.

Dog Talk

These boxes contain definitions or explanations that I consider important for all Rottie owners to keep in mind.

Watch Out!

These are warning boxes. They tell you what you should be extremely careful to avoid (or, in some cases, things you really *must* do).

Word to the Wise

Here are some real pearls of wisdom. Perhaps cultured pearls in some instances, but pearls nonetheless.

Bet You Didn't Know

These are tidbits of information that may not cause you to revolutionize your life or the way you take care of your Rottie, but are certainly interesting and worth reading.

Part 1

Finding and Acquiring Perfection in a Rottweiler Suit

Questions, questions, questions—who would have thought? First you have to decide if you really want a dog. Then you agonize over what seems to be a billion different breeds, and finally you come to the dog of your dreams—a Rottweiler. But still the questions aren't over. What age? What sex? What personality? What, what, what? Too confused to go on?

Fear not my reader! The answers are all here—or if not the answer itself, you'll find all the material that will help you arrive at the best answer for yourself. Everyone's needs and personalities are different, and what I will attempt to do here is match you up with the absolutely perfect Rottweiler of your dreams—sort of a canine Dating Game, if you will.

Knowing a little bit about the history of the Rottie will give you some idea of the how and why of the breed's temperament. Knowing that temperaments and personalities range significantly within a litter will guide you to the right pup. Knowing breed pitfalls will steer you away from places that specialize in production-line puppies. The dog you choose is going to be your pal for many years to come. This section serves as your road map to the right Rottie.

Chapter 1

Were You Really Meant for Each Other?

In This Chapter

➤ Why not a goldfish?

➤ Learning to get real

➤ A Personal Suitability Test for you

➤ Do you have all the right stuff?

Today it seems as though everyone wants a Rottweiler. When the American Kennel Club (AKC) issued its most recent official count (in 1998), there were more than 55,000 Rotties registered in that year alone. That gave Rottweilers the number four spot out of the 146 breeds the AKC registered that year.

Just a few decades back hardly anyone had even heard of Rottweilers; and then, all of a sudden—pow!—up the popularity ladder they shot. Rotties are not just popular here in the United States, they have become one of the most popular breeds in the entire world.

Rottie ownership has become a status symbol, an ego boost, a style trend and an outward symbol of a macho attitude. All of these are reasons that people have decided to bring Rottweilers into their lives, but none of them are good reasons. Nor, as you will see as we move along, would any of the people who were inspired by those reasons provide a suitable home for a Rottie.

The Top Ten Breeds

Breed	Number of Dogs Registered in 1998*
Labrador Retriever	157,936
Golden Retriever	65,681
German Shepherd Dog	65,326
Rottweiler	55,009
Dachshund	53,896
Poodle (Toy, Miniature and Standard)	51,935
Chihuahua	43,468
Yorkshire Terrier	42,900
Pomeranian	38,540

In 1998 the AKC registered a total of 1,220,951 dogs.

There is no doubt the well-bred and well-trained Rottweiler has qualities that have made the breed one of most highly admired in world. What too many would-be Rottweiler owners don't stop to consider is how difficult life can be coping with a Rottie who hasn't had the benefit of an owner committed to giving the dog the care and training it requires.

If more prospective owners took the time to investigate the breed's history and understood the kind of owner a dog of this character requires, they might reconsider bringing a Rottweiler into their homes. On the other hand, for the person who does the research and understands the Rottie's temperament and needs, there could be no better choice. There are few breeds with a greater capacity to learn or to be better pals to their owners and their owners' families.

Dog Talk

It's either **Rottweilers** or **Rotties** (the singular is **Rottie**), never Rotts or Weilers.

Before dashing out to buy yourself a Rottweiler, there are a number of important things you have to do.

*The Rottweiler is
extremely popular
these days.
(D. Gallegos)*

First, be very clear about how you deal with responsibility. Think
back on your past experiences with pets. How those characteristics
and experiences interact with the Rottie's needs and behavior will
determine if yours will be a match made in heaven or a remake of
Hell's A'poppin. Having a 100-pound-plus problem child on your
hands is not exactly fun and games, and the best way to avoid that
situation is to be sure, very sure, that the Rottie is the right dog for
you and that you are the right owner for the breed.

First Try a Goldfish

There are as many different sizes and shapes of pets as there are sizes
and shapes of people. I have friends who seem determined to have at
least one representative of every animal species in the world. What's
more, they seem to thrive on all the work required to maintain the
menagerie. I have other friends who find having to feed a goldfish
once a day or throw a handful of cedar shavings into the hamster cage
beyond the pale. Know which end of this spectrum you call home.

Once a pet enters the household it will be there all day, every day. It
will rely entirely on you for care and comfort, and that's not even
counting the training necessary for some pets, including dogs—that
is, if you want to protect your sanity and the sanity of those you live
with. If the pet was your idea in the first place, don't rely on someone else in the household to step in and help. Unless the other person has already volunteered to do so (and *meant* it), you might be
very disappointed.

If the kids in the family promise, promise, promise not a day will go
by without the pet taking first priority, don't believe it! Not that they

Watch Out!

If feeding the goldfish or buying liner paper for the birdcage seems like drudgery, dog care is going to be a monumental task. Better think twice (or four times?) about this one!

don't believe it themselves—they do. Children don't intend to mislead you (well, not always), but first priority means one thing today and another thing tomorrow.

Pets can't grab a snack out of the refrigerator when they're hungry. They don't clean up their own messes, and if they require exercise they are not going to hire a personal trainer. All that is up to you, you and only you. If your plan is to hire someone to do all those things for you just so you can have some ears to scratch, save yourself the time, the aggravation, and the money—get a stuffed toy.

So You Were Expecting Maybe a Whiz Kid?

If you believe what you read in some of the "I Love My Dog" kinds of books written today, you would swear some breeds can do all that needs doing. Doggie brags, particularly those about Rottweilers, would have you believe that a Rottie is the one breed that can do it all, plus eliminate your need for a security system and teach your kids their algebra on the side.

No Rottweiler—no breed of dog, for that matter—can do everything. In fact, your brain-trust Rottie is not going to be inclined to do anything outside of misbehave without the benefit of a leader who can teach the dog what to do and when to do it. Rottie puppies have a great *capacity* to learn, but they do not come preprogrammed. Guess who is going to help the dog fully realize that capacity? You!

As puppies begin to venture out of the little nest their mother made for them, they are looking for two things:

1. A pack leader.

2. The pack rules and regulations that let them know what they can and cannot do.

In nature, mama wolf and her relatives provide what the pup seeks without thinking twice. Since your Rottweiler puppy is not living in the great North Woods, but in your home, it is you who is elected to perform all the duties of the pack. If you do it, you will have a great companion. If you do not, you could have more headaches than you could ever imagine.

Watch Out!

Get real! Don't have un-realistic expectations of your dog. Your puppy will arrive with a blank slate; the only writing that will appear on it is what *you* write or what the puppy writes—and it's wise to remember puppies can't spell!

Your PST (Personal Suitability Test)

Buying a dog, especially a Rottweiler, before you are absolutely sure you are ready to make such a major commitment can be a serious mistake. A new dog owner must clearly understand the amount of time and work involved in the project. Again, if feeding the goldfish or watering the philodendron proved to be something you did grudgingly and only because you had to, a Rottweiler is going to make you feel like you're responsible for the national debt.

Can you pass the Rottweiler PST? Unless you can pass with flying colors, you may not qualify to own one! Before you leap into this, sit down with a pencil and sheet of paper. Answer these questions as honestly as you possibly can. The final results will tell you a lot.

➤ Does the person who will actually care for your Rottie really want a dog?

➤ Is everyone you live with as anxious as you to have a Rottie in the home?

➤ Does your lifestyle allow the time for the Rottie's care and training?

➤ Is your living environment suitable for a dog of this size?

➤ Do you have the endless patience required for your Rottie's training regimen?

➤ Are you physically strong enough to handle a fully grown Rottie?

➤ Is your own character and personality strong enough to establish the proper relationship with a Rottie?

➤ Can you afford the cost (purchase, upkeep, veterinary, food) of Rottweiler ownership?

Don't laugh. Affirmative answers are required for every one of these questions. There are other breeds that might not require a "yes" to every single question, and there are other pets for which hardly any of the questions require an answer in the affirmative. But for a Rottweiler owner, all eight points need an emphatic yes!

Do You Have All It Takes?

After you have taken the PST, think about each point carefully. It's a foregone conclusion that the dog needs a primary caretaker. Is that you? Is that your significant other?

If you live alone, the answer is simplified; naturally, you will be the caregiver. On the other hand, if you live alone you probably have to trudge off to Wall Street or a movie studio each day so you can earn the money to keep Brutus in dog biscuits. Then who will sit and hold your growing giant's paw all the day long?

Word to the Wise

Owning a Rottweiler requires **time** (feeding, exercising, training), **space** (fenced yard, dog run, indoor private space) and **money** (there's no such thing as a bargain Rottweiler, nor can you skimp on care).

Leaving this bundle of curiosity home alone all day will do nothing for its personality and less for your household goods. You might think worrying about the personality and friendliness of the dog you obtained to guard you and your belongings is irrelevant, but think again. A guard dog is one thing, an uncontrollable beast is another. Young Rotties left home alone day after day will begin to see life on their own terms and solely their own terms. This can include how strangers will be dealt with and who the dog decides it should protect you from.

If you live alone, you need to make sure you have a strong enough desire to make the necessary commitment dog ownership entails. If you share your life with a significant other or an entire family, other opinions will have to be considered as well. Your significant other may not be interested in having your twosome become a threesome.

In many households, mothers—even working mothers—are the automatic winners of the daily drawing in the Who-will-take-care-of-Gretchen-when-we're-all-away contest. Regardless of whether or not mom

Word to the Wise

Rottie pups have a huge storehouse of energy that must be expended in the course of day. This can be done constructively with exercise and games or destructively by snacking on your shoes or excavating for lost treasure in the middle of your antique Persian rug.

works away from home, all too often she's saddled with the additional chores of feeding and trips to the veterinary hospital. She might not be entirely keen about adopting yet another needy child—especially if it was not her idea in the first place.

Time for Training

And don't forget about training. Gretchen and Bruno both need lots of it as youngsters. Training takes time and patience (with a very strong emphasis on the latter). This is something that should take place every day. It *has to*. Not feeling up to it doesn't count here. Not only must you *feel* up to it, you must *be* up to it. By that I mean your state of mind will have a great deal to do with how well your training sessions go.

Losing patience and taking it out on your Rottie doesn't work. A properly raised and educated Rottweiler understands and accepts correction, but the breed does not tolerate abuse. If it is continually subjected to abusive treatment, even the most amiable and temperamentally sound Rottie can become neurotic and unpredictable.

This doesn't mean you should be passive in raising and training your Rottie. On the contrary, a Rottweiler puppy has to start learning the household rules on the very first day it comes to your home. If the

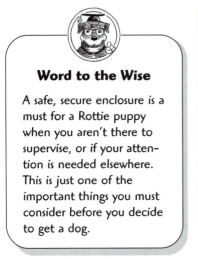

Word to the Wise

A safe, secure enclosure is a must for a Rottie puppy when you aren't there to supervise, or if your attention is needed elsewhere. This is just one of the important things you must consider before you decide to get a dog.

puppy is to believe you and learn to avoid certain behavior, the "no!" command must mean no all the time, not just most of the time or when the dog decides it wants to respond.

Climbing up on the sofa will never be a forbidden zone for your Rottie if you relent and allow the dog to climb up and cuddle with you on the days you feel in need of comfort. Rotties have a great deal of difficulty relating to the very human concept of changing minds. If mama wild dog were teaching her offspring to stay down in the den while she was gone, she would enforce the rule all the time, not just on rainy days or days she felt up to correcting the little ones.

Rule enforcement is one of the important reasons to have a place to stash Gretchen or Bruno when you are too busy to insist the rules be obeyed. A securely fenced yard, a fenced and gated outdoor run or a secure indoor crate will keep your Rottie contained and out of mischief when you are involved in activities that take your attention elsewhere.

Let's say you decide it's no problem to set aside time for your Rottie's training. Surely you can squeeze those training sessions in somehow, and then your life's your own again. Right? Wrong!

Plenty of Exercise

Training is one thing, exercise is another. For your Rottie to grow and develop both mentally and physically, it needs plenty of exercise. Think about human children and the never-ending fountain of energy they all seem to be blessed (blessed?) with. Now multiply that by about five and you have the activity level of the average Rottie pup.

Not only do Rottweiler pups have an amazing energy capacity, they use it! Pups will either unload all those energy molecules under your supervision in some acceptable activity, or they will devise activities of their own.

A Rottweiler pup needs someone and something to keep him busy.

Believe me, what these little guys can think up on their own will make you wonder why on earth you decided to bring a dog into your life in the first place. Fashioning hideouts in the new sofa cushions, removing baseboards from the walls, digesting the contents of your most prized literary masterpieces—these are activities any self-respecting Rottie puppy has all the energy in the world for and needs no training in at all.

Can You Afford It?

Even the well-exercised Rottie pup may suddenly decide the time has come to redecorate the family room or help you get rid of all those shoes in your closet. (You only have two feet—why keep so many?) These are fun things to do for your growing Rottweiler. Until the two of you have gone through all these activities together and you have convinced your young friend that they will not be tolerated, it may take more than just a dollar or two to repair the damage.

That cost must be added to fencing the yard or building a secure run so that little Bruno doesn't wander off down the street. Then there are those costly trips to the vet for shots, breaks, bruises and to remove the balloons Gretchen ate after the kids' birthday party. Add that to enrollment in puppy kindergarten and, and, and . . . !

And we haven't even talked yet about how much it will cost to get Gretchen or Bruno in the first place. Your Rottweiler must be purchased from a breeder who has earned a reputation over the years for consistently producing dogs that are mentally and physically sound. Reliably sound dogs of this kind are not cheap.

Watch Out!

Beware a breeder who offers a bargain basement price. Highly recommended breeders usually have waiting lists for their puppies. Don't allow someone to unload their problems onto you. Expect to pay at least $800 to $1,000 for a companion-quality Rottweiler puppy.

The only way a breeder can earn a reputation for producing quality dogs through the years is by maintaining a well-thought-out breeding program. Responsible breeders rigidly select the individual dogs they will use in their breeding programs. Selective breeding is aimed at maintaining the virtues of a breed and eliminating genetic weaknesses.

It takes a great deal of time, space and testing to effectively conduct a breeding operation of this kind, and all this is extremely costly. Therefore, responsible Rottweiler breeders protect their investment by providing the utmost in prenatal care for their *brood matrons* and maximum care and nutrition for the resulting offspring.

Once the puppies arrive, the knowledgeable breeder initiates a well-thought-out socialization program. Only when these breeders feel the puppies have been given the benefit of the best care, nutrition and sufficient human contact do they even begin to look for the proper homes for each and every puppy in the litter. This may mean keeping one or even all the puppies in a litter until they are four, five, even six or seven months of age.

Dog Talk

Brood matrons, or **bitches** (it's okay to say it!), are the female dogs a breeder uses in their breeding program. The males are called **stud dogs**.

The only way a breeder can continue to breed and raise Rotties in this responsible way is to charge a realistic price for their puppies. Naturally, a puppy with all these advantages is going to cost more than a puppy from a litter whose mother was never tested for any of the breed's genetic weaknesses or who was bred to a male of unknown mental stability. There are always people who are ready and willing to jump on the bandwagon and exploit a breed for financial gain. These people give no thought to the breed's health or welfare, or to the homes in which the dogs will be living. But could you even consider bringing a Rottweiler into your home that was not given these important advantages? It is hard to believe you would. It may cost more initially, but in the end that sound investment could save you thousands of dollars in veterinarian bills and professional training to cope with inherited health and temperament problems.

Yes, you will have to pay a respectable price for a well-bred Rottweiler puppy. Only you know what you can afford, but like anything else in life, you only get what you pay for.

Think Again

Have I discouraged you from owning a Rottweiler? Good!

No one who isn't at least 110 percent sure a Rottweiler is what he or she wants should think about the venture. The Rottweiler is not a breed for just anyone, and never a breed that should be purchased on a whim. But if you've thought this all out and you are still with me, we can get on to the great joy, challenge, companionship and devotion Rottweiler ownership entails.

The Least You Need to Know

➤ There are many pets that do not require nearly as great a commitment as a dog does.

➤ As great as the Rottweiler's capacity is to learn, nothing but bad behavior results without training.

➤ Using the Personal Suitability Test will very quickly let you know if you are the right kind of person for a Rottie.

➤ Think about how owning a Rottie will affect the other people in your life and in your household.

➤ Raising healthy, stable puppies is expensive. Don't go out looking for a bargain or you may wind up getting far less than what you paid for.

Chapter 2

What Is a Rottweiler?

In This Chapter

➤ Why is the Rottie so special?

➤ Living up to the breed standard

➤ Over the Alps to you: A history of the Rottweiler

➤ The Rottie at work

Currently the AKC offers the prospective dog owner 145 breeds to choose from, and there are probably upwards of 400 breeds recognized worldwide. They range from Chihuahuas, one of the tiniest toy breeds weighing in under six pounds, to the giant breeds that include man-sized Great Danes and Irish Wolfhounds. Practically every one of these breeds was developed with a specific purpose in mind. The reasons may have been very different, but there was a reason for each of them.

The toy breeds were meant to be companions, in most cases for the ladies who wanted a dog small enough and light enough to be carried around easily. As you move up the size scale, canine duties range from hunting small game to hauling large loads. The size, shape and temperament of each breed has been carefully manipulated though many generations to conform to an ideal. To this day, if a purebred dog is going to be a good example of its breed, the dog must not only have a specific look, but must also behave in a fashion typical of the breed.

Dog Talk

Most breed standards will tell you how tall the average dog of the breed you are considering will grow by giving a height at the **withers**. That measurement is taken from the top of the shoulder to the ground. Some standards will also give the average weight of full-grown dogs and bitches.

Let's face it, if someone went out to buy a laid back, ho-hum kind of a dog like a Basset Hound and the dog behaved like a busybody Jack Russell Terrier, it would be somewhat upsetting. If you brought home a dog to guard the family jewels and it met intruders at the door with its tail wagging and a road map to the safe in its mouth . . . well, I think you see the point I'm trying to make.

If you are taking the time to read this guide, you've obviously either seen a Rottweiler in the flesh or at least have seen pictures of the breed. You know what the breed looks like. But the Rottie is much more than its looks. As I take you through this and the following chapters, you will begin to see not only why the Rottweiler looks the way it does, but also why it is able to perform in the many capacities that are assigned to it. How a Rottie behaves and its high level of trainability are as important as, if not more important than, what the individual dog looks like.

Rottweiler Is Spelled U-n-i-q-u-e

When a Chihuahua says, "Yo quiero Taco Bell," people laugh. If a Rottie were to say the same thing, most people would give him all the Taco Bell he craves and then ask if he wants more! The Rottie has a reputation for being one tough taco, and deservedly so. That doesn't mean the breed is, or should ever be, mindlessly mean. The ideal Rottweiler's character and temperament are the result of generations of controlled breeding and rigorous testing by the breed's German developers.

Mature Rottweilers can be as strong as most men, and probably a lot more agile. In the right hands a Rottie can be the best security system in town, and at the same time be a good friend the entire family can rely on for fun and games. The well-bred, well-trained Rottweiler has the courage of a lion and is as willing to obey as the best-behaved child. In the wrong hands, the very same dog could just as easily be a complete menace. This is a breed that has an amazing capacity to learn, but it is also a breed that requires a capable teacher.

Everything in the Rottie's history, including the guys in Germany who formulated the first breed standard, demands that the breed be bold, courageous and protective. Yet standing right alongside those requirements are demands that the breed be

Word to the Wise

Although the Germans who framed the Rottweiler breed wanted a dog that was courageous and protective, the last thing they had in mind was a dog that couldn't be controlled or one that went off half-cocked.

peaceable and of good nature—cooperative and possessed of a willingness to learn and to abide by a master's wishes. If the scale tips more to one side or the other, the essence of the Rottweiler is lost. However, if balance is achieved, you have Rottweiler perfection.

What Are Breed Standards?

That may sound like a *Jeopardy* answer, but it is probably what a lot of you are wondering about now. With all of this talk about what the Rottweiler should and shouldn't be and how it should and shouldn't act, you might be wondering, "Who says so?"

The presiding kennel club of each country in the world has a system for registering the purebred dogs that are born and bred in that country. The AKC is the recognized authority here in the United States. These clubs issue certificates of registration that are probably best described as canine birth certificates. These canine birth certificates are just as important as ours. The only way a dog can be considered a purebred and be registered is if the dog's father and mother (*sire* and *dam* in dog parlance) are registered, and the only way they could have been registered is if their parents were registered and . . . well, I'm sure you get the picture.

Bet You Didn't Know

Many breeds have changed so drastically in both form and temperament from the original concept that they are barely recognizable. It is to the great credit of Rottweiler breeders in the United States and throughout the world that they have made every effort to maintain the essence of the breed. A truly outstanding Rottweiler is respected and appreciated anywhere it might go—truly an international citizen.

For a breed to be accepted by one of the registering sources in the first place, the supporters of the breed must form a club and provide credentials certifying their dogs had been bred true to form and free of *outcrosses* (the introduction of other breeds) for at least five generations. Rottweilers were granted recognition by the AKC in 1936.

Before a breed is given official recognition, the sponsoring club is also required to submit a written description of the breed that gives a word picture of both what the breed should look like and how it should interact with humans. This written description is called the *breed standard*.

The German Standard for the Rottweiler

In Germany, dog breeding was never a case of taking Little Nell down the street to get her hitched to the neighborhood Lothario. As new breeds were created, German fanciers organized clubs to improve and protect their respective breeds. If people wanted to breed dogs, they had to join the club dedicated to the breed and abide by the club's rules and regulations.

The club that was organized to oversee the breeding of Rottweilers was the Allgemeiner Deutscher Rottweiler Klub (the General German Rottweiler Club, or ADRK). The ADRK wrote a standard of perfection for the Rottweiler upon which all other standards, including the American and British, are based.

The ADRK has never had any qualms about amending or adding to its standard and has created a great deal of supplementary material to accompany the original standard. Following are the basic characteristics of the Rottweiler as advocated by the ADRK. It is followed by the main points of the American (AKC) standard, which you will see follows the original in essence. A complete copy of the Rottweiler standard is worth studying. You can get one from the AKC or the American Rottweiler Club.

As you read through both the German and AKC standards of the Rottweiler, you will begin to see what is described is a dog of great power and grace. Sheer bulk does not give a Rottie the strength and agility to perform as the breed was intended.

Word to the Wise

Few titles earned by dogs in foreign countries engender as much respect as those earned by the Rottweiler in Germany, the breed's country of origin. This is largely due to Germany's great reputation for breeding highly intelligent working dogs, and the training ability of the people who work with those breeds.

Size and Appearance

"The Rottweiler is a medium-large, robust dog neither gross nor slight, nor spindly. In correct proportion he is compactly and powerfully built indicating great strength, maneuverability and endurance," begins the German standard. In other words, don't judge your Rottie puppy by the pound. The Rottweiler is a medium-large breed, not a giant breed. Huge Rotties are often far more prone to joint diseases and other ailments.

Being German, they're very specific about what "medium" means: 24 to 27 inches high and 100 pounds for dogs; 22 to 25 inches and 92 pounds for bitches.

The Head

The head is medium long and broad in the back. The dog should have pronounced cheekbones and strong jaws, and the upper incisors should close like scissors over the lower teeth. Rottweilers should have a full complement of 42 teeth. The eyes should be dark and shaped like an almond. The ears should be triangular and set high on the skull.

The head sits atop a powerful, moderately long, well-muscled neck that is slightly arched.

The Body

The Rottweiler should have a straight and strong back, a broad chest and a short docked tail.

Both front and rear legs are straight and not set close together. The feet should be round and hard, with black nails and no dewclaws. The thighs are powerful and heavily muscled.

The coat actually consists of a outer coat and under coat. The outer coat is medium long, coarse, thick and straight. The under coat must not show through the outer coat. A Rottweiler should be black with sharply defined dark reddish-brown markings on the cheeks, muzzle, under the neck, on the chest and legs, over the eyes and under the tail.

Dog Talk

Docking means artificially cutting the tail. A **dew-claw** is an extra claw on the inside of the front leg—a kind of rudimentary fifth toe.

When it moves, the back remains firm and relatively motionless. The gait is harmonious, positive, powerful and free, with long strides.

Faults

There's no such thing as a dog with no faults. Every dog deviates from the ideal in some way. Still, the standard has a long list of faults that judges and breeders are asked to take note of. These include looking less than solid and strong, having a narrow or long head, light eyes, a back that dips down or humps up, crooked legs, a coat that is too long, too short, too soft or of the wrong color and various faults of the ears, eyes, nose, cheeks, lips, feet, legs, tail, back, chest and just about every other part of the body.

These faults should be weighed carefully when a dog is being judged, either in the show ring or in a breeding program. But they don't eliminate a dog from contention. However, some faults do. These are called *disqualifying faults*.

Disqualifying faults include dogs that look like bitches (and vice versa), having yellow eyes or various eye conditions, missing molars, missing testicles, a long and curly coat, white markings or grossly incorrect colors.

A dog that is nervous, shy or vicious also has a disqualifying fault. "He is descended from friendly and peaceful stock and by nature loves children, is affectionate, obedient, trainable and enjoys working. His rough appearance belies his ancestry. His demeanor is self-reliant, with strong nerves and fearless character. He is keenly alert to, and aware of, his surroundings," says the German standard of the Rottweiler's character.

Word to the Wise

Although not all breed disqualifications (flaws that eliminate a dog from being shown) necessarily eliminate a Rottweiler from being a happy, healthy companion, there is one that does. Any Rottie of unsound temperament should not be shown, bred from or ever owned as a pet.

This beautiful Rottweiler meets the requirements of the standard.

The AKC Standard for the Rottweiler

The AKC standard for the Rottweiler has much more detail than the German standard. That's because the German standard is accompanied by official statements of requirements that are not necessarily contained in the standard. The German standard and its accompanying statements are far more likely to be amended or changed over time than is the AKC standard. Changing an American standard requires serious consideration by both the AKC and the American Rottweiler Club (ARC), and the membership of the ARC must put any change to a vote.

Size and Appearance

"The ideal Rottweiler is a medium large, robust and powerful dog, black with clearly defined rust markings. His compact and substantial build denotes great strength, agility and endurance. Dogs are characteristically more massive throughout with larger frame and heavier bone than bitches. Bitches are distinctly feminine, but without weakness of substance or structure," begins the AKC standard. Sound familiar?

Height is the same as the German standard for dogs and bitches, but no weights are given. The standard then goes on to say, "Correct proportion is of primary importance, as long as size is within the standard's range." The formula for figuring correct proportion is that the ratio of height to length should be 9 to 10.

The Head and Body

The head and neck are described with much of the same language as in the German standard. However, there are two additional points. The first is that the underline of a mature Rottweiler has a slight tuck-up, which means there is an upward arch to its belly. The second is, "The back remains horizontal to the ground while the dog is moving or standing," which provides a lot of information about proper structure.

The coat and markings are pretty much the same as well. But the AKC standard tells us that the Rottweiler is to be exhibited in the natural condition with no trimming—in others words, there's no fudging a coat that's a little too long.

Faults, both disqualifying and not, are also much the same in both standards.

Temperament

The AKC standard has this to say about the Rottweiler's temperament:

Bet You Didn't Know

A long-coated Rottweiler cannot be shown at AKC shows, but they are born into some litters. This does not change the character of the dog, and inasmuch as the pet owner has no intention of showing or breeding a long-coated Rottie, it makes just as good a pet as its short-coated littermates.

"The Rottweiler is basically a calm, confident and courageous dog with a self-assured aloofness that does not lend itself to immediate and indiscriminate friendships. A Rottweiler is self-confident and responds quietly and with a wait-and-see attitude to influences in his environment. He has an inherent desire to protect home and family, and is an intelligent dog of extreme hardness and adaptability with a strong willingness to work, making him especially suited as a companion, guardian and general all-purpose dog. The behavior of the Rottweiler in the show ring should be controlled, willing and adaptable, trained to submit to examination of mouth, testicles, etc. An aloof or reserved dog should not be penalized, as this reflects the accepted character of the breed. An aggressive or belligerent attitude towards other dogs should not be faulted. A judge shall excuse from the ring any shy Rottweiler."

Most established breeders anticipate that at least 95 percent of the Rotties they breed will spend their lives in homes as family companions. Therefore, the one thing they will not make concessions on is temperament, and that applies to not only what they keep to show and breed but also to the majority of their dogs who will be household pets.

However, temperament is a two-way street. A well-bred Rottweiler puppy comes to you with a sound and stable temperament, but you must return the efforts of the breeder by making sure your puppy is properly socialized and given the proper amount and kind of training. Otherwise, the best efforts of the breeder are doomed to failure.

The majority of Rottweilers make great pets. (Beth Fitzgerald)

Does Your Dog Have to Fit the Standard?

The answer is both yes and no. The standards I have been talking about are guidelines. Since nothing in nature is ever perfect, these guidelines or word pictures act like carrots in front of a good breeder's nose—perfection always just out of reach. The best of a breeder's efforts are what he or she uses to perpetuate the line and what often becomes show stock—the dogs that are campaigned to achieve Championship status.

There are, of course, dogs that fall just a bit too short of this elusive perfection to be either show stock or breeding stock. They are the Rotties, both male and female, who are intelligently bred and of sterling temperament but who just don't have what it takes to come home with all the blue ribbons.

A highly recommended breeder will give you the assurance that the puppy or young adult you buy will meet the

Word to the Wise

If you are looking for a Rottie that you wish to show or breed, it's quite a different story. You must discuss this with the breeder so that he or she can help you choose a puppy that qualifies both temperamentally and physically.

highest physical and temperamental standards of the breed. That must be your top priority in the purchase of a Rottweiler. Minor cosmetic shortcomings will not change the breed's compatibility or temperament. When you are going to live with a dog for many years, a tiny blemish here or there is not going to make one iota of difference.

Over the Alps to You: Rottweiler History

By the time Romans were attending games in the amphitheaters, humans had developed a level of sophistication that was reflected in many ways. Classes of society had developed so that there were those who did the work and those who sat around and thought up all kinds of work for everyone else to do. One of the things thought up was how to further meddle with nature and make more breeds of dogs out of those that already existed.

The noble ladies of Rome had tiny dogs to sit on their laps and keep them company, but real men (the ones who didn't eat quiche) had dogs that were large enough and fierce enough to fight lions, tigers and assorted other wild beasts in the arena. Only the largest, strongest and fiercest of these dogs were allowed to fight in the Roman arenas. These brawny beasts were known as the Mollosus, and although there were undoubtedly many candidates for the honor of tearing everything in sight limb from limb, not all of the dogs qualified. From the same litters that produced the arena dogs came the dogs that became guards, protectors and draft (as in hauling) dogs for the Roman legions. Ancient writings that describe these military dogs reveal dogs that were similar to the Rottweiler as we know the breed today.

Since the Roman armies were constantly on the move, their dogs had to serve a more diversified purpose than the fighting dogs of the arenas. Their great courage was employed to ward off wild animals that threatened

Word to the Wise

Bravery and protectiveness have been selected for throughout the Rottweiler's history, and they are qualities the breed is respected for to this day. Owners should also respect the great efforts that those who love the breed have expended in developing a dog that uses these qualities wisely.

the livestock that accompanied the legions, but the dogs had many other duties as well. The speed and agility of the dogs made them excellent drovers for the cattle that accompanied the troops. Their large size and great strength made them capable of hauling carts loaded with weight that often far exceeded their own.

Bet You Didn't Know

The Roman Legions that set off to conquer the world as they knew it were veritable moving cities. Since they were often gone for years at a time, everything that was needed became a portable part of the troop movements: livestock, harvested crops, shoe repair shops, pottery makers, blacksmiths, shop keepers, servants for the officers and sometimes even their wives.

There is no recorded proof that these Mollosus dogs were, in fact, the ancestors of today's Rottweiler. However, it is known that dogs of this type existed throughout every region of Europe where the Roman legions traveled—including Germany.

As early as 2000 B.C. the Romans occupied a town in southern Germany that they called Arae Flavia. It was an isolated but strategic town militarily and politically. For this reason, Arae Flavia became a highly developed administration and social center. The town had a large enough population and sufficient activity to encourage setting up the fun and games facilities the Romans were accustomed to back home. Baths and brothels proliferated, along with the more serious aspects of the Roman lifestyle such as temples and aqueducts.

All this activity called for building administration centers. The more important of these centers had red-tiled roofs, and the town eventually became known as Rottwil—translated, it means "red villa."

Through the ages Rottwil (later Rottweil) endured invasions and occupations that decimated the Roman populations, and their dogs along with them. The surviving dogs found mates among the local breeds, and as time passed two distinct types of dog emerged. One type was very large and was used primarily for draft work. Those dogs also doubled as guards to insure the safe arrival of what the carts they pulled contained.

The ancestors of the Rottweiler were hard-working draft dogs. They also guarded what they transported—would you try to hijack a Rottie? (Beth Fitzgerald)

The other type of dog that developed in Rottwil was a more moderate but versatile variety. No less courageous an animal, the smaller dogs were initially used for herding, but as time passed they became known as the Metzgerhunde, or butchers' dogs, because so many of the people who made their living as butchers kept the dogs. Eventually, though, the two types of dogs merged and became known simply as Rottweilers.

Changing Times

In spite of the unique adaptability of these dogs, they were not exempt from being affected by the social changes of the following years. With the arrival of the twentieth century, many of the jobs that had been performed by the Rottweiler were eliminated. Industrialization began to make the existence of the dogs an expense rather than an asset. By 1905, breed history discloses, there was only one dog, a female, of this type left in Rottweil.

Bet You Didn't Know

Folklore tells us in the Middle Ages Rottweilers were known as the butchers' dogs of Rottweil. The name developed from the fact that butchers of the area tied the money they would use to buy cattle around the dogs' necks for safekeeping. What thief would dare take it off?

Elsewhere, because of the German fondness for the Rottweiler, efforts began to save the breed from extinction. A short-lived International Club for Leonberger and Rottweiler Dogs was established. The first written standard for the breed was published by that organization in 1901. This was followed in 1907 by the organization of The German Rottweiler Club in Heidelberg, and through that club's efforts the breed prospered and was recognized as a service dog for use with the police and the military. With this formal recognition, the breed's situation really started to improve.

By 1920 the Allgemeiner Deutscher Rottweiler Klub (we'll just call it the ADRK, or General German Rottweiler Club) was formed to protect the Rottweiler's physical and mental health. Strict codes of conduct were established for Rottweiler owners, including making sure all dogs had hip X-rays performed to prevent hip dysplasia. Only the very best dogs were allowed to be bred.

The members of the ADRK were dedicated to preserving and enhancing the health and welfare of the Rottweiler. Their purpose was to eliminate from the gene pool any dog that did not mentally, physically and genetically live up to the extremely high standards of the organization. The ADRK was highly successful in its efforts to preserve the best qualities of the breed, and it was not long before the rest of the world began to take an interest in this rugged protector.

Anchors Aweigh!

The first Rottweilers were imported into the United States in the 1930s and the breed was given full recognition by the American

Kennel Club in 1936. The breed was also registered with the Kennel Club in England in 1936.

The first Rottweiler litter recorded as having been born in the U.S. was bred in 1930 by Otto Denny, a German immigrant who had already established himself as a breeder before he left his homeland. Denny's litter was not registered with the AKC, but instead with a German-based breed club—not an unusual occurrence at the time.

Stina v Felsenmeer was the first Rottweiler to be registered with the AKC, and when she was bred to Arras v Gerbermuhle, Stina's was the first AKC-registered litter. From that point on, interest in the breed began to grow in America—very slowly at first, but over the next 60 years the popularity of the breed grew to what dedicated fanciers saw as alarming proportions.

When World War II came to a close, America began to forget its anti-German sentiments and Americans had more money to spend than many knew what to do with. Sports and hobbies like dog breeding and dog showing began to attract interest. In 1960 the AKC registered 77 Rottweilers. Thirty-seven years later the tally was nearly 77,000!

Amazingly, for a breed that was to soar to such heights of popularity, it was difficult to find American supporters in the early days of the breed. It wasn't until the 1960s that the first failed attempt was made to organize a national club. After several stops and starts, the American Rottweiler Club found enough support to become the first national club for Rottweilers in the United States.

Bet You Didn't Know

The breed's first American conformation Champion was Zero, a male belonging to Paul Jones. Zero's sister, Zola, became the first female Rottweiler champion. Jones became a founding member of the American Rottweiler Club, which was the first national club for the breed in America. Jones also handled the first Rottweiler to win a Working Group first in this country. The first all-breed Best in Show was won by Ch. Kato v Donnaj, CD, TD, owned by Jan Marshall.

Initially, the Rottweiler earned itself a place of respect with American dog trainers and in obedience circles. It was only a matter of time, however, before the breed also began to catch the eye of those who were showing dogs in the conformation rings.

A lot of credit for maintaining the level of quality that had been established in the Rottweiler's homeland can be attributed to the efforts of Clara Hurley and her Powderhorn Press in California. Hurley translated and published the many important books written by the breed masters in Germany, giving Americans the benefit of all the work that had already been done in the breed's behalf. Hurley was also instrumental in establishing the Rottweiler Registry to chart the status of hip dysplasia, a degenerative joint disease that is prevalent in the breed.

But Can Bruno Adapt to Everyday Life?

In the event you have no immediate plans to cross the Alps, send Bruno off to gladiator school or tie your life savings around Gretchen's neck, you might be wondering what you can give your talented, energetic dog to do?

The size, agility and intelligence level of your Rottweiler open doors to you both that you may never have even considered. The following list barely scratches the surface of areas in which the Rottweiler has excelled:

➤ Obedience programs

➤ Hospital therapy volunteer programs

➤ Search and rescue work

➤ Herding trials

➤ Carting trials

➤ Watch dog

➤ Schutzhund training

➤ Tracking tests

➤ Agility competition

If you want to cheat and go ahead of the class to see what these intriguing activities might be all about, go directly to Part 4, "One Life to Live." But put a bookmark here, because a great deal of what I will be telling you before I get to Part 5, "Tapping the Rottie's Resources," will enable both you and your Rottie to be even better at the activity you decide to pursue.

The Least You Need to Know

➤ The Rottie will probably have far more brainpower, brute strength and ability to learn than any dog you have ever owned.

➤ The Rottweiler breed standard describes the ideal mental and physical characteristics of the breed.

➤ The Rottie's history is one built around bravery, protection and discipline.

➤ A Rottweiler is extremely adaptable to a wide variety of activities and services.

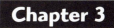

Chapter 3

Finding the Rottweiler That Has What It Takes

In This Chapter

➤ Rottie personality types

➤ Is a male or female better for you?

➤ What age is best?

➤ Where to find the right Rottie

➤ Picking your particular puppy

It's important to understand that each dog has a different and distinct personality. Some of the differences are the direct result of which end of the gene pool a pup emerged from, and some are influenced by the other dogs and the humans the pup interacts with. But the nature-nurture argument is really moot. What is important to know is all dogs are different and they are different in many ways.

This is true even for dogs of the same breed. Still, all Rottweilers share certain breed characteristics. You can be fairly certain, barring unforeseen accidents or unfortunate treatment, that each pup in a litter will grow up with some pretty similar characteristics:

➤ All the pups will grow up to be on the medium-large end of the canine size scale.

➤ Your pup will be the same color and same general shape when it grows up as it is on the day you bring the little fellow home.

➤ As an adult, the dog will have a relatively strong inclination to protect you and your family.

➤ Your Rottie will be territorial and will not welcome trespassers.

What most people don't stop to consider is that any of those characteristics can be graded on a scale of 1 to 10. Your Rottie pup can grow up to be big, or it can grow up to be BIG! The adult can maintain its proportions, but pack a little or a lot of muscle in that package. Even more important, the dog can be reasonably protective and territorial, or it can grow up to be a dog militia protecting you and yours from situations and people you haven't the least desire to be protected from!

Word to the Wise

Purebred dogs perform and behave the way they do because of generation upon generation of selective breeding. Expecting a purebred dog to behave against its basic nature leads to frustration for both dog and owner.

The breeder of a litter is most apt to know at which end of the temperament scale an individual puppy stands. There is always a range, even within a breed known for its courage and aggressiveness, as to how an individual manifests these characteristics.

It is important to sit down and talk to the person who bred the litter. They have been observing the pups as they were growing. If the breeder you are visiting is an experienced person, they know best how to mix and match the pups from the litter with the right owners. One pup is going to need a Marine drill sergeant as an owner, while the next might be just the ticket for the 90-pound weakling who just needs a good friend to lean on.

Mars or Venus? (Male or Female?)

Men are from Mars and women from Venus, or so current literature would have us believe. That might apply to Rotties as well. There are many breeds in which the sex of the dog makes little difference when it comes to pet ownership. This may not be the case with the Rottweiler.

While both the male and female Rottweiler are capable of becoming excellent companions and are equally trainable, do consider the fact that a male Rottie will be larger and heavier than his sister, and he will have all the muscle power to go with the extra weight. Give serious consideration to your own strength and stature.

There are also sexual differences totally apart from size and weight. The maternal instincts of the girls serve to make them a bit sweeter and gentler, and they are inclined to be less boisterous. Boys will be boys, and most of them grow bigger and faster than they are aware of themselves; this can make for some clumsy fellows! When those hormones start raging, the boys are inclined to be somewhat challenging, too—not unlike most male human teenagers.

There are other sex-related differences to consider as well. While the Rottweiler is a clean breed and relatively easy to housebreak, the male dog of any breed has a natural instinct to lift his leg to mark his territory with urine. The amount of effort involved in training the male not to do this varies with the individual dog, but what you must remember is a male considers everything in the household to be a part of his territory and has an innate urge to establish this fact. Unfortunately, this may include your designer drapery or newly upholstered sofa.

Word to the Wise

All too often people who have purchased purebred pets will say, "We're only going to breed her once and then have Gretchen spayed," or "Bruno needs a girlfriend to relieve his frustration." I assure you, neither dog needs sex to make their lives complete. Actually, in Bruno's case, breeding will only increase his frustration rather than relieve it.

Rottweilers are not beyond getting into arguments with other dogs, and the tendency in males may be considerably stronger. A male Rottweiler is all male and has no qualms about making a point of this.

The girls have their own set of problems. Females have their semi-annual heat cycles that begin at about one year of age. These heat cycles last about 21 days, and during this time the female has to be confined to avoid soiling her surroundings with the bloody discharge that accompanies estrus. There are "britches" sold at pet supply shops that assist in keeping the female in heat from soiling the area in which she lives. She must also be carefully watched to prevent males from gaining access to her, or she will become pregnant. Do not expect the marauding male to be deterred by the britches!

A good many of these sexually related problems can be avoided or at least reduced by having the pet Rottie altered. Spaying the female and neutering the male saves the pet owner all the headaches of sexually related problems without changing the basic character of your Rottweiler. If there is any change at all in the altered Rottie, it is in making the dog an even more amiable companion. Above all, altering your pet precludes the possibility of its adding to the unwanted pet problem that exists worldwide.

Granted, there are smaller, very docile males and larger, considerably dominant females, but generally speaking the male Rottie is larger, stronger and of a more dominant personality. There again, dominance will range from the "I prefer not to do that" kind of dog on up to the "just you try and make me!" attitude.

There are proper ways of dealing with variations on the personality scale. The secret is knowing what kind of personality a pup has and knowing yourself well enough to know if you are able to provide that particular Rottie with the care and training it will require.

Word to the Wise

Don't discount the older dog. Sometimes an old fellow loses his loving owners and needs another good home to finish out those golden years. These dogs can make great pets.

Time Takes (and Gives) Its Toll

Your Rottie's age when it first enters your household determines how you will handle the arrival and what you'll have to deal with in the following weeks and months. You may decide that a very young puppy will not work under your particular circumstances. A young adult, a mature dog or even an old timer might be your best choice.

Like all living things, Rotties have different needs at different stages of their lives. They will react to their new environment accordingly, and you should be prepared for this.

In the Nursery: Zero to Seven Weeks

During these first few weeks of life, there is nothing a Rottie pup has greater need for than its mom and littermates. They provide sustenance, comfort and warmth. During this period the pups find out other creatures exist and they have to be coped with. At first, it's just mom and her milk bar, but shortly the pup finds it must compete with other pups for what it needs.

Rottie moms also teach their offspring a great deal during these first weeks of life. It is extremely important to a pup's development that it has this time with mother and littermates.

The Diaper Brigade: Seven to Eight Weeks

This is the perfect time to introduce baby Bruno or little Gretchen to their new home. At this age they are mature enough to readjust easily, but not old enough to have developed strong attachments. Puppies that remain too long as part of a litter, rather than getting on to their individual homes, may identify with their siblings rather than transferring this relationship to humans.

The Terrible Twos: Eight Weeks to Six Months

As with children, this stage stretches on for a bit. It's not only the stage that is stretched—you'll wonder how elastic your patience can be! Anyway, from eight weeks to almost six months of age you may wonder at times if the pup has taken leave of its senses with its nonsensical behavior and arbitrary balkiness.

Word to the Wise

When you have decided upon the breeder your Rottie will come from, discuss your situation. You know best what you will be able to do for the new dog and what you won't be able to do. Then, the breeder can best decide the best age for you to take home your puppy or young adult.

Everything in life is an experiment at this stage, and there is no end to the pup's curiosity. This is the time when all electrical wires must be pulled, all fences must be climbed and all objects tested to determine their chewability.

At the same time, your Rottie pup is pretty much dependent on you and wants to be with you all the time, wherever you go. This is the proper time for the puppy to learn the good puppy basics. Confidence begins building as this stage, and the early dependency that was so typical may diminish almost overnight.

Rottweilers need to start their training early. At three months, Ante learns to jump as part of her Puppy Kindergarten Class. (Beth Fitzgerald)

Rebels with (and Without) a Cause: Six to Twelve Months

Anything you can do they can do better, or at least Bruno and Gretchen think so. Large breeds grow quickly and mature slowly. Maturity seems to manifest itself spontaneously and in awkward stabs at independence. What were cute puppy antics are beginning to be obnoxious behavior if you have not corrected them by this time. If those early bad habits haven't been curbed, you may have to deal with variable degrees of rebellion. This stage can be hardest on the boys and their owners—hormones raging and all that. It is critical that these young rebels understand clearly who is in charge.

Legal at Last: The Adult Rottie

The well-adjusted adult Rottweiler is confident and devoted, protective without being rash. If you get an adult Rottie that hasn't had the benefit of good training, you've got some serious work to do. However, a well-trained adult can adjust to a new home and will make a great pet.

Where All the Right Stuff Is Made

So I haven't dissuaded you so far. You've decided the time and commitment involved in owning a dog, especially a Rottweiler, is worth the effort. You scored a perfect eight on your PST and find that you are an ideal candidate for Rottweiler ownership. The breed's history and origin are firmly implanted in your repertoire of canine knowledge. You are practically an expert in how a Rottie should and shouldn't look and act. So, you're done—out the door and get that puppy, right? Wrong!

Yes, you have done your homework, and this does make you a potential candidate for Rottie ownership. But trust me, there are lots of people who own the breed, and even people who profess to be breeders, that couldn't tell a Rottie's left foot from its right. There are responsible breeders and there are not-so-responsible people breeding Rottweilers.

Unfortunately, there are also Rottie puppies born that should never have seen the light of day. Hidden recessive traits in pedigrees can produce health and temperament problems that make dog ownership an incredibly expensive and complicated experience, to say nothing of the toll it can take on your emotions.

If you have ever lived through the recuperation of a seriously ill dog, you know what a helpless and frustrating feeling it can be. The dog cannot tell you what the problem is, and you are seldom able to guess. You only know your buddy is sick and there doesn't seem to be much you can do to help. There are also some very debilitating and painful skeletal diseases Rotties are prone to that would bring tears to the eyes of a stoic.

There is no way to predict these problems when all you have to look at is a litter of very young puppies. Unless the breeder can show you that the parents of the litter have been proven clear of potential problems, it is all a case of let the buyer beware! No one can predict the future, but the fact that the breeder has taken pains to guard against potential disasters is at least some insurance that the puppy you take home has a better than average chance of being healthy as an adult.

Who Pours the Purest Water?

Rottweilers are a popular breed. You're going to find ads in the newspapers, puppies at the pet store, even litters at a friend's or neighbor's home. As hard as it is to believe, I have even seen what are supposedly purebred Rottweiler puppies in a box with a forlorn looking little youngster standing outside the supermarket.

If you've read anything at all about buying a puppy, you have undoubtedly come across a couple of warning statements published by the AKC or by concerned owners and breeders of purebred dogs. The advice is sound and is not to be taken lightly:

1. Buy from an experienced and *recommended breeder*.

2. Beware the backyard breeder.

One of the questions I'm frequently asked is how someone determines the difference between a recommended breeder and a backyard breeder. Can't a breeder keep his dogs in the backyard? If someone does keep their dogs in the backyard, does that mean the pups aren't any good?

Dog Talk

A **recommended breeder** is a person who is a member of the American Rottweiler Club and has agreed to abide by its code of ethics. The AKC can put you in touch with recommended breeders.

Actually, the name "backyard breeder" was invented to save dog buyers a lot of head- and heartaches. And, in the case of Rottie buyers, to save them from bringing a 100-pound wrecking ball into their home. It refers not so much to a place (the backyard), as to an experience level and an attitude about breeding.

You need to know how to tell the difference between a responsible breeder and a backyard breeder. So, here's a list to help you decide if the person you are talking to or visiting is the real thing, or someone to be avoided at all costs.

➤ **Responsible breeders** belong to Rottweiler or all-breed dog clubs and participate in many activities that support the breed. In the case of Rotties, just about every breeder I know is involved in training organizations of some kind. The Rottweiler is a breed that has such a great capacity to learn that dedicated owners would feel as though they were negligent in not providing the opportunity for the dog to develop. Participating on this level also provides the Rottie with the socialization and discipline the breed must have.

➤ **Backyard breeders** do nothing else with their dogs except breed and sell. Their dogs have no special titles or accomplishments and the owners do no training, nor do they participate in activities designed to protect and preserve the breed.

➤ **Responsible breeders** are delighted to set up an appointment so that you can come and visit their home or kennel and meet their dogs. They want you to see their puppies and their parents and have a look at the environment in which the dogs are raised.

➤ **Backyard breeders** may offer excuses why you can not see the mother or father of the puppies, perhaps because "they don't like strangers." They hesitate to take you into the area where the puppies and grown dogs spend their time.

➤ **Responsible breeders** know a great deal about the dogs they have bred and their pedigrees, and are ready and willing to discuss any of the problems that could conceivably exist in any Rottie pedigree.

➤ **Backyard breeders** are quick to assure you their dogs have no problems. They seldom know much about anything in the genetic makeup of their dogs.

➤ **Responsible breeders** will show you certificates that certify the health tests that have been performed on the puppies' parents before the breeding took place.

➤ **Backyard breeders** do not perform health tests on the parents. If you ask about them, they'll assure that the puppies are "perfectly healthy."

➤ **Responsible breeders** will ask you so many questions that you'll think you are being investigated for Top Secret clearance. They'll ask questions about your home, your family and the conditions under which the puppy will be living.

➤ **Backyard breeders** are willing to sell you a puppy with no questions asked.

Holding Up Under the Third Degree

Word to the Wise

The amount of time a breeder spends interrogating you as a potential owner of one of their puppies and the degree of their involvement in outside activities with the breed are strong indicators of the health and stability of their breeding stock.

Responsible breeders aren't invading your privacy with all their questions, but they are extremely discerning about where their puppies go. Expect to answer a lot of questions about why you want a Rottweiler and how you intend to care for the puppy. Get over the idea that you are doing a responsible breeder a favor by taking a puppy off their hands. If you do get that impression—scoot!

Here are some questions most breeders will ask. Really, you should be asking yourself these same things, because they are all bottom-line important for anyone who wants to own a Rottie.

➤ **Why do you want a Rottweiler?** A good breeder will want to know what experience with the breed made you decide that a Rottie is right for you.

➤ **Do you have a home with a fenced yard?** If not, will you or someone in your family be there to take the dog outdoors on a leash as many times as age and circumstances require?

➤ **Are you prepared to have the pet Rottie you buy spayed or neutered?** Most breeders will either require this before releasing registration papers to you or will sell the pet-quality puppy with a Limited Registration. That means the AKC can't register any puppies your dog might produce.

➤ **Are there children in the family and, if so, how old are they?** Most breeders will want to meet the children to get a sense of how well behaved they are. Households with children who do not mind well are not good environments for a Rottie to grow up in.

➤ **Do you have other pets?** Breeders will want to know what other kinds of pets are already living in your home, and if these other pets can adjust easily to a new dog or puppy.

Health Tests and Guarantees

Before you even ask, a responsible breeder will usually tell you what kind of testing they've done and what kind of guarantees they offer with any dog or puppy they sell. These are things that you should check against your own list, just to make sure that nothing has been missed or that you have not misunderstood what they are responsible for.

Testing for health and temperament are, of course, extremely important to everyone concerned with Rottweiler breeding and ownership. There are other things as well that will assure you of a happy transition for your new Rottie, regardless of age.

Health Concerns

Look for:

✔ Tests and certification that the parents of the litter are free of hip and elbow disorders.

✔ Appropriate eye and heart checks to establish that the parents are regularly tested and are clear of problems.

✔ A veterinary examination revealing the current state of health of the puppy or adult being considered, and a complete list, by date, of all inoculations given and due.

Temperament Testing

Make sure:

- ✔ The parents are certified as having passed character tests for stability of temperament.

- ✔ You have been allowed to meet and handle both parents if they are on the premises. If they're not present, their whereabouts should be established.

Guarantees

Make sure you understand:

- ✔ The conditions under which you may return the dog or puppy for a full refund.

- ✔ The conditions under which you may ask the seller to replace the dog or puppy with another dog or puppy.

- ✔ The kind of continuing care, advice and assistance the breeder offers.

Which Puppy Would the Breeder Choose for You?

Word to the Wise

If you put your trust in what the breeder feels would be the right puppy for you, it could easily lead you to that absolutely perfect friend and companion in a Rottweiler suit you have been hoping for.

You may well have digested everything in this guide so far and now consider yourself something of an authority on all things Rottweiler. You may be. However, no one knows more about the individual Rottie you are considering than the dog's breeder. A good breeder has not only observed each puppy in the litter from birth, but also knows the important characteristics in the puppies that should be given attention. They know the bullies, they know the cry babies; they know which of the puppies will require an exceptionally stout heart and a firm hand.

When you honestly answer all the questions the breeder asks about you and your family, they will also know which of the puppies in the litter would be the best choice for you. The bravest and boldest of the litter may come bounding out to greet you and may even be secure enough to give you a cute little "woof" to let you know your presence is being challenged. A winning personality? Perhaps. It may also indicate early aggressive tendencies that should be handled in a special way in order to produce good temperament.

This even applies to grown dogs. People experienced in the breed know what to look for when it comes to character, and although your first impression may be entirely positive or entirely negative, the long-time breed authority may know things about the dog you would never think to question.

The Rescue Option

In addition to recommending established and responsible breeders, there is every possibility that you can find the Rottie of your dreams and help a deserving Rottie find the home of its dreams in the process. There are all kinds of reasons why there are so many Rottweilers around the country that need new homes. Chief among them is the buyer who sees one of these magnificent creatures and thinks how protected or how fashionable life would be with a dog like that. What they do not stop to do is exactly what you have been doing—trying to find out if a Rottie is right for them and if they are right for a Rottie.

A Rottweiler with an owner who has not been able to provide the leadership this breed needs can become a terrible nuisance—if not a menace. Usually, no one is willing to accept responsibility or blame, and it is the neglected Rottie that must bear the consequences.

Irresponsible owners are not the only reason Rotties sometimes find themselves homeless. What otherwise was a perfect home can be disrupted by

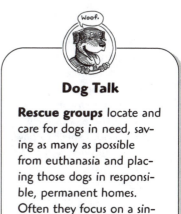

Dog Talk

Rescue groups locate and care for dogs in need, saving as many as possible from euthanasia and placing those dogs in responsible, permanent homes. Often they focus on a single breed of dog.

divorce or serious illness, and it can become impossible to maintain and properly care for a dog the size of a Rottweiler. As unfortunate as these scenarios are, it is far better that a new home be found for the dog than that a loved companion is neglected.

If you're looking for a Rottweiler, a *rescue organization* or animal shelter may be just the place to find one. Shelters, of course, will not always have Rotties, but you can put your name on a waiting list. And Rottweiler organizations will sometimes only have adult dogs. On the other hand, adult dogs can make super pets.

American Rottweiler Club Rescue

For all the reasons given and more, nicely bred Rotties that can become treasured members of a second home are often available through the many rescue agencies throughout the country. The American Rottweiler Club (ARC) has a Web site (webmaster@ amrottclub.org) that will guide you to the National Rescue Coordinator, who will be able to put you in touch with the rescue chapter groups that are affiliated with the club throughout the United States.

If you don't have access to the Internet, you can call the American Kennel Club at (919) 233-9767 and ask for the Rottweiler National Rescue Coordinator. They'll give you the name and number. (I've chosen not to give that information here because the coordinator does change from time to time.)

Watch Out!

When you're working with an independent rescue group, ask for references. There are many, many groups of goodhearted souls out there, and a few not so good. Expect to pay a fee to help defray the costs of rescue, but if the group seems more interested in making money, beware!

Independent Rescue Groups

There are also many independent Rottweiler rescue organizations that are maintained by people who simply love the breed. These individuals cannot stand by and allow a Rottie to be euthanized in an animal shelter because no one has taken the time to find out if a good home can be found.

Most of these bona fide Rottweiler rescue organizations or individuals have resources to trace the background of the abandoned dogs and observe and test character and temperament. Naturally, this is an extremely important consideration when adopting an adult Rottie.

Humane Societies and Animal Shelters

Countless numbers of healthy, well-bred Rotties also end their lives in our nation's animal shelters. (This is why a responsible breeder will insist all dogs they sell be returned to them if the buyer is unable to keep the dog.)

Watch Out!

Most dogs wind up in shelters because the former owner says he or she is moving and cannot take the dog with them. Sometimes this is so, and sometimes it is not. It is extremely important that you check this out, particularly if you have young children or if the Rottie will be around young children.

If you're considering adopting a dog from a shelter, it is extremely important to investigate the background of the dog and find out just why it wound up in the shelter in the first place.

This information may be readily available at the shelter, or it may take a bit of private investigating. Regardless of how much time it takes, it is time well spent. You are looking for a mentally and physically sound friend and companion, not someone else's problem pooch. Often local Rottweiler organizations can assist you in your search for information. Taking the time to investigate the dog's circumstances and history could easily result in your finding an outstanding dog that desperately needs a new home.

Other (Not So Great) Options

On more occasions than I care to remember, I have received a phone call from a friend who wants me to help them search for a Rottie puppy. Before I can even begin my search among responsible breeders, I will get a follow-up call from the friend telling me the "perfect" puppy has been found! Without even asking, I know it has come from a litter bred by the fellow down the street or by a friend of a friend. That is all well and good if the neighbor or the friend knows what they were doing when they planned the breeding and if they are knowledgeable enough to help you select the right puppy for you.

There are many, many Rottweilers waiting for good homes.

This also applies to classified ads in the newspapers and sweet-looking little puppies you may see staring out the window of a mall pet shop. Only here the unknowns are even greater. Classified ads can state what they want to state, but you do not even have the recommendation of friends and neighbors to rely upon.

There are, no doubt, sincere and responsible pet shop owners who sell live animals, but you can rest assured that of those who qualify in reliability and integrity, very few (if any) would prove to be Rottweiler breeders. More often than not, the dogs offered for sale in pet shops come from a source that the pet shop owner knows nothing about. There is absolutely no way to determine the character of the pet shop puppy's parents. There is no way to check what kind of care the puppy had from the time it was born until it reached the pet shop. Even with a guarantee of the puppy's current state of health, how could you possibly know what the genetic makeup of the pup will bring in the future when it comes to health issues?

And health is not the only issue in a large, powerful breed like the Rottweiler. Unreliable temperament in miniature and toy breeds can prove to be a nuisance. In a Rottweiler, unreliable temperament can result in danger to you or your family and even to lawsuits from those outside your home.

The Least You Need to Know

➤ All dogs have different personalities. Make sure your Rottie's and yours are compatible.

➤ Male and female Rotties have different mental and physical characteristics that you should be aware of.

➤ A well-established reputable breeder is your best bet for finding the right Rottie puppy.

➤ A Rottweiler rescue organization run by responsible and knowledgeable people in the breed can be another source for a puppy or adult Rottie.

➤ Buying a Rottie pup from the guy down the street or from the friend of a friend can be a risk if the owner of the litter does not have the background to do pedigree research and the experience to help guide you through proper care and training.

➤ Classified advertisements in newspapers or pet shop puppies present the greatest risk of all, because there is no real way to check up on early care or genetic problems.

Chapter 4

Picking Your Particular Puppy

In This Chapter

➤ Good health must be a priority

➤ Making a personality match

➤ Behaviors that can tell you how your pup will turn out

➤ Who makes the final decision—you or the puppy?

➤ Some important papers you need

By this time you are probably wondering if we will ever get to the point when you can actually go out and pick your puppy. Well, the time has arrived. But don't get carried away. You have to give just as much thought to selecting *the* puppy from a litter as you did to finding just the right litter to select the puppy from.

So far, the deck has been stacked in your favor: You have determined you are right for a Rottie and that the breed is right for you. You have located a breeder who comes with a long history of producing really top-notch Rottweilers, and you've set up an appointment so that the breeder has plenty of time to spend with you and the puppies. The big moment has arrived—you've graduated *magna cum laude* and now you are going to put all that knowledge to work for you.

Good Health Comes First

Above all, the Rottie puppy you buy should be a happy, playful extrovert. Don't even think about taking a puppy that appears sickly because you feel sorry for it and just know you will be able to nurse it back to good health. There's nothing but heartache there. Responsible breeders would never dream of letting a sickly puppy go, anyway.

Well-bred Rottweiler puppies with positive temperaments are not afraid of strangers. In fact, they love the world. Do not settle for anything less. Under normal circumstances you will have the whole litter in your lap if you kneel and call them to you.

Even if your puppy is eventually going to be entrusted with guarding the crown jewels, never consider a puppy that acts shy or suspicious of you. Nor should the pup act threatening or aggressive. The protective nature of the Rottie establishes itself with maturity. If a puppy shows any signs of an aggressive nature, something is definitely wrong. Puppies are babies, and properly socialized babies do not threaten—ever!

Word to the Wise

No matter what kind of a future you have planned for your Rottweiler, chief on your list of considerations must be mental and physical health. The Rottweiler was bred to be an asset to its owners, and you do not need to settle for anything less.

Later we will discuss temperament and personality tests that can tell you a lot about a puppy, but first let's look at what makes a healthy puppy. One quick look at the conditions the puppy is living in will tell you a great deal. The puppy you select may smell perfumed and sweet, but if the environment in which the puppy is living is dirty and unsanitary, all the perfume in the world will not be able to cover up the stench of neglect.

If one puppy in particular appeals to you, pick it up and ask the breeder if you can carry it off to an area nearby where the three of you can spend some time away from the puppy's littermates. As long as a puppy is still in a fairly familiar environment where scents and sounds are not entirely strange, the pup should remain relaxed and happy in your arms. Avoid the puppy that becomes tense and struggles to escape.

Playing Inspector General

Do not be afraid of offending the breeder by thoroughly inspecting your prospective puppy. Good breeders want you to be as pleased with the puppy you select as they are with the home their puppy is going to. Knowing what to look for to get a sense of the pup's overall health will assure the breeder that the puppy will get the care it deserves.

When you have the puppy away from the rest of the pack, here's what to look for:

➤ **The coat** should be clean and soft—jet black with tan markings.

➤ **Conformation** is important even at an early age, and you do want a puppy that represents the breed well. Rottie puppies should have a fair amount of skeletal substance and strength, and the legs should be straight. The back should be strong and level. The well-made Rottie's head is powerful looking even as a puppy, with a broad skull and strong muzzle. (Do realize, though, that female puppies will be finer in structure than their brothers.) Movement should be free and easy. All in all, the baby Rottie does not go through the extreme metamorphosis that some other breeds do. You can expect the Rottie puppy to look much like a miniature version of the adult.

Dog Talk

Conformation means how well the dog's structure conforms to the breed standard.

➤ **Ears** should be pink and clean, and there should be no odor. Lift the ear flaps and check inside.

➤ **The nose** of a Rottie puppy is black and should not be runny.

➤ **The lips** should be black should not droop, allowing the puppy to drool.

➤ **The teeth** should be clean and white. They should meet in a *scissors bite*—that is, the lower incisors touch the inside of the upper incisors. If you have any questions at all about the alignment of the teeth, discuss them with the breeder.

Bet You Didn't Know

An adult dog has 42 teeth (22 in the lower jaw, 20 in the upper jaw). However, until a puppy is about three months old it has only 28 temporary or baby teeth. With this first set of teeth come 12 incisors in the puppy's mouth. The incisors are the six small teeth at the front of both the upper and lower jaws. These are the teeth that should mesh in what is commonly called a **scissors bite**.

➤ **The eyes** should be dark, but clear and bright. Even very young Rottie puppies have a distinctly intelligent expression.

➤ **In body**, Rottie puppies should feel compact and substantial to the touch. A puppy will be a bit more *cobby*, or square, in appearance than an adult, but it should never be short-legged or long in body. Don't mistake puppy clumsiness for unsoundness though. Rottie pups aren't the most graceful things in the world—they need a while to become accustomed to those big feet and chubby bodies.

Danger Signs

Avoid a puppy that seems bony and undernourished or one that is bloated; a taut and bloated abdomen is usually a sign of worms. However, a rounded puppy belly is normal. Check the belly button for lumps, which could indicate a hernia.

Coughing or signs of diarrhea are danger signals, as are skin eruptions. Flaky or sparse coats can be signs of both internal and external parasites. Although the puppy coat will be softer and finer than the adult's, the hair should not be long or fluffy.

Any odor or dark discharge from the ears could indicate ear mites, which in turn suggests poor general care. A crusted or running nose is another sign of possible serious problems. There should be no malformation of the mouth or jaws.

Running eyes can indicate any number of problems. Check to see if the eyelids are turned inward, as well. This creates a condition called *entropion*, where the lid brushes against the cornea. This is damaging to the eye and usually requires surgery later on.

Questions You Need to Ask

Puppies are too young to have had any conclusive tests for genetic complications, but it's important for their parents to be tested *before* they are bred. The parents' good health strongly suggests that the puppy will follow suit.

Dog Talk

Two eye abnormalities that can be observed even in young puppies are entropion and ectropion. With **entropion** the eyelids turn inward and the eyelashes irritate and damage the cornea. **Ectropion** is the opposite—the eyelid droops down and outward, exposing the eyeball and subjecting it to irritation and damage.

Look for a pup that seems healthy, confident and exuberant. (Martha Kay Turner)

The parents of the litter should have been X-rayed to show they are free of hip and elbow disorders. The X-rays are then examined by certified orthopedists at either the Orthopedic Foundation for Animals (OFA) or PennHip. A certificate will be issued, stating that the parents are clear of these problems. The parents should also be certified as

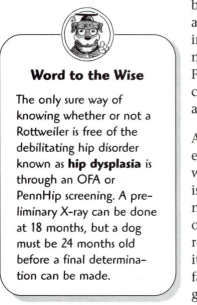

Word to the Wise

The only sure way of knowing whether or not a Rottweiler is free of the debilitating hip disorder known as **hip dysplasia** is through an OFA or PennHip screening. A preliminary X-ray can be done at 18 months, but a dog must be 24 months old before a final determination can be made.

being free of eye abnormalities such as progressive retinal atrophy, an inherited disorder that causes blindness. The Canine Eye Registry Foundation (CERF) issues the certificates, and testing must be redone annually. Ask to see these certificates.

Ask when the puppy had its last veterinary health check. You will also want to know if the sale of the puppy is contingent upon your own veterinarian giving the puppy a clean bill of health. Ask if the puppy will be replaced if it is found to have a hereditary fault. Discuss what kinds of faults are included in the breeder's guarantee and the age limitations for when they turn up.

Ask what inoculations have been given and how soon the next ones are due. Although it is not at all unusual for puppies to have roundworms, even from the best of breeders, it is necessary to know when and if the puppy has been wormed and what product was used.

Personality Patrol

There's an inscription in the temple of Apollo at Delphi that says, "Know thyself." (Actually, it says, "Gnóthi seautón," but who can read Greek?) No one knows for sure just who wrote those memorable words, but I wouldn't be the least bit surprised if the guy who did was writing to someone who was about to buy a Rottweiler. The more you know about yourself, the more apt you are to get the right pup for you.

Will your personality meld with that of your Rottie? Laugh not, gentle reader—this is important. By meld I mean, will the way you handle life's little (and not so little) problems work for the Rottie puppy you are going to bring home?

If you are the type who handles problems by waiting until they disappear, forget about owning the little bruiser in the litter who is bound and determined to be king of the hill. Although he might appeal, that little pink-tongued cutie you bring home is a lot smarter than you think. It won't take the little fellow long to figure out you are a *laissez faire* kind of a guy or gal, and the day he steps on the scale and realizes he is no longer a 90-pound weakling—watch out! Someone is going to be in charge, and it could well be the dog!

Some Rotties are going to require a much firmer hand than others. The breed has a great capacity to learn, but each puppy learns at a different

Word to the Wise

It is wise to remember that bigger is not necessarily better when it comes to choosing your Rottie. Aside from the physical problems an oversize Rottweiler can develop, consider what your home and family are able to accommodate.

rate and one puppy may be a good deal slower to catch on than another. If you have patience that stretches from here to eternity, this won't bother you at all. But if you are equipped with a very short fuse, you may want to reconsider taking little Pokey home.

Breeder Knows Best

There's little doubt you know how you prefer to handle situations, but how much can you know about a puppy's personality when you only have a few minutes together? Probably not much. Aside from those pups who register at opposite ends of the temperament scale, it's pretty hard to tell a great deal about the rest of the litter.

An experienced breeder will be able to give you a pretty good evaluation of the puppy you are considering. The breeder has been observing the litter since birth and has been through the growing-up process of Rottie pups time and time again. The breeder knows a great deal about what to expect from each puppy in the litter. If you give the breeder even a general idea of your own personality, he or she can help tremendously in directing you to the right puppy.

Looking at Behavior

We have already established what the key characteristics are in an adult Rottweiler's character—bravery, protectiveness, confidence and devotion to family. By and large, you are going to find these characteristics in any well-bred Rottie. However, these characteristics are rooted in basic behaviors that can be seen even in youngsters.

Although definitive temperament testing can't be done on very young puppies, there are characteristic puppy behaviors that can indicate how suitable a particular puppy will be for you and you for it. Please understand I am not trying to suggest the following are characteristics are good or bad, because the same characteristic can be an asset in one situation and a liability in another. These are simply some of the factors you need to consider:

➤ **Dominance.** How the puppy interacts with its littermates is a strong indication of how dominant or submissive it will be as an adult.

Word to the Wise

Although a good part of how your Rottie behaves will be determined by how well the puppy is raised and trained, there is much that can be predicted in the way the puppy interacts with its littermates.

➤ **Dependence.** One puppy will be the first out of the nest and rush out to meet every stranger that comes by. Another may only do so with the rest of the gang. The more dependent dog will usually be more eager to please and easier to train. The more independent dog may prove to be stronger willed, but may not need as much attention and reassurance.

➤ **Energy.** Some puppies play until there is absolutely no littermate willing to go on, and then will be the first awake to start over again. Other pups like to nap frequently and may be completely content to sit on some high perch for long stretches of time just observing the world.

➤ **Determination.** There are puppies that seem to have only one thing in mind, and that is what they are trying to accomplish at the moment. Nothing seems able to distract them. Yet, others in the same litter can be redirected quite easily.

➤ **Aggressiveness.** There are puppies in a litter that will not tolerate having their possessions tampered with and will respond angrily or by biting. This response can be directed toward littermates and/or toward humans. Uncontrolled aggressiveness can lead to serious problems, but harnessed it can serve a definite purpose.

But He Picked Me!

Some Enchanted Evening applies in plays, love songs and movies. The two protagonists spot each other across a crowded room and somehow they know—it's happiness forever after. Good for songs and movies, but not so good when it comes to picking out your Rottie.

Undoubtedly, the aggressive little fellow who knows no strangers will be the first one out of the chute and over to you. He or she will probably be happy to follow you to the ends of the earth, or if not there at least to the end of the hall. Does this mean you were meant for each other? In a good number of breeds I might unhesitatingly say yes, but in Rotties I would want to reserve judgment.

Make no mistake, I am not discounting friendliness and self-confidence—not by a long shot. But beware the absolutely reckless pup that plows straight ahead without thinking twice. Obviously you don't want a shrinking violet or you wouldn't be considering a Rottie. At the same time, you don't want a dog incapable of using a bit of Rottweiler discretion. Puppy bravery is all well and good, but it should be tempered with *some* good sense.

Ask breeders for their opinions. If the person who knows the puppies best assures you that the puppy you want is a sensible one and has become totally smitten with you, the two of you (you and the puppy that is) can start singing love songs.

My Friend Told Me Always to Pick . . .

Friends, many of whom have never even owned a dog and who know

Watch Out!

Do not bring the entire neighborhood with you when you visit a breeder. This creates confusion and is a distraction for the breeder, who has a great deal to discuss with you. Even if you have a very large family, it would be much better to make several visits with just two or three members of the family in attendance each time.

absolutely nothing about Rotties, will usually offer all kinds of sage advice about how to pick a puppy. But when the big day comes, remember you are choosing this puppy for yourself and your family, not for anyone else.

Your pals down at the bowling alley may look at you with a bit more respect if you own the biggest, toughest Rottweiler on the block, but they don't have to live with the dog. For reasons I have already outlined, you know the biggest, toughest puppy who comes streaking out of the whelping box to chew your shoes or swing on your pant leg may not necessarily be the right pup for you.

If you think this tiny tornado will grow up to provide you with that macho tough-guy image, think again. Joining a gym, buying a gym and reinventing yourself as a latter-day Arnold Schwarzenegger could prove far less of a challenge than living with a Rottie you aren't able to handle.

Then there are all those romantic stories about the sickly runt of the litter who grows up to be the dog that wins New York's Westminster Kennel Club dog show. Were it only so! Taking home the forlorn little runt of any litter might well earn you a prize—for spending the most money on veterinary bills.

What you should be looking for is a healthy, happy Rottie puppy that the breeder feels would be just right for the kind of guy or gal you happen to be. If Bruno and Gretchen are going to be members of the family, the most easy-going, nicely adjusted pup in the litter is the only one you want to consider. If you use good sense in selecting your Rottie puppy, you'll have a friend whose intelligence and devotion will be everything the breed was intended to be.

Important Papers

Before you leave with young Gretchen tucked under your arm, there are some very important transactions that have to take place. First, the seller will want to get paid. Cash is always appreciated, as is a cashier's check or money order. If your payment is a personal check the seller may want you to come back to pick up your puppy when the check has cleared the bank.

Don't feel this is because you look untrustworthy or because the breeder is a suspicious old coot. What recourse does the breeder have once you are gone with the puppy if the check keeps bouncing right back no matter how many times it's deposited?

On the day the actual sale is completed you are entitled to four very important documents:

➤ A health record, including an inoculation schedule

➤ A copy of the dog's pedigree

➤ The registration application

➤ A sales contract

These are the papers that will ensure little Bruno or Gretchen is a real Rottweiler. There should be no extra charge for these documents. Good breeders supply them with every puppy they sell.

Health Record

Most Rottweiler breeders have begun the necessary inoculations for their puppies by the time they are seven or eight weeks old. These inoculations protect the puppies against adenovirus, distemper, parainfluenza and canine parvovirus. These are all deadly, communicable diseases that will be dealt with at greater length in Chapter 10, "Nutrition and Exercise." At this point it is important to understand that these are diseases that can kill your puppy seemingly overnight.

A rabies inoculation is also necessary, but in most cases it is not administered until a puppy is four to six months of age or older. Local ordinances may require that the rabies shot be given before that time. Check with your veterinarian, who will know what the law is in your area.

Watch Out!

If you want to be sure you are buying a purebred Rottweiler, do not be maneuvered into buying a "bargain pup" whose parents were "purebred but we never got around to registering them" or "the mother was purebred and registered, but the people who owned the sire lost the dog's papers." The only way you can be sure you are getting a purebred Rottie is if the pup comes with an official registration application and at least a three-generation pedigree.

A puppy should never be taken away from its original home before these initial inoculations have been at least started. There is a pre-scribed series of inoculations developed to combat these infectious diseases, and it is extremely important that you obtain a record of what shots have been given to your puppy, and when. You must also have the type and make of serum used, so your veterinarian can continue with the appropriate inoculations as needed.

The health record should also say what kind of veterinary treatment the puppy has been given since birth. This will include records of exams, along with dates and type of medication used for each worming.

Bet You Didn't Know

The chances that your dog will be infected with rabies by another pet dog are very remote. However, this doesn't preclude the possibility of your Rottie coming in contact with wild animals, which frequently carry the rabies virus. Do not overlook the importance of inoculating to protect your dog from this possibility.

Pedigree

The pedigree is your dog's family tree. The breeder of every AKC-registered dog should supply the buyer with a copy of this document.

The pedigree lists your puppy's ancestors back to at least the third generation by giving the registered names of each dog.

Dog Talk

A puppy's **sire** is its dad, and the **dam** is its mom. Going back in the genera-tions, there's **grandsire** and **granddam**, and so on.

A pedigree is read from left to right. The names are presented in pairs, and the first pair of names in the first col-umn on the left are the puppy's sire and dam. The sire's ancestry, reading left to right, occupies the top half of the pedigree. The dam's ancestors appear on the bottom half. For each pair of names, the sire is on the top and the dam is on the bottom.

In most cases, pedigrees are hand-written or typed by the breeder. These unofficial documents tell you your puppy's ancestry, but like any document prepared by a human, they can contain spelling errors and other assorted mistakes. If you wish to obtain an Official Pedigree, you'll need to contact the AKC. The information contained in an AKC document is taken from its computerized files. The registration application will contain a box you can check off if you want to order an Official Pedigree (which costs $17, in addition to the $10 registration fee).

A pedigree is just a list of ancestors. It is no guarantee of quality. If there is anything that indicates one pedigree is better than another, it is the titles the individual dogs in the pedigree have earned. Most of these titles will be indicated on the pedigree. The titles can be earned for excellence of conformation and achievement in a host of sports and activities. There may also be titles awarded for producing many Champion puppies.

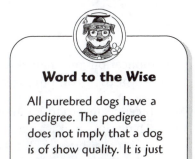

Word to the Wise

All purebred dogs have a pedigree. The pedigree does not imply that a dog is of show quality. It is just a chronological list of ancestors—nothing more, nothing less. Don't let anyone tell you otherwise.

Even if you have not yet decided what the future holds in store for your puppy, you should understand that the titles on the pedigree tell you the dog's ancestors have excelled in certain respects—that they represent true Rottie character and intelligence. They also tell you the people who owned the title-holders were responsible individuals who felt an obligation to help their Rotties achieve their highest potential.

Registration Application

The registration certificate is the canine world's birth certificate. When a breeder has a litter of puppies, the first thing he or she must do to get them registered is submit an application to register the entire litter with the AKC. The information about the litter's sire and dam is checked, and the AKC issues individual registration applications for each puppy in the litter.

Dog Talk

Breeders refer to these individual applications as **blue slips**, just because they've always been that color.

Breeders can either use the blue slip to transfer ownership of the puppy directly to you, or they can individually register all the puppies in the litter in their own name first. Most breeders will give you the blue slip when you buy the dog, and you will be responsible for sending it in. As with the Official Pedigree, the registration certificate is issued by the AKC. When the breeder sells you a Rottweiler, an official record of the transaction is entered on the registration application and mailed to the AKC, where it is permanently recorded in their computerized files.

Most breeders like to insert an official registered name for the puppy on the blue slip, or at least a prefix. This permanently associates that puppy with that breeder. Actually, it is a compliment to the puppy that the breeder thinks enough of it to ensure the association. However, once a dog is individually registered with the AKC, the registered name can never be changed. You can, of course, call the puppy anything you choose.

Dog Talk

A **kennel name** is the prefix or suffix used to identify the breeder or kennel that bred the dog. This kennel name is registered with the AKC and no other breeder may use it. Most breeders add this to a dog's individual name, so that ends up being Happy House Gretchen or Bruno of High Acres.

When you buy a puppy, the registration application is transferred to you. This blue slip must be completed and returned to the AKC with necessary fee ($10 when I wrote this book) no later than 12 months from the date of the puppy's birth. The puppy's birthdate is printed on the blue slip.

Never, never, *never* accept a purebred puppy without either the blue slip or the actual registration certificate. Don't take anybody's word for it, don't accept any promises that the papers will be along later and don't listen to any excuses. Responsible breeders have all their papers in order.

Sales Contract

A reputable breeder will supply a written agreement that lists everything that he or she is responsible for in connection with the sale of your Rottweiler. The contract will also list all the things the buyer is responsible for before the sale is actually final. The contract should be dated and signed by both the seller and the buyer. Sales contracts vary, but all assurances and anything that is a condition of the final sale should be itemized. Some of these conditions might be:

➤ Sale is contingent upon the dog passing a veterinarian's examination within 24 to 48 hours after it leaves the seller's premises. There should be a clear statement of the refund policy if the dog does not pass the vet's exam.

➤ Any conditions regarding the seller's requirement to spay or neuter the dog.

➤ Whether a Limited Registration accompanies the dog. (That is, the dog is ineligible to have offspring registered by the AKC.)

➤ Arrangements that must be followed if at any time in the dog's life, the buyer is unable to keep the dog.

➤ What conditions will apply if the dog develops genetic bone or eye diseases at maturity.

Diet Sheet

Your Rottweiler is the happy, healthy youngster it is because the breeder has properly fed and cared for it every step of the way. All established breeders have their own experienced way of doing so. Because they have been successful in breeding and raising their puppies, most breeders give the new owner a written record of the amount and kind of food a puppy has been eating. They will normally give you enough of the food the puppy has been eating to last until you are able to go out and buy some yourself. Do follow these recommendations to the letter, at least for the first month or two after the puppy comes to live with you.

Word to the Wise

Some breeders add vitamin supplements to their dogs' and puppies' diets as a matter of course. Other breeders are adamantly opposed to supplements when well-balanced and nutritious food is given. Be sure you understand what your breeder's thoughts are on this issue and act accordingly.

The diet sheet should indicate the number of times a day your puppy has been fed and the kind of vitamin supplementation or additions to the food it has been receiving. Following the prescribed procedure will reduce the chance of upset stomach and loose stools.

Usually a breeder's diet sheet projects the increases and changes in food that will be necessary as your puppy grows from week to week. If the sheet does not include this information, ask the breeder for suggestions on increasing the size of meals and the eventual changeover to adult food.

In the unlikely event the breeder does not give you a diet sheet, your veterinarian will be able to advise you about what to feed your puppy. I'll also talk more about Rottweiler nutrition in Chapter 10.

The Least You Need to Know

➤ When picking puppies, health comes first.

➤ Make sure you and the pup were, in fact, meant for each other.

➤ Always ask to see the health certificates of the puppy's sire and dam.

➤ Ask the man (or woman) who really knows for advice about choosing the right puppy for you. That's the puppy's breeder.

➤ Make sure you get a registration application and a pedigree when you buy your dog.

Part 2

The Life Can Be Beautiful Tool Chest

You wouldn't start building a house without the right tools, would you? Well, don't expect to build a solid relationship with your Rottweiler if you don't provide yourself with the means to do so. Don't wait until after you bring the little one home—be prepared!

This section will help you plan ahead so that you have all the toys and tools you'll need before that plump little pup arrives. One of the things you'll learn in a hurry is that preventing a bad habit from ever beginning is far easier than trying to erase the habit from your Rottie's mind.

Puppies are babies. Baby dogs, yes, but still babies, and all babies are concerned with is what they want and when they want it. It is up to you to figure out what in all those "wants" is for the good and what simply won't work for the two of you. Whether or not you had planned on having children, you definitely have a child now—a little black-and-tan bundle of needs that will look to you to supply every one of them.

Lest you think this section will tell you your pup is really a little person, forget it. Dogs, large or small, young or old, are not little people—they're dogs, and this section will help you decode their language and behavior so that you can set about the basic training that will make your Rottie a canine good citizen.

Chapter 5

What the New Puppy Needs

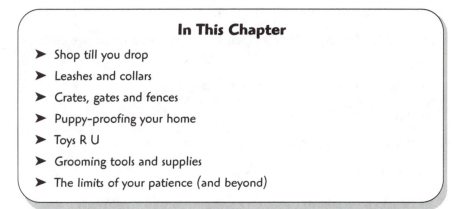

In This Chapter

➤ Shop till you drop

➤ Leashes and collars

➤ Crates, gates and fences

➤ Puppy-proofing your home

➤ Toys R U

➤ Grooming tools and supplies

➤ The limits of your patience (and beyond)

He's the King of the World, and he (or maybe it's she) is coming to live with you. Wonderful! If your friends really loved you, they would already have given you a puppy shower, and you'd now have everything you need to make the king or queen as comfortable as possible. If so, you can skip right to the next chapter—that is, if you are positive you have everything you need. If, by some chance you never got that puppy shower, read on.

Perhaps next time you should register at the local pet emporium and send out announcements to friends and family. But for now you had better get down to making that list and checking it twice, because having everything in place *before* Gretchen or Bruno arrives will save you some hectic days and sleepless nights.

You are going to need equipment to keep that little tyke busy, other equipment to keep him in and still other equipment to keep him out. There has to be a place for the pup to play and a place to sleep. You'll need some toys for training and some toys just for fun. The one thing you won't be able to find in any shop is patience. That you will have to supply yourself—and believe me, there will be times when you will have need to have far more than you ever imagined possible. First, let's make the list—then we'll go shopping.

The New Puppy Shopping List

If this is your first dog, you will probably need to start from scratch and buy everything on this list. If you've had a dog before, check to make sure that what you have will suit the size and needs of your Rottie puppy. More expense? But of course—remember what I said about the high cost of dog ownership?

➤ Paneled fence partition or pen to cordon off a living area for the puppy

➤ Fiberglass kennel crate or metal wire cage

➤ Feeding bowls and water dishes

➤ Food prescribed by the breeder

➤ Brushes, combs and nail clippers

➤ Doggy quick bath

➤ Special dog shampoo

➤ Collars and leashes

➤ Toys

➤ Household odor neutralizer and cleaners

➤ Chewing deterrents

All of this equipment can be purchased from local pet supply stores or the larger pet emporiums. Many supermarkets now carry a very extensive line of pet products as well, and if you have the opportunity to attend a dog show, you will find trade stands selling all the products you will need.

Leashes and Collars—More Than One

The collar you buy that fits little Gretchen today will probably just go around her wrist next week. Perhaps that's a bit of an exaggeration, but like shoes for kids, collars for young Rotties seem to be outgrown on the way home from the store.

You'll probably end up buying:

➤ **Baby collar.** This is just to get your puppy used to having a collar around its neck. Buckle collars made of soft leather or sturdy cloth work well. They are adjustable to about 14 inches, and even after the initial introduction period they can be used to carry the puppy's identification and rabies tags. The operative words here are *soft* and *light*. This will be the first collar to go around the puppy's neck, and the less noticeable it is, the better.

➤ **Training collar.** You will definitely need this link chain collar (also called a slip collar) by the time your Rottie pup is three to four months old, when basic training is about to begin. At that point, you can take the puppy with you to the store get the proper size collar. The pet supply shop or trade stand owner will be able to demonstrate how to measure and put on the link-chain training collar. (If they can't, do your shopping elsewhere.)

Word to the Wise

When you go puppy shopping be sure to tell the shop owner or clerk that you are getting a Rottie. Toys and equipment suitable for a Chihuahua will not work for your Rottweiler. The person that takes care of you may even have suggestions that will eliminate your having to replace all your equipment because your little Goliath has outgrown what you buy.

A link-chain training collar is a must for basic training.

➤ **Leashes.** The first leash should be flexible and lightweight. (Actually, you can survive those first few days with a piece of light cotton clothesline.) When you first attach it to the puppy's collar, expect the little tyke to act as if he or she is being pursued by a king cobra. Fear not, your little treasure will get over seeing the leash as a death threat fairly quickly. Obviously, avoiding a leash that's big and heavy will aid in the transition. Eventually you are going to need a four-foot leather training leash, so my advice is to move right on up to that piece of equipment just as soon as little Bruno graduates from the clothesline.

Hold That Tiger!

I strongly recommend creating a partitioned-off living area for the puppy. Wire paneled fence partitions, called exercise pens, are available at most pet supply shops. The panels are three or four feet high, and are well worth the cost. The kitchen is an ideal place to confine your puppy, as it will miss its mother and littermates very much and will almost immediately transfer this dependence to your and your family. There is usually some member of the family in the kitchen to keep the puppy company, and kitchen flooring is usually easiest to clean up in the event of an accident.

This fenced-off area provides a safe place for the puppy, as well. Not only does it keep the puppy out of mischief, but it also protects it from being bothered by (or bothering) older or larger dogs in the household (if there are any). It can also be a place where the children are told to leave the pup alone.

Puppies that have not been raised with small children may find these miniature humans very frightening. Most puppies love children, but it may take a bit of time for the puppy that is not used to children to feel comfortable around them. The fencing keeps the children at a safe distance and gives the puppy an opportunity to accept them gradually.

A Crate Is Great

I always place a wire cage or the rigid fiberglass crate inside the fenced-off area with the door open. This quickly becomes the dog's sleeping den. These crates or kennels come in various sizes, and although the one that will accommodate the fully grown Rottweiler may seem terribly oversized for a very young puppy, you will be amazed at how big your puppy will grow in just a few weeks.

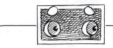

Watch Out!

Kids and puppies were meant for each other, but make sure the initial introduction takes place slowly, especially if they have never met before. Rottie puppies are inclined to chase anything and anyone that runs. When children are frightened, they run and scream. This incites a puppy's chase instinct and even creates the urge to bite at the child's heels.

The crate will prove invaluable for both housebreaking and travel. When I have recommended crates to some first-time dog owners, you would think I had suggested locking their precious one in a trunk and throwing away the key. At first, they considered the crate method of confinement (especially during housebreaking) to be cruel. But when they did as I suggested anyway, they invariably came back to thank me over and over. They agree the crate is one of the most valuable training tools they have ever used.

Using a crate of the proper size reduces the average housebreaking time to a minimum, and eliminates all the stress of constantly correcting a puppy for making mistakes in the home. Then too, there are those days when everything and everyone in the house seem to be working at odds. The children need time out, you need time out. At those times there is no better place for the family dog than its own little den with the door closed.

Crates provide a sense of safety and security. Most adult dogs use their crates voluntarily as a place to sleep. It becomes their cave or den, and in many cases a place to store their favorite toys or bones.

The fiberglass airline-type crates are ideal for Rotties. They can be purchased from almost any pet supply shop. Do check to see if the manufacturer's warranty states the crate is "airline approved"—just in case you and Bruno decide to visit the relatives in Oshkosh. When traveling by air, this is a requirement. Even when you decide to have Bruno or Gretchen accompany you in the car, they are safest in the crate.

Word to the Wise

Dogs learn to look at their crates as safe and private quarters. Those of us who live on the earthquake-prone West Coast find our dogs make a bee-line for their crates at the first rumble. With some, it takes a good deal of coaxing to get them to come out of their shelter.

Buy the extra-large crate (40 inches long × 27 inches wide × 30 inches high). That size will accommodate the average full-grown male and allow him to stand up and turn around. Should your Bruno decide to grow beyond the norm, there is a giant-size crate available—but do remember, this is not a home gym, it's just for sleeping. Your dog should be able to comfortably stand up and turn around in the crate. It doesn't need to walk around.

Naturally, this size is much too roomy for a very young puppy, especially one you are trying to housebreak.

Dogs do not like to relieve themselves where they sleep, so if the crate is large enough they will eliminate at the far end of the crate. A plywood partition can be cut to reduce the inside space, as needed. If you don't want to bother with the cut and paste routine, inexpensive smaller size crates can be purchased and discarded or sold at your next garage sale as the dog outgrows them.

In warm climates, some Rottie owners prefer the metal wire type crates, as they provide better air circulation. The wire crates come in all sizes, as well, and some have the additional advantage of being collapsible so that they can be folded flat if you need to transport them.

Outdoor Runs

A securely fenced yard is the ideal place for your Rottweiler when it is outside. If you don't have a fenced yard, or if you do not wish to see your rose bushes transplanted every few days, a dog run can be a godsend. Some of the larger pet emporiums carry very strong portable sections of chain-link fencing from which you can create any size run you choose.

Puppy-Proofing

Bruno and Gretchen will not spend their entire lives inside the partitioned-off area, but trust me, sometimes you'll wish they did. Your puppy's safety and your sanity depend upon your ability to properly puppy-proof your home. As you do so, remember that what a Rottie puppy can't reach today, it will easily be able to dash off with tomorrow.

Mouth-size objects, electrical outlets, hanging lamp cords and a host of other things you never looked upon as dangerous can be lethal to an inquisitive and mischievous puppy. Think of your Rottie puppy as one part private investigator and one part vacuum cleaner. That way, you will be much better equipped to protect your puppy and your belongings.

Puppies can get into places that defy the imagination. You'll need latch ties to keep the cupboard doors closed. Yours wouldn't be the first puppy to find a 10-pound sack of flour and decorate the kitchen with it. More dangerous for the puppy is trying to digest a few

Word to the Wise

Along with the fire department and police emergency numbers next to your telephone, it is wise to have the emergency number for your local veterinarian. Rottie puppies are constantly scooping up every item they find on the floor, and if it's an object that fits into the mouth it's also an object that should be swallowed (or so they think). Getting the pup to the vet quickly may save the little tyke's life.

sponges or the contents of a plastic bottle that can be chewed open. Many cleaning products, gardening supplies and medicines can be poisonous and must be kept in securely latched or tied cupboards out of a puppy's reach.

Chewing Deterrents

A product called Bitter Apple (it tastes just like it sounds!) is available at pet supply stores, hardware stores and some pharmacies. It's actually a furniture polish, but it is nonpoisonous and can be used to coat electrical wires and furniture legs. In most (but not all) cases it will deter a puppy from damaging household items. I have also seen it applied to itchy spots to keep a dog from chewing itself.

If Bitter Apple does not deter your puppy, there is plastic tubing available at hardware stores called PVC that can be placed around electrical cords and some furniture legs. The fencing panels I recommended will also help keep your puppy out of dangerous situations. And a daily puppy-proofing patrol will help you and your pet avoid damage and danger.

Toys R U

Rottweilers love toys and games. There is seldom any problem in enticing them to play, and after a Rottie learns a game well, it becomes a master at coaxing you into playing it. The trick is in finding the right toys and teaching your dog games that are fun but that will not lead to complications or accidents.

Chew Toys

Puppies have a strong need to chew. So if you don't want your puppy to chew on the furniture, what can it chew on? Chew toys help puppies through their teething periods and help them strengthen their jaws.

Providing your puppy with fun and interesting chew toys will save a great deal of wear and tear on your chair legs and encyclopedias. But you have to be careful about what kind of toys you select. What is safe and fun for your neighbor's Chihuahua could be swallowed or splintered (right along with the Chihuahua) by your Rottie before you can even say "Call the vet!"

Pet supply stores carry all kinds of toys. Some provide hours or days of chewing pleasure, while others are not much more than a quick snack. The dinosaur-size rawhide bones are good, as long as you keep your eye on the pup. Some puppies worry and chew these rawhide bones for days. Other pups become masters at chewing off chunks and swallowing the pieces. The chunks can get caught in the throat, so don't take the risk.

Cured cattle and horse hooves are enjoyed by Rotties, but the size of the hoof is important. If your big guy is the chew-and-swallow type, nothing smaller than an elephant hoof (if there is such a thing) is safe, but since harboring anything less than the entire elephant is illegal anyway, that pretty much eliminates hooves entirely.

A big fresh knuckle bone is a great idea, and your Rottie will love it and you. Just make sure it is the bone of an animal that had very large knuckles.

For the vegetarians among you, there are things that have never lived that you can buy for your Rottie to chew on. These are excellent manufactured substitutes that have different names, Nylabone and Gumabone among them. These hard nylon chew toys are next to indestructible, and puppies, even adult Rotties, can chew away to their hearts' content. Just make sure you buy the large sizes.

Watch Out!

Be careful of those toys sold in the pet section of your supermarket. Just because a toy is marketed for dogs does not mean that it is safe for your Rottie pup—who has jaws that seem capable of chewing through concrete!

Play Toys

There are other things besides the chew toys that will keep Gretchen or Bruno happy for hours. Kongs are super-tough rubber toys that are all but impossible to break.

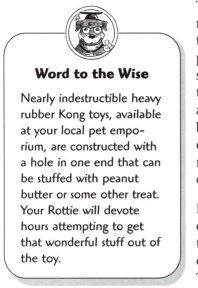

Word to the Wise

Nearly indestructible heavy rubber Kong toys, available at your local pet emporium, are constructed with a hole in one end that can be stuffed with peanut butter or some other treat. Your Rottie will devote hours attempting to get that wonderful stuff out of the toy.

The large Boomer Balls are made of nylon can keep your Rottie entertained by the hour. They can be pushed and chased all over creation, so it is best only to allow your Rottie to play with Boomer Balls in a fenced area. Some dogs are so focused on the balls they don't realize they have chased the thing a mile down the road or into the middle of 5 p.m. commuter traffic!

Rope toys take a tremendous amount of punishment before they give up the ghost. They are washable and come in all kinds of shapes and sizes. The rope toys are shakeable and very throwable, so outdoors is probably the best place for playing with them. You wouldn't want the rope toy to go flying into your objet d'art collection.

No-Nos

Don't think you are saving money by giving your pup an old sock or discarded slipper. Everything you and your family wear or have worn has your special smells, and dogs care not that you bought those socks or shoes last week if they are accustomed to playing with the older versions. A dog is unable to tell the difference between a discarded old loafer and your new dancing shoes. Don't confuse the issue.

Painted things are also no-nos. The toy may be as colorful as Disneyland itself, but make sure the coloring agent is nontoxic.

Teddy bears and other stuffed toys are not a good idea either. Your Rottie can treasure and care for a favorite Teddy bear for months on end, then one day, for some transgression on the part of little Teddy that we know nothing about, the bear winds up inside Gretchen's tummy. When this happens, the three of you will be at the vet's office facing surgery.

Even before that happens, your Rottie is going to feel duty bound to remove the eyes, nose and squeaker from any stuffed toy immediately. That is part of being a dog. So is swallowing whatever is removed. Your Rottie is better off not eating little plastic parts, so don't offer them.

Keeping Your Puppy Pristine

You don't have long hair to deal with as a Rottie owner, but that does not mean short hair never sheds. On the contrary, if you neglect to brush Gretchen she will drop every unwanted hair exactly where you don't want it to be. There is a bit of shedding all through the year, and there are major shedding periods in the spring and fall. Females tend to have a major shed when they come into heat, as well.

Neither does the short hair mean that your digs will be free of doggie odor. All dogs have doggie odor—some more, some less.

Still, having a dog in the house, even a dog the size of a Rottweiler, does not mean the place has to smell like a stable or even a dog house. I seriously doubt you would enjoy that, and you can rest assured your guests will not. If you keep your Rottie's skin and coat clean, you will minimize the amount of odor that is present.

Realize of course, that if Bruno has the run of the house and you aren't diligent about keeping him clean and shiny bright, his doggie odor is being transferred to every carpet, every chair and every bedspread he rests on. Neglecting your Rottie's hygiene means extra work for whoever has the responsibility of keeping the house suitable for the human occupants.

A thorough five-minute brushing every couple of days will suffice most of the year, but seasonal shedding and those special times of the year demand daily brushing to keep the hair from flying.

Required Tools

A slicker brush works well to remove all debris and loose hair. A slicker brush has bent wire bristles set in a flat rubber base. Removing the loosened hair from the brush is done easily with a fine-tooth comb. Greyhound combs have fine teeth on one side and wider teeth on the other. This makes them useful for both removing hair from the brush and running through little tangles or mini-mats on the dog. For shedding periods, a shedding rake is very useful because it removes more loose hairs.

Word to the Wise

Rottweilers have an intimidating habit of grumbling about what they don't like. This does not necessarily mean they are angry, but if you react in fright or stop a grooming procedure, your Rottie will quickly relate his grumbling to getting his way. You must let Bruno know you are the one who makes decisions about what the two of you will do.

Nails have to be attended to, and you'll find a variety of nail clippers and nail grinders on offer. The value of each will be discussed further in Chapter 11, "An Ounce of Prevention."

When a brush and a promise are not quite enough, you can bathe your dog with a good shampoo made especially for dogs. Special dog shampoos are highly recommended, because their pH balance is set for a dog's needs—which are significantly different than a human's.

A wet bath is not the only approach to getting the coat clean. There are many dry bath products that are extremely effective as well. You quickly rub in these products, and then wipe or brush them out, eliminating the mess and time involved in a wet bath.

Household odor neutralizers and cleaners should also end up in your shopping basket. As fastidious as you are, sometimes the doggie odors just get ahead of you. Supermarkets carry sprays, candles, liquids and plug-ins that help in these cases, but the pet emporiums often carry products that really work better for pet odors. Also, many of the products you can buy at the grocery store may irritate and animal's skin, while the products you buy at the pet supply store are more likely to be dog-friendly.

Not at Any Price

There are two more dog owner necessities that are as important as everything I have discussed so far, but they can't be purchased at any pet emporium or supermarket. They are patience and persistence. The other intangibles, like experience, respect and a resounding sense of humor, come with time. Long-time dog owners know the importance of these three, but they also know that without patience and persistence you can never achieve them.

Patience is a must, with both kids and Rottweilers. (Dede Brownstein)

The Least You Need to Know

➤ Do your dog shopping before you bring your new dog home.

➤ For your puppy's safety and your sanity, a fiberglass kennel crate or wire cage and escape-proof pens can go a long way to keep your puppy safe and out from underfoot.

➤ Puppy-proofing your house before your pup comes home and gets into trouble will help make the transition much smoother for both of you.

➤ Dog toys come under the heading of safe and unsafe. Be sure you know the difference.

➤ Regular grooming will keep your Rottie clean and smelling sweet.

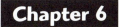

Chapter 6

Bringing Up Baby

In This Chapter

➤ The best time to bring home your new dog

➤ The first week at home

➤ Puppy behavior you can't avoid

➤ When "baby" isn't a baby

Good parents, or people with good parenting potential, make good dog owners. Why? Because owning and caring for a dog is pretty similar to raising a child. The main difference is that with a child you do eventually reach a point where you can wipe your hands and say, "Well, I've done a good job and now you are on your own." That day never comes with a dog. And although Rottweiler lovers make extravagant claims for their dogs at times, they do realize that in the end the owner is completely and totally responsible for his or her dog.

The puppy doesn't learn until you teach it. A puppy, or grown dog for that matter, cannot eat until you feed it or turn on the faucet when it wants a drink of water. Dogs cannot let themselves out of the house to take care of bodily functions, and they don't have access to over-the-counter remedies when they are ill.

You have to do all these things over and over—for the rest of the dog's life. And that is so whether you feel you are up to doing those things or not.

The first few weeks and months after your new Rottie puppy arrives, it needs the same kind of care and attention all babies need. When you finally get through that stage and adolescence sets in, you have to call upon all the patience in the world to work your way through that difficult time.

Bringing Home Baby

The safest way to bring your puppy home is to get a pet carrier or cardboard box big enough for the puppy to stretch out comfortably with sides high enough so it can not climb out. Put a layer of newspapers at the bottom in case of accidents and a soft blanket or towel on top of that.

Ideally, another family member or friend should accompany you to do the driving or to hold the carrier that the puppy is in. All the better if you can hold the box on your lap. That way it will be your reassuring hand that will be the first to stroke the puppy as it becomes accustomed to the strange and ever-changing new world.

It is not always possible, but do your best to have your Rottie puppy come to live with you when you or another family member has a week or at least a few days off to be there most of the time. By the time a week has gone by, your puppy will have begun to forget all about littermates and will begin to become a member of your family, even if the family is just the two of you.

If you can't manage a week off, try taking a Friday off and picking the puppy up early that day. It will give the two of you a full three days to get past that difficult transition.

The breeder may have started a housebreaking routine with your puppy. If so, check carefully to learn just how this was being done so that you can follow suit. If the puppy has been accustomed to relieving itself outdoors, don't expect the youngster to understand you want it to use newspapers indoors. If the situation is the other way around and the breeder has started the puppy using newspapers, take newspapers out with you at first and put them down where you want the puppy to take care of its duties. You can eliminate the papers later.

Ideally, you should try to collect your puppy from the breeder in the morning so that the newcomer has at least one full day to acclimate to the overwhelming new world it is thrust in to. Then it won't be quite as bad when night falls.

Facing the Facts

As you've probably begun to suspect, a new puppy is capable of finding its way into situations you never thought possible for any dog to think up, much less one so young. And just in case you think you can eliminate all the problems of puppyhood by getting an adolescent or a more mature Rottie—forget it. Granted, you won't have the baby puppy problems; you'll only have the problems a more experienced adolescent will present.

Give in and face facts: Bringing a new dog of any age into your home is going to present transition problems that have to be dealt with. It wouldn't be any different if you were bringing another human being into your home for the first time. If the new arrival was a baby, you would have infant problems. An adolescent would have all the challenges of that enigmatic stage, and certainly there's no need to tell you what having an adult move in with you would be like.

The Two Ps come into play here: preparation and patience. Think, read and ask for advice from your puppy's breeder. Breeders have lived through this transition many times, and if anyone can give you workable suggestions it is the person who has gone through it all before.

Not only do breeders understand how Rotties react in most situations, they know how the dog you are taking home is inclined to behave. Believe me, having input on those two things alone can save you a good many headaches.

Keep in mind that everything in your home the new Rottie comes in contact with is entirely strange. To make matters worse, there is no one familiar around to assure the newcomer that all is well. Beginning with the

Word to the Wise

If you allow Gretchen and Bruno to sleep in bed with you the first few nights because they appear sad and lonely, don't expect them to be happy about banishment to their crate in the kitchen later. They will probably advise you in no uncertain terms that those arrangements are not acceptable.

very first day your new Rottie enters your home, there are two very important points to keep in mind:

1. Do not let your Rottie do anything on the first day or days that you will not want it to do for the rest of its life.

2. Never be severe in correcting unwanted behavior.

Don't start off doing something you will not wish to continue. Think ahead—feeding little Bruno buttered toast while he sits on your lap through breakfast may be fun when Bruno is a tot. Where, however, will Bruno sit and what will he eat when he weighs more than 100 pounds? For that matter, where will *you* sit?

Try to avoid nagging and correcting a new pup every time it turns around. New dogs, regardless of age, will make mistakes simply because they do not know the rules yet. Since this is the case, you're probably wondering how you can prevent bad habits from being established yet still avoid constant corrections. The answer is actually quite simple: Avoid putting the new dog into situations where it will be breaking the rules.

Don't let your dogs sleep with you as puppies, unless you intend to share your bed when they're adults. (D. Gallegos)

A pup that is asleep in its crate when you can't be there to supervise or is confined in a nearby enclosure where it can see you but can't get underfoot is being protected, not mistreated. By gently confining the pup, you don't have to be a nag and the pup doesn't have to be confused about what is okay and what is not.

The Difficult First Week

This is the tough one, especially for a very young puppy. When you take a puppy away from its littermates and put it into an entirely strange environment, the baby is going to be confused and lonely. No warm bodies to snuggle up to. No playmates for games. During the day it's bad enough, but the nights seem even worse.

As brave as Bruno was in the midst of his littermates, this is all very new and very bewildering for him. Expect some mournful complaints the first few nights. Usually, with a bit of help from you, the puppy will settle in and sleep the night through after that. However, there are some pups that will keep up the lonely crying and howling night after night until you, your family and the entire neighborhood are ready to move to another county. You may be amazed at how loud and how persistent a Rottie puppy can be when it comes time to announce to the world that it is homesick and lonely.

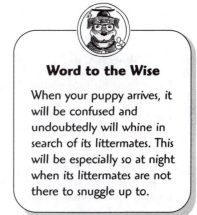

Word to the Wise

When your puppy arrives, it will be confused and undoubtedly will whine in search of its littermates. This will be especially so at night when its littermates are not there to snuggle up to.

For the first few nights after the new puppy arrives, I put a box next to the bed and let the newcomer sleep there. Should the puppy wake up crying, a reassuring hand can be dropped down into the box without getting out of bed. The box-by-the-bed method teaches the puppy two important lessons:

1. The pup is really not alone in the world.

2. It helps the puppy transfer its dependency from littermates and mother to you.

When you find the puppy has learned to sleep through the night without waking you up, you can first change the puppy's sleeping quarters to the crate or cage you have purchased. Then, when the puppy is accustomed to that minor change, you can move the crate to the part of the house you prefer. You can do this more easily once the puppy has learned to be by itself for increasing periods of time.

Inevitable Baby Behavior

Remember, everything is new for the puppy and every household rule has to be learned. Make everyone in your home understand that it is a critical part of your Rottie's education to be consistent with the rules. A puppy is not going to understand that it is all right to lounge on the sofa with the kids but not all right when mom is looking.

Watch Out!

No begging for food at the table means no begging at any table, any time, from any member of the family. Your first week with your Rottie, use a firm but gentle hand to consistently correct this behavior. Do you want a full-grown Rottweiler snatching your dinner from your plate?

Stop the Music!

Human babies cry. There are fretting cries, needy cries and angry cries. Puppies are no different. They cry for all those same reasons, and they cry to express anxiety at being left alone. It is important to teach your Rottie that it will live through periods of being alone. Some puppies fret a bit and then settle down. Others are determined that you are going to give them the attention they want—or else. Do not let your Rottie get the idea that if it is persistent enough, salvation will come. Once you teach your puppy this is so, life becomes a nightmare because the little monster will apply what it has learned to everything it wants or doesn't want.

Begin the training by confining your pup to its crate while you are in the same room. Some pups will be fine as long as they can see you. Others may decide they can only be happy under your feet. If the puppy begins to whine or bark, give a sharp "quiet!" command. Usually that does the trick. If not, you may have to rap the crate with the flat of your hand when you give the command. Almost invariably the noise and simultaneous command will make the puppy pause, if not stop entirely.

You must have the last word, and if you are persistent you definitely will. Do not take the puppy out to comfort it. This is exactly what the complainer is after, and you will be teaching the puppy that the way to get what it wants is to be vocal about it.

Sometimes, with the more persistent little fellows, sterner measures are necessary. Purchase a plastic spray bottle or water gun and fill it with water, adjusting the spray to a steady stream. The minute the barking or whining begins, command "quiet!" and give the pup a shot directly in its face. No harm is done, but puppies (even grown dogs) hate this. A few rounds with the water treatment usually get the message across.

Bet You Didn't Know

Some dogs are determined not to be left outdoors alone at any time. While I absolutely do not advocate banishing any dog at any age to the backyard, a little time alone outside in a securely fenced yard is not a bad thing. A friend of ours exhausted every known method to keep his young Rottie from standing at the fence and barking. Finally, in desperation, he rigged up a sound-activated water hose system so that the dog received a good blast of water every time he began barking. The Rottie learned very quickly that the consequences far exceeded the pleasure of vocalizing his unhappiness.

Another effective correction for puppies or barking adults is the shake can. A small aluminum soft drink can is ideal. First, empty the can. Then put a dozen pennies in the can and shake it—the noise is surprisingly loud, and if thrown at or near the puppy's crate it will surely startle the complainer. Be sure to give the "quiet" command first, and immediately follow the command with the shake can if the dog does not comply.

Once the puppy understands what the consequences are for whining or barking, you can stand in the next room. Just as soon as the racket starts, dash into the room and give your "quiet" command. Follow up with the water or shake can, if necessary, but make sure you intervene each time and always use the same command. Don't make the mistake of saying "no" one time, "quiet" the next and "stop" another time. This does nothing but confuse the dog.

Word to the Wise

Dogs have a hard enough time learning English as it is. Always use the same command for the same action, for the life of your dog. And make sure everyone in your family knows and uses the commands consistently.

House Training Problems

Some puppies get the housebreaking message right off the bat. Others may require all the patience reserves you have. You just never know how quickly (or slowly) your pup will get the message. But be patient, and eventually it will. Rotties are basically very clean, and when the breeder gets them off to a good start, housebreaking is a breeze. Still, accidents can and do happen. Remember—they're babies!

Avoiding the problem is the easiest way to approach this particular phase of your puppy's training. When it's time to go, a puppy will be inclined to return to the same area where it has previously relieved itself. If that's in the middle of your new white Oriental rug, so be it. The puppy won't mind. But if the proper spot (with all the right smells) is outdoors, the puppy will begin to develop a yearning for that spot.

A puppy will let you know when it has to go. It will pace and circle and begin sniffing the ground. You'll see a mild sort of distressed expression and perhaps hear a little whine, seconds before "it" happens. As puppies begin to associate eliminating with that spot outdoors, they will become more and more insistent that they be given access to that spot. I'll deal more with housebreaking in Chapter 7, "If the Student Hasn't Learned, the Teacher Hasn't Taught."

Chewing

Puppies will chew. Grown dogs will chew. The difference is that your adult Rottie has already learned what it can and cannot chew. The puppy hasn't learned this yet. While Rotties are not as compulsive about chewing as some other breeds, when your Rottie does chew, you won't miss it. Never underestimate the power of those jaws.

A Chihuahua owner might return home to find their dog has left a tooth mark or two on the leg of the prized Chippendale table.

A Rottie owner will wonder where the whole leg went. A word to the wise— bored Rotties are capable of reconstructing an entire household in a relatively short time. Be kind enough to your puppy to avoid leaving temptation in its path, especially during teething time.

Yes, Bitter Apple, Tabasco sauce and other taste deterrents can help, but you can't cover your whole house with these products. Confinement with an enjoyable chew toy when you can't keep an eye on your pup is the wisest approach. In fact, you should always have something handy that the pup can chew on even when you are there.

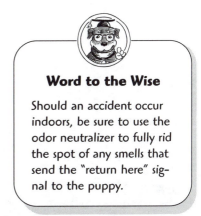

Word to the Wise

Should an accident occur indoors, be sure to use the odor neutralizer to fully rid the spot of any smells that send the "return here" signal to the puppy.

Energy Bursts

I have always wondered what goes through puppies' minds when they suddenly decide to take off on a mad dash through the house as if the devil himself was right on their tails. You know, those headlong gallops 'round and 'round the dining room table or through the halls. If nothing else, it is a way for the pup to burn up some of that excess energy that all puppies seem to have.

After they have one of those Indy 500 tears around the house, most pups immediately flop down and take a good long snooze. There is nothing wrong with the puppy. Just be careful that the pup doesn't crash into something and hurt itself—or that the older dog doesn't crash into something and hurt the thing. Also watch out for puppies that attempt to snap and grab at things as they go tearing around. This is definitely a no-no of the most serious kind!

Play Biting and Growling

Although a little tough-guy growling and chewing on your hand may be cute in two- to three-month-old puppies, these are *extremely* dangerous habits to encourage. Rotties have an inherent desire to guard and protect. This trait has to be managed and directed by you.

Watch Out!

Remember the Rottie's herding heritage—you do not want to awaken a Rottie's need to snatch at moving objects. This can lead to chase-and-grab at joggers and cyclists. I can assure you none of them will appreciate being pulled down by your 100-pound cowboy out on a roundup!

Growling and attempting to snatch back things from your hand gives a Rottweiler puppy the idea that this behavior is just fine any time. This is not so, and it is your responsibility to make your Rottie understand it is never permissible—not even "just for fun." Stop the behavior before it becomes a problem. A Rottweiler must learn to relinquish anything it may be holding in its mouth or standing watch over.

Begin this training very early by removing a play thing or food dish when the puppy is using them with the appropriate, "Bruno, leave it!" Do not tolerate any objections on the dog's part. You may even want to use your spray bottle here. I can not stress enough the importance of your being fully in charge at all times.

Watch Out!

No dog as large and as purposeful of character as a Rottweiler should ever be allowed to decide for itself what it can and cannot do!

Inevitable Adolescent and Adult Behavior

As I have already mentioned, your Rottie puppy will pass through all the stages of maturity that all dogs go through. When you finally get through the dependency of infancy and the incessant curiosity of the Terrible Twos, you will plunge head on into adolescence. With some Rotties, particularly the boys, this period can be extremely challenging. It is a critical phase during which you must be especially wary of bad habits setting in and be persistent and consistent in training and maintaining the upper hand.

This doesn't mean every Rottie is going to start challenging you when it reaches adolescence. Some males have no great interest in becoming the leader of the pack. But a lot of them do. Females are less inclined to be rebellious, but can easily become over-protective.

It is up to you to make sure your Rottie doesn't get the ill-conceived idea that he or she is making the decisions.

Although dogs can't talk back, they can and do growl back. If you let puppy growls slip by uncorrected, you'll have a lot more difficulty trying to correct this behavior in adolescence. Even the Rottie who tried it in puppyhood and was corrected may take another shot at voicing disagreement in adolescence. The puppy that was permitted to get by with growling and puppy biting knows it's possible to rebel and escape unpunished. The big difference now, however, is that Baby Bruno weighs a hulking 100 pounds.

Word to the Wise

If you've raised children, you'll recognize the signs of oncoming adolescence: grumbling, reluctance, inattention, sullen attitude. If you haven't raised children, try thinking back on how you viewed the world at that same stage of your life.

The Instincts Emerge

Your Rottie's bold attitude is as much a part of its genetic makeup as its black and tan color the breed sports. A brave heart is an inherent part of the breed's character—or at least, it should be. You can't change it, but you can direct and channel those instincts.

Guarding

The poor adolescent Rottie has a great deal to cope with just keeping those hormones from raging out of hand. On top of that, the young dog is constantly flipping back and forth between puppyhood and maturity. There are new and unaccustomed feelings developing. At this stage the guarding instinct also begins to develop, and no one is less confident about what to do with it than the Rottie itself. At this stage of their lives something deep within stirs and tells Gretchen and Bruno they should do something about the gardener coming around the side of the house, but they aren't sure of just what that "something" is.

Usually the budding guard dog will bark and then run off to hide. Another time your protector may beat a hasty retreat behind you and peek out between your legs, barking furiously to let you know the two of you are in danger. There's a problem, but the inexperienced Rottie just isn't sure what the problem is or what to do about it.

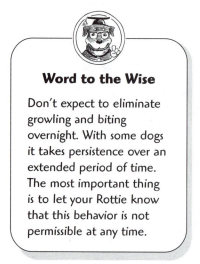

Word to the Wise

Don't expect to eliminate growling and biting overnight. With some dogs it takes persistence over an extended period of time. The most important thing is to let your Rottie know that this behavior is not permissible at any time.

This is the time you have to step in and teach your protector that not all strangers intend harm, nor does the dog necessarily have to do anything about a stranger. If someone is to be a frequent visitor, introduce the person to your dog and get the two familiar with each other.

If you are the stranger (or even if you know a neighbor dog), discretion is definitely the better part of valor. I would not enter a friend's home or yard where a Rottweiler is on duty if the owner was not there, simply because I know the Rottie's first instinct is to protect and it may have a brief lapse of memory in regard to our friendship. I wouldn't want to be waiting around until the dog regained its lost memory.

I would certainly advise friends and workers to come calling when you are home. Posting your yard or home with a "Guard Dog on Duty" warning of some kind would be entirely appropriate. Signs of this kind can be purchased at most hardware stores and pet supply shops. The merchants at dog shows often carry "Rottweiler on Duty" placards that are very effective for warding off unwelcome strangers. In many cases, these signs are posted even when there is no Rottweiler at home. Most would-be thieves are not particularly interested in testing the veracity of such a warning.

Dominance

Think again about the Rottweiler's origins and the characteristics insisted upon by those who shaped the breed: positive attitude, bold, courageous and determined. These are characteristics that do not come without willpower and an inborn sense of superiority. Neither are we able to pick and choose which of these qualities that are a part of the breed's character. They come together, and together they can be molded into the fantastic animal the Rottweiler was meant to be. Without direction, they can result in a dog that is the absolute antithesis of what was intended.

The German breed standard points out that the Rottweiler has a strong instinct to retaliate when danger threatens. This characteristic was developed and encouraged in the breed. It is a good part of the reason Rotties are so well respected. Do note I said "a good part," and not "the whole story." This trait, combined with a unique level of trainability, makes the Rottie what it is—a discerning and highly controllable protector.

This is why a well-informed owner and a well-devised training regimen are so important to the Rottweiler's stability and reliability. A Rottie that flies off the handle at any situation it deems threatening is useless as a companion and a menace to society. Behavior of this kind should not be tolerated and would never be considered acceptable by knowledgeable and experienced breeders.

Throughout this book, I will stress the importance of order in Rottie ownership. You and your human family are collectively your Rottie's pack leader. There must be no exceptions to this rule. If it is enforced, your Rottie will always look to you and your family for guidance in all things and you will not have a problem with dominance.

A Rottie who is pampered, whose every whim is catered to, begins to see itself as leader of the pack. Rotties who balk at giving up their playthings or who won't relinquish their spot on the sofa are trying to find their place in the order of things. It is up to you to let your dog know where this is.

The pack leader does not arbitrate— the pack leader demands. There is no compromise. The members of the pack never have to wonder where their place is. Should any member forget its place or challenge the authority, the offender is quickly put back in line or ousted from the pack. There is no democracy in pack government, nor should there be in dog ownership.

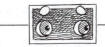

Watch Out!

Although kindness, respect and tolerance must prevail in your relationship with your Rottie, there can never be a doubt as to who is in control. Anything less is a real disservice to your dog.

Stress

When a dog is unable to cope with the conditions it is experiencing, stress results. Sound familiar? In fact, all the things that stress you can also stress your dog. I don't mean going to work or driving in traffic, but being asked to do things we don't understand, being separated from a loved one or sudden, unexplained changes can stress us all—canine and human.

Pressure

As I have explained, all Rotties, while somewhat similar, have individual personalities. They are no different than children in this respect. Some respond to a gentle reprimand, others don't seem to get the message unless three Marine drill sergeants are shouting out the order.

Each personality type requires an entirely different approach to training. The rough and ready, perhaps dominant, male needs to be handled differently than a quiet, compliant little female. (Please realize I am only using these as examples—not all males are bound to be bullies, nor are the girls sure to be little angels!)

The more passive pup is a lot more anxious to comply and will not need or be able to handle the same kind of tough approach required for the extrovert. Bearing down too hard on the pup that was ready to comply in the first place can create a great deal of stress and confusion and interfere with learning. The passive puppy's first reaction to a command could then be fright rather than enthusiasm about being given an opportunity to perform for you.

Too much training before a pup is ready, or being taught with too heavy a hand can upset some youngsters to the degree they too can become neurotic and destructive. Pay attention to what your dog actually needs. Just because you once owned a dog that had to be run down by a bulldozer before the message got through doesn't mean you have to treat every dog that way. An observant owner very quickly learns which techniques work best with his or her dog.

Separation Anxiety

Separation anxiety is a far greater problem than most dog owners realize. This anxiety can be manifested in extremely destructive or neurotic behavior when the owner is absent. All too often this is dismissed as a temper tantrum, done out of spite or because the dog is just plain destructive. But in fact, Gretchen or Bruno's destructive tendencies when their owners are away may be the result of a stress condition called separation anxiety.

Bet You Didn't Know

Animal shelter managers say destructiveness caused by separation anxiety is the problem most likely to cause owners to abandon their dogs. This is especially sad because it is a problem that can be solved with a little training and patience.

In most cases, behavior of this kind is due to the dog's uncontrollable fear of being left alone. The behavior is almost to be expected from dogs that have been abandoned at some point in their lives. Some dogs who have been forced to undergo an extreme change in their living conditions will also exhibit this neurotic and destructive behavior.

Unwittingly, owners create or compound the problem by their own behavior. Do not add to your dog's insecurity by making your departure or return comparable to a soap opera cliff-hanger. Going to the store is not The Exodus, so don't make it that. Just go. When you return, don't carry on like a reenactment of the Return of the Prodigal Son. In fact, with a dog that is manifesting symptoms of separation anxiety, it is wise to completely ignore the dog for 10 or 15 minutes after you get back.

It is best to confine all dogs to a safe area while you are gone, but it is imperative to do so with a dog

Word to the Wise

The new drug Comicalm helps to relieve that anxiety so that gradual retraining can take place. The drug is actually an antidepressant that works in much the same way as Prozac. If your Rottie is experiencing stress of this kind, discuss the problem with your veterinarian.

experiencing separation anxiety. Rather than giving the dog yet another opportunity to reinforce its neurotic behavior—prevent it!

The Least You Need to Know

➤ The best time to bring your new dog home is just before a vacation or a long weekend.

➤ Certain doggy behaviors are unavoidable. Puppy-proofing your home before the new arrival will help head off some trouble. Be prepared!

➤ The first week is the toughest for both you and your Rottie. Be considerate, consistent and understanding.

➤ Baby Rotties, like all babies, do things that are typical for their age. Some of what they do can be overlooked, but other behaviors need to be nipped in the bud—before they become major problems.

➤ As the puppy passes through adolescence, certain problem behaviors are bound to emerge. It is up to you to watch for these changes and deal with them appropriately.

GRRR...

Chapter 7

If the Student Hasn't Learned, the Teacher Hasn't Taught

In This Chapter

➤ How you think, how your Rottie thinks and what science tells us to think

➤ The power of positive reinforcement

➤ Why socialization is so important

➤ Preschool for the precocious puppy

➤ Understanding dog body language

While a Rottie can be a brilliant dog, Gretchen and Bruno aren't born knowing all the things you want them to know. Rottweilers have a tremendous capacity to learn, but if there is no one around to teach them or no one who can teach them properly, they will not be able to achieve that great potential. Every Rottie is born with a clean slate. It is you who will do the writing. Just make sure you write clearly and spell everything correctly!

Unfortunately, the things that work best for teaching humans cannot always be transferred to our dogs. What seems reasonable and logical to us may not apply to our dogs because (I know you're ahead of me here) they're dogs, not people! We all know this, of course, but once we accept our new pooch as a member of the family we tend to endow the dog with human qualities. Love your Rottie, be fair and kind to your Rottie, but do your Rottie a favor and remember that a dog is a dog and not a human. If you remember that, it will be easier for both you and your student.

Same Destination, Different Routes

You and I obey the law because we know swift and unpleasant consequences could result if we do not. We do not have to actually experience the consequences to know this is so. Then how do we know? We know it because someone may have explained the consequences to us, or we may have read about what happens to lawbreakers, or perhaps we saw what might result in a movie or on television. We have the ability to conceptualize—to imagine, if you will.

Now, when it comes to our dogs' learning to obey the laws of the house, there are some things we know: Dogs understand things differently (sort of), and we can not explain things to them the way we would to another human (most of the time).

If it sounds like I'm waffling, it's because I am. Some dog behaviorists tell us that all the canine world's behavior is purely instinctive and offer all kinds of proof for why this is so. Other behaviorists insist scientific studies prove dogs learn in a rational manner, much the same way young children do. We'll find out for sure, I guess, when we are able to teach our dogs to talk. I do believe, however, when and if that day arrives, how our dogs learn will be the least of what they'll have to tell us!

At any rate, what I tell you here about your role as teacher and your dog's role as student is based upon three things:

1. What the instinctual behaviorists believe

2. What the rational learning clan believes

3. What living with dogs has taught me

Pure Instinct

Let's make this as simple as possible. All dogs have some instinctive behaviors because they are, in fact, dogs. Great granddaddy wolf, from whom all the dogs of the world have descended, gave his descendants certain genes that have just hung in there through the

Bet You Didn't Know

Words have no real meaning to a dog. It is what they associate the word with that counts in their minds. Actually, things are the same for us. We believe "sit" means "bend your knees and rest your behind on a chair" because somebody taught us that's what it means. If you were taught that the word for it was "martini," you'd sit down every time someone offered you a cocktail! The point is, always use *exactly* the same word or phrase for what you want your dog to learn. If "sit" means sit and "sit down" means sit and "sit, sit, sit" means sit and "sit, dammit" means sit, your dog is going to get very confused.

ages. Once humans recognized these hereditary inclinations, they manipulated the gene pools to either eradicate certain characteristics or to cultivate them.

A purebred dog will have some instinctive behaviors peculiar to all dogs and some that are specific to its own breed. We don't expect the Bulldog to have a burning desire to herd sheep, but we do know the Border Collie will. Border Collies herd because this is something passed down from wolf ancestors that has been selectively encouraged and refined. Granted, wolves had a much different purpose in mind when they herded together a group of animals, but humans took care of that by adding a pinch of reserve and a dash of trainability to suppress the desire to dine on the livestock.

You can't teach a dog to be something it's not, but you can train a dog to channel its instincts into productive activities. (Judy Butler)

Border Collies don't go to herding school to develop the desire to herd. They attend to learn how to do it to our liking. Guarding and protective breeds like our Rotties aren't sent off to school to give them the desire to protect—they already have that. They are given lessons in how to control and channel those protective instincts in a manner that will be both suitable and beneficial to their owners.

Word to the Wise

It is practically impossible to eliminate a dog's breed-related behavior and responses. You can and should train your Rottweiler not to aggressively discourage strangers from entering your property, but it is against the breed's nature not to stand guard. It is pointless to buy a breed that is naturally inclined to behave in a certain manor and then expect it to react contrary to that natural instinct.

Thinking Creatures

With all that said about instinct, the only people I know who are willing to say dogs are unable to think things out are people who have never lived with a dog. When Gretchen starts hunting up her leash to let you know she's decided it's time for a stroll, or when Bruno stands between your child and the street and refuses to budge, it's obvious dogs are rational, thinking creatures.

This is not to say a dog will always use the good sense it has. (Humans don't either!) Dogs are inclined to be as wise as Methuselah at one time and absolutely witless at another. Don't expect Bruno not to run off to romance the girl dog across the street just because it's rush hour. Left to his own devices, the instinct that takes Bruno across the street will outweigh any sense he possesses and any love he might have for you. In other words, unless he has learned there are consequences to breaking the law (your law), Bruno will follow his instincts.

How Behavior Gets Reinforced

Bruno and Gretchen learn to avoid breaking a specific law because every time they break that law they experience something unpleasant: a snap of the leash, a harsh tone of voice from you, a correction. Breaking the law results in this unpleasant experience. To associate the unpleasant experience with the lawbreaking act, the experience must occur immediately upon breaking the law.

This unpleasant experience must happen every time a certain behavior occurs—not some of the time but all of the time. Some of the time does not really mean much to the student dog. Negative experiences then become things that "just randomly happen," rather than being the consequences of a specific behavior.

You and I do the right thing because we have been lead to believe that "good" people do it this way and "bad" people do it that way. We understand the concept of good and bad—at least as it is taught to us. We do not need a piece of candy to encourage us as adults to eat our veggies. We eat them because they are good for us.

Gretchen and Bruno, on the other hand, are suckers for bribery. When Bruno barks on command, he gets a doggie yum-yum. He quickly learns barking equals yum-yum. Gretchen, on the other hand, learns she cannot bark her head off any time she wants because that will lead to a rebuke or a squirt in the face rather than a yum-yum or a pat on the head.

Why then, you will certainly get around to asking, does Gretchen insist upon doing things that will get

Word to the Wise

Some young dogs are so wild and exuberant that it is almost impossible to get their attention long enough to get a point across to them. Food treats seem to work best with the enthusiastic types. The promise of some delicious tidbit will usually get the pup to concentrate.

her into trouble? She knows you will scold her when she empties the trash can and scatters its contents all over the kitchen, but she keeps doing it. The answer is really not simple. Evidently, Gretchen got some reward (a pork chop?) the first time she emptied the trash. She was able to topple the can again at another time and, lo and behold, she was rewarded with half a bag of potato chips.

Now, what is worse in Gretchen's mind—your being upset or missing out on those gourmet treats? She hates the scolding, but her burning desire for those delectable morsels is satisfied when she raids the trash can. After several successful trash can raids Gretchen knows for

Watch Out!

Each time your Rottie repeats an undesirable act, it will be more difficult to remove that behavior from the dog's repertoire. That's why the best cure is prevention. Keep a tight lid on the trash can, and never allow behaviors to begin that you don't want to see repeated.

certain there is a pot of gold at the end of that rainbow. Forget the scolding! That comes later; the golden pork chop comes now.

Gretchen should not have been allowed to get at the trash can the first time. When she was able to do it the second and third time, she became satisfied that the thrill of victory was worth the agony of getting caught!

I'm using this common example to give you some idea about why a dog does or doesn't do what we think it should. Understanding how your dog gets from here to there will greatly increase your chances of success in teaching household rules or anything else you want your dog to learn.

Vengeance Is Thine!

Knowing why dogs do what they do is one thing, but that understanding doesn't make Bruno being splattered across the highway or Gretchen's spreading the contents of the trash can all over the house any more acceptable. In both cases, the situation has to be handled before it gets out of hand. And when it comes to Rottweilers, this can take more than a whispered, "no no, sweetheart."

Don't forget the breed's long, cultivated history of courage, determination and fearlessness. That doesn't all go away because your Rottie senses you are unhappy about something. There are times when punishment is entirely appropriate but the punishment itself must be appropriate as well. Some things your Rottie does will be mildly upsetting, other things may make you furious. Don't make the mistake of interpreting your dog's actions in human terms. Vengeance and retaliation are human characteristics. What you may interpret as retaliation on the part of your dog is far more apt to be instinct or even anxiety and frustration. Although it may seem so, your Rottie did not diabolically plan to get back at you.

Separation anxiety, as I discussed in Chapter 6, "Bringing Up Baby," can manifest itself in many ways. Dogs mildly affected will often seek out an object that is very personally "you." A shoe, an undergarment or a glove are as close as your dog can get to you when you're gone, and your absence can best be endured through the dog's highly developed art of chewing. You come home and find your Bruno Maglias in shreds and assume Gretchen has done this to you because she is angry that you left her behind. But you have entirely misunderstood why she did what she did. She missed her lord and master, and got as close to him as she could in the best way she knew how. What you call retaliation, she calls devotion.

If you respond with rage when your Rottie acted out of anxiety, you are only compounding the problem. When punishment is warranted there are three things you must always remember:

1. **Be calm**

2. **Be fair**

3. **Be consistent**

If you are unable to interact with a Rottweiler on that basis all the time and no matter what the circumstances, you should definitely not be a Rottie owner!

Socialization

Right on the heels of your Rottie's need for food and water comes a need for early and continual socialization. Our dogs no longer live in the wild, and if there is one lesson they all must learn, it is how to get along with humans. This does not necessarily mean the dog has to love every stranger that crosses its path. But it does mean the dog must understand that humans lay down the rules and regulations and the dog must learn to abide by them without hesitation.

Watch Out!

Assuming your Rottie has intentionally done something to spite you is a foolish error in judgment on your part. Flying off into a rage because of the behavior is both unfair and dangerous. Unfair because dogs are not vengeful creatures, and dangerous because a Rottweiler is not a breed whose history makes it willing to accept that kind of treatment. There is a vast difference between punishment for an infraction of rules and abuse.

Temperament is both hereditary and learned. Poor treatment and lack of socialization can ruin inherited good temperament. A Rottweiler puppy that has inherited bad temperament is dangerous as a companion or as a show dog and should certainly never be bred. But a well-bred dog that is not socialized can present just as many problems, and they are almost as difficult to overcome. It is therefore critical that you obtain a happy puppy from a breeder who is determined to produce good temperaments and has taken all the necessary steps to provide the early socialization necessary.

But just because the puppies in a litter are the result of such care does not mean socialization and temperament are a finished product. Not by a long shot! The responsible Rottie breeder begins the socialization process as the puppies enter the world. Constant handling, exposure to strange sights and sounds, weighing and nail trimming are all experiences that help the growing Rottie understand that this is a human's world and that it is entirely safe and secure when it is with human beings. The puppy is learning that after mom, the best care and comfort comes from people.

Word to the Wise

Everything puppies experience with people at this early age must be positive. Inoculations, a toenail nipped a bit too short—anything that causes discomfort for the puppy should be followed by reassurance and comfort to assure the youngster that all is well and that the discomfort was not intended.

Secluded, sheltered puppies who never see a stranger until they are ready to go off to their new homes are a poor risk in the temperament department. Their ability to take strangers and strange situations in stride has not been cultivated. That's why, after the puppies have had their first inoculations, they should be given the benefit of as many strange sights, sounds and people as is possible.

Breeders will also make it a point to introduce their puppies to strange environments—if the gang has been raised in the kitchen, a trip outdoors is arranged (weather permitting). One puppy at a time gets special attention in the family room.

Kids Do It Best

A household with dog-wise children is a fantastic environment for puppies to spend the first several weeks of their lives. Puppies and children have a natural affinity, and children who are well trained in puppy care and sufficiently supervised have no equal in the socialization department. Children seem able to teach puppies things like eating from their own dish and behaving during clean-up with relative ease. They have a knack for breaking up puppy squabbles, and it seems to take children minutes to leash train a puppy while the same pup will balk and refuse when an adult tries the same thing.

Ongoing socialization works especially well with kids. (Armstrong)

We have friends that come to visit with their young daughter, who brings a whole wardrobe of doll clothes to dress our puppies in. The puppies even have the opportunity to get rides in the doll carriage. The pups adore all the attention, and go to their new homes thinking that children are the greatest playmates in the world.

The Continuing Process

At this early stage, puppies are becoming accustomed to different tones of voice and inflections. It is never too early for a puppy to learn the meaning of "no." Never followed by punishment of any kind, of course, but gently guiding a puppy away from danger with a firm "no!" prepares the pup to understand it cannot do just anything it may want to.

The socialization must continue when the puppy arrives at your home, as well. In fact, socialization must continue through the rest

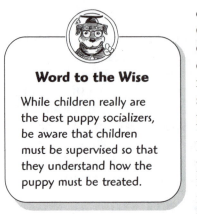

of the puppy's life with you. Granted, you will not want the entire neighborhood waiting with a drum and bugle corps when the pup first arrives, but increase the new sights, sounds and people with each passing day.

It is also important to realize a Rottie puppy may be as happy as a clam living at home with you and your family, but if the socialization begun by the breeder is not continued, that sunny disposition will not extend outside your front door. From the day the young Rottweiler arrives at your home you must be committed to helping the puppy meet and coexist with all human beings and animals. Do not worry about the Rottweiler's protective instinct. This comes with maturity. Never encourage aggressive behavior on the part of your puppy, nor should there be any reason for the pup to fear strangers.

Your puppy should go everywhere with you: the post office, along busy streets, to the shopping mall—wherever. Be prepared to create a stir wherever you go. The public seems to hold a special admiration for the Rottweiler, and while they might not want to approach a mature dog, most people will be quite taken with a Rottie baby and will undoubtedly want to pet your youngster. There is nothing in the world better for the puppy!

Carry treats with you when you go out. Should your puppy back off from a stranger, give the person one of the little snacks and have that person offer it to your puppy. Insist your young Rottweiler be amenable to the attention of any strangers you approve of, regardless of sex, age or race. It is not up to your puppy to decide who it will or will not tolerate. You are in charge. You must call the shots.

All Rottweilers must learn to get along with other dogs as well as with humans. If you are fortunate enough to have a puppy preschool or dog training class nearby, attend regularly. A young Rottie that has been exposed to other dogs from puppyhood will learn to adapt and accept other dogs and other breeds much more readily than one that seldom ever sees other dogs.

The Gang's All Here

This is the time when your Rottie pup will meet everyone in the family and eventually everyone on the block and even everyone in town. Do not think for a minute that you should isolate your pup to ensure the Rottweiler's guarding or protective abilities. Meeting everyone in town with wagging tail will have no affect whatsoever on the territorial character of the adult Rottie. Believe me when I tell you the maturing Rottie will definitely know what is yours and will be as protective of it as you are.

This is the time your Rottie puppy will meet the family cat or other dogs in the household. Remember though, that previous occupants deserve seniority treatment. Don't confine the pets who have already established residence. It is the puppy that is invading their territory. If you invested in the fence panels on your initial shopping list, this is the perfect time to set up the puppy enclosure in the kitchen. Let the previous residents check out the pup at their leisure and at the pace they choose.

The Name Game

Decide on a name for your puppy before you bring the little guy home, because it is one of the first things the pup should become familiar with. Name recognition is the puppy's first step in identifying with its new home. Notice that after just a couple of days of hearing that familiar word, the pup will respond by wagging its little tail and giving you that "you mean me?" look.

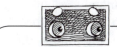

Watch Out!

Puppies don't use a great deal of sense in who they go rushing up to or who they will challenge to a puppy duel. A puppy's unsophisticated overtures of friendship might be entirely misread as aggression by an adult cat or dog and cause some very negative reactions.

Use the name as often as you can. "Bruno, come!" "Bruno, outside?" Preface everything you say to your puppy with the puppy's name.

Bet You Didn't Know

The subject of talking to your dog reminds me of an old English dog training book I have in which the author is asked if a dog owner should talk to his dog—if it makes any sense to do so. The author's reply: "Bloody well do talk to your dog. Just make sure what you say makes sense!"

Adorable/Deplorable Puppy Antics

After the first day or so of unfamiliarity, your Rottie pup will begin to regain its confidence and start showing you a complete repertoire of antics that only puppies and kittens are capable of.

Unfortunately, as cute as some of these little behaviors are, many of them have to be curbed. The play biting, chewing, jumping up, dragging the sofa pillows off into the next room—all those things that are too cute for words now will not be things you'll appreciate in your adult Rottie. You'll have to harden your heart, be a killjoy and nip bad habits in the bud.

Look at it this way—doing so will actually be teaching the pup those first two very important lifelong lessons: name recognition and the meaning of the word "no!"

Housebreaking

Rottweilers generally are very easy to housebreak, because the breed is an exceptionally clean one. However, if you are inconsistent or lackadaisical in your approach, the Rottie gets a mixed message and as a consequence may well decide to do what has to be done wherever.

As you learned earlier, young Rottie puppies have an amazing capacity to learn. It is important to remember though, that these young puppies also forget with great speed unless they are reminded of what they have learned by continual reinforcement.

The method of housebreaking I recommend is avoidance. I think the task gets progressively harder with each time a puppy is allowed to have an accident indoors. Take your puppy outdoors to relieve itself after every meal, after every nap and after every 15 or 20 minutes of playtime. Carry the puppy outdoors to avoid the opportunity of an accident occurring on the way out.

Housebreaking your Rottweiler becomes a much easier task when you use a crate. Begin by feeding your puppy in the crate. Keep the door closed and latched while the puppy is eating. When the meal is finished, open the crate and carry the puppy outdoors to the spot where you want the pup to learn to eliminate.

If you do not have outdoor access, or if you will be away from home for long periods of time, begin housebreaking by placing newspapers in some out-of-the-way corner that is easily accessible for the puppy. If you consistently take your puppy to the same spot, you will reinforce the habit of going there for that purpose.

It is important that you do not let the puppy loose after eating. Young puppies will eliminate almost immediately after eating or drinking. They will also be ready to relieve themselves when they first wake up and after playing. If you keep a watchful eye on your puppy, you will quickly learn when this is about to take place. A puppy usually circles and sniffs the floor just before it relieves itself.

If you are not able to watch your puppy every minute, it should be in its crate with the door securely latched. Each time you put your puppy in the crate, give it a small treat of some kind. Throw the treat to the back of the crate and encourage the puppy to walk in on its own. When it does, praise the puppy and perhaps hand it another piece of the treat through the wires of the crate.

Word to the Wise

Do not give your puppy an opportunity to learn that it can eliminate in the house! Your house-training chores will be reduced considerably if you avoid bad habits in the first place.

Do understand a Rottweiler puppy of eight to twelve weeks will not be able to contain itself for long periods of time. Puppies of that age must relieve themselves often. Your schedule must be adjusted accordingly. Also, make sure your puppy has relieved itself at night before the last member of the family retires.

Your first priority in the morning is to get the puppy outdoors. Just how early this takes place will depend much more upon your puppy than upon you. If your Rottie is like most others, there will be no doubt in your mind when it needs to be let out. You will also very quickly learn to tell the difference between the puppy's emergency signals and just unhappy grumbling. Do not test the young puppy's ability to contain itself. Its vocal demand to be let out is confirmation that the housebreaking lesson is being learned.

Should you find it necessary to be away from home all day, you will not be able to leave your puppy in a crate. That is just not fair to the pup. On the other hand, do not make the mistake of allowing it to roam the house or even a large room at will. Confine the puppy to a small room or partition off an area and cover the floor with newspaper. Make this area large enough so that the puppy will not have to relieve itself next to its bed, food or water bowls. You will soon find the puppy will be inclined to use one particular spot to perform its bowel and bladder functions. When you are home, you must take the puppy to this exact spot to eliminate at the appropriate time.

You're probably wondering if your Rottie will eventually get to a level of maturity where it can let you know what is needed. The answer is yes—sort of. You will have to make allowances for those times when you don't fully understand what it is Bruno or Gretchen is trying to tell you. There are days when your Rottie will give you the "I need to go outside" signal, and the minute you let it out it will turn around and demand to be let back in. Instead of accusing your Rottie of not telling the truth, you'll simply have to mark it down as just another thing you're failing to understand.

When Your Rottie Speaks, Listen!

You and I are accustomed to learning about each other by listening to what the other person has to say. The more attention we give the speaker and the more we dismiss our own preconceived notions and prejudices, the more apt we are to understand what the other person is really all about. Your relationship with your Rottweiler is based on exactly the same principle.

Dogs in the wild have communicated with each other through the use of growls, squeaks and barks since the days when they were still wolves. Their major form of communication though, is body language. The canine world's body language is a much simpler and far less ambiguous one than our spoken language. A good part of it can be learned very quickly by understanding two of a dog's basic attitudes: active and passive.

Active Versus Passive Behavior

Generally speaking, the active dog leans forward and up, while the passive dog moves backward and down. The challenging Rottie will step forward, stiff legged, often with the hair on the back of its neck and shoulders standing up. The dog's head is up and it looks directly forward, staring at who or what is being challenged. A snarl emerges through clenched teeth. The tail is stiffened and carried in a semi-erect position. Everything about the dog's stance and attitude will indicate it plans to move ahead with whatever action must be taken.

Bet You Didn't Know

If you believe your brother when he says he talks to cats and there's no doubt in your mind the Horse Whisperer holds two-way conversations with his four-hoofed friends, you aren't entirely wrong. These people may simply have highly developed powers of observation and are able to interpret the nonverbal messages animals transmit.

Another dog would recognize the aggressive attitude this body language indicates and act accordingly—either actively or passively, depending on its status in the pack. The dog reacting passively does so with body language that is just the opposite of the active dog. The passive dog moves back and crouches down. The head is lowered and the ears are pinned back.

More to Say

A Rottweiler's communication skills go far beyond just active or passive, and it is up to you to learn the language. The degree of success you will have in training and socializing your Rottie is in direct proportion to how much you understand of what Gretchen or Bruno is trying to tell you. A Rottie seldom acts or reacts without giving some advance notice. Sometimes this is done in very subtle ways, but if you have made an effort to understand what these signals tell you, you will be fully prepared.

None of us may fully understand the reasons for every single thing our dogs do, but being attuned to the fact that they do have reasons will get us at least halfway there. For instance, let's look at something as basic and apparently meaningless as Bruno's wanting to lift his leg on every tree and fire hydrant you pass on the evening walk. He does not do this simply because he wants to prolong the walk or because he has a leaky faucet.

We watch television or read newspapers to learn what's going on. We discuss what we've seen or heard with our friends and neighbors. When Bruno sniffs the fire hydrant, he is reading the evening news by way of a scent-o-gram. He is finding out who passed by, when they passed by and whether the passerby was a friend or not. When he lifts his leg, he is also leaving a note to say he stopped by.

What Your Body Says

Dogs are born with the ability to read body language—Rotties it seems, particularly so. They do it so well at times that some owners are willing to swear the breed is blessed with Extra Sensory Perception. We will leave ESP to canine behaviorists, but do realize that your Rottie is reading you every step of the way—probably far better than you read your dog.

Many owners new to training will get very upset and angry if their dog doesn't perform in exactly the prescribed manner. Dogs read anger very easily. Gretchen can learn to dislike a command very quickly because you fly off the handle if she doesn't perform as soon as you think she should. She associates the anger with the lesson and anticipates that immediately after you give the command, you will become angry with her.

She becomes confused because she is being given a command and then the commander gets hot under the collar, even though she is responding. Gretchen will have no idea your anger is a reaction to the manner in which the command is obeyed.

The Least You Need to Know

➤ Your Rottie doesn't learn in the same way you do.

➤ When your Rottie misbehaves, punishment may be necessary, but be sure that the punishment fits the crime.

➤ Ongoing socialization is as important to your Rottie as food and water.

➤ Introduce your new Rottie to prior animal occupants slowly!

➤ That "cute" puppy aggressiveness is a major no-no! Let your pup know you won't tolerate it.

➤ Basic training should be a matter of avoidance rather than correction.

➤ In order to teach, you must also understand. Make the effort to learn your dog's body language.

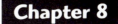

Chapter 8

Basic Training

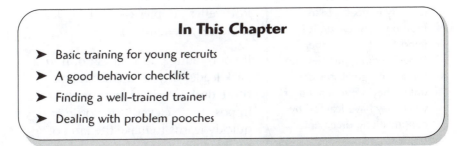

In This Chapter

➤ Basic training for young recruits

➤ A good behavior checklist

➤ Finding a well-trained trainer

➤ Dealing with problem pooches

A Rottie puppy's attention span is very short, and a youngster is not going to understand the more complex commands that an older dog will eventually learn to respond to. Still, this does not mean you should delay simple basic training. As soon as you bring your puppy home, household rules begin. It will be much harder on the puppy to be reprimanded today for something it was perfectly okay to do yesterday.

Leader of the Pack

Puppy boot camp begins on the day the pup arrives, and guess who the drill sergeant is? Right—it's you! And there are a few things you should know that will help you accomplish all the goals you've set for your little trainee.

Using the proper approach, any dog can be taught to be a good canine citizen. Many dog owners do not understand how a dog learns, nor do they realize they can and should be breed specific in their approach to training.

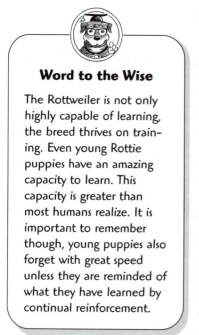

Word to the Wise

The Rottweiler is not only highly capable of learning, the breed thrives on training. Even young Rottie puppies have an amazing capacity to learn. This capacity is greater than most humans realize. It is important to remember though, young puppies also forget with great speed unless they are reminded of what they have learned by continual reinforcement.

As a Rottie puppy leaves the nest, it begins to search for two things: a pack leader and the rules of the pack that the leader has set down. The mentally sound Rottweiler mother fulfills both of these needs unhesitatingly. However, a puppy's new owner often fails miserably in supplying these very basic needs. Instead, the owner immediately responds to the demands of the puppy, and Rottweiler puppies can quickly learn to be very demanding.

If your young puppy does not find its pack leader in you, it will assume those duties itself. If there are no rules imposed, the clever little Rottie puppy quickly learns to make the kind of rules it likes. The longer this goes on, the more difficult it will be to change.

If your Rottweiler finds a growl or a snap is the means to its end, rest assured that behavior will continue. In fact, the behavior will only increase. If that same challenge is met with a stern, uncompromising correction, your Rottie quickly learns bad behavior does not accomplish anything good.

When the pack leader talks, Rottweilers listen. Don't forget that. Through all your training you must remember to go about your business with an authoritative and commanding attitude. Your Rottie will respect this and learn much more quickly.

If you don't give your Rottie the leadership it wants and needs, your chances of winding up with a well-behaved dog are very slim at best. This doesn't mean you can't praise and pet your dog when it responds correctly. You can be as enthusiastic and jolly as you want

118

to be when you get what you want, but be direct and forceful at all times when you are giving your commands.

The Power of Positive Reinforcement

The Rottweiler is easily trained to almost any task. It is important to remember as you train that the breed does not comprehend violent treatment, nor does a Rottweiler need it. Positive reinforcement is the key to successfully training a Rottie, and it produces a happy, confident companion. Your Rottweiler puppy should always be a winner.

Word to the Wise

Make sure you are in the right frame of mind for training sessions. Training should never take place when you are irritated, distressed or preoccupied. A quiet place away from the maddening crowds is where you should begin.

Good Behavior Checklist

If you own a Rottweiler, there are basic behavior minimums you should aim for right from the first day your puppy enters your home. The rewards of owning this great breed are practically limitless, but to gain access to what has earned Rotties their great reputation you must provide the framework within which your dog will reliably operate.

Here is a checklist that all Rottweiler owners should consider a basic part of their dogs' education.

➤ Walk on a leash quietly at your side, even on a crowded street.

➤ Allow any stranger to pet your dog when you give the okay.

➤ Come immediately when called.

➤ Sit and lie down on command and remain in position until you say otherwise.

➤ Be tolerant of other dogs and pets.

➤ Show no unprovoked aggressiveness toward any person.

119

These are things that every companion Rottweiler must be taught and consider an ordinary, everyday way of behaving. Your Rottie is more than capable of mastering all of the items on this checklist, and it is up to you to make sure the dog is given the opportunity to do so.

"No!" and Puppy's Name

The two most important early lessons your Rottie puppy will learn are the meaning of "no!" and its name. (Name calling here is good, not bad!) Use your pup's name in conjunction with every command you give.

Word to the Wise

Always include your puppy's name in every command you give and every time you speak to the little fellow. "Want to go outside, Bruno?" "Come Bruno, come!" Repetition counts, and soon just saying the pup's name will make that little stub of a tail wag.

"No!" is the command the puppy can begin learning the minute it first arrives in your home. It is not necessary to frighten the puppy into learning the meaning of "no," but it is critical that you never give this or any other command you are not prepared and able to enforce. The only way a puppy learns to obey commands is to realize that once issued, commands must be followed.

Say "Gretchen, no!" just as soon as she grabs the end of the tablecloth or eyeballs the electric plug on the wall. Screaming "no" *after* the damage is done does nothing to further her education. Dogs do not associate a reprimand with something they've done in the past. In fact, reprimands after the fact will probably confuse Gretchen rather than teach her that you do not approve.

Collar and Leash

It is never too early to accustom your Rottie puppy to its leash and collar. The leash and collar are your fail-safe way of keeping your dog under control. It may not be necessary for the puppy or adult Rottweiler to wear its collar and identification tags within the confines of its own home, but no dog should ever be outdoors or in an unsecured area without a collar around its neck and the leash held securely in your hand.

It is best to begin getting your puppy accustomed to this new experience by leaving a soft collar around the puppy's neck for a few minutes at a time. Gradually extend the time you leave the collar on. Most Rottweiler puppies become accustomed to their collars very quickly, and after a few scratches to remove it, they forget they are even wearing one.

While you are playing with the puppy, attach a lightweight leash to the collar. Do not try to guide the puppy at first. The point here is to accustom the puppy to the feeling of having something hanging from the collar.

At first, follow the puppy while holding the leash. After a bit, try to encourage the puppy to follow you as you move away. Should the puppy be reluctant to cooperate, coax it along with a treat of some kind. Hold the treat in front of the puppy's nose to encourage it to follow you. Just as soon as the puppy takes a few steps toward you, praise it enthusiastically, give the pup a tiny bit of the treat and continue to do so as you move slowly along.

Make the initial sessions short and fun. Continue the lessons in your home or yard until the puppy is completely unconcerned about the fact that it is on a leash. With a treat in one hand and the leash in the other, you can begin to use both to guide the puppy in the direction you wish to go. Begin your first walks in front of the house and eventually extend them down the street and around the block. Try to encourage the pup to walk on your left side—it will come in handy later.

Come Here, Baby

The next most important lesson for a Rottie puppy to learn is to come when called. Learning to come on command could save your Rottweiler's life when the two of you venture out into the world. "Come" is the command a dog has to understand must be obeyed without hesitation, but the dog should not associate that command with fear. Your dog's response to its name and the word "come" should always be associated with a pleasant experience, such as great praise and petting or a food treat.

121

All too often, novice trainers get very angry at their dog for not responding immediately to the "come" command. When the dog finally does come, or after a chase, the owner scolds the dog for not obeying. The dog begins to associate "come" with an unpleasant result.

Once again, it is much easier to avoid bad habits than it is to correct them. Avoid at all costs giving the "come" command unless you are able to make sure your puppy comes to you. Begin teaching the "come" command when the puppy is already on its way to you or while walking or running away from the youngster. Clap your hands and sound very happy and excited about having the puppy join in on this "game." Be reasonable though—don't expect the just-learning young puppy to come dashing over to you when it is engrossed in some wonderful adventure.

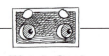

Watch Out!

Never allow your puppy to associate the "come" command—or any command—with anger or punishment. If you call your pup to come for a scolding or a trip to the vet or to be dragged inside after a play session, why should the dog come when you call? Remember, I said Rottweilers are *smart.*

If you save "Bruno, come" for when he's already headed toward you, and use lots of praise when his majesty arrives, soon the royal rascal will learn the word is associated with his being absolutely wonderful and that coming to you brings many pats and hugs.

Later, as a puppy grows more self confident and independent, you may want to attach a long leash or rope to the puppy's collar to ensure the correct response. Again, do not chase or punish your puppy for not obeying the "come" command. Doing so in the initial stages of training makes the youngster associate the command with something to fear, and this will result in avoidance rather than the immediate response you desire. It is imperative that you praise your puppy and give it a treat when it does come to you, even if the pup takes its time in getting to you.

"Sit" and "Stay"

These commands are just as important to your Rottie's safety (and your sanity!) as "no!" and "come." Most Rottie puppies learn to sit easily, often in just a few minutes—especially if it seems to be a game and a food treat is involved. Your puppy should always be on collar and leash for its lessons.

Give the command "Bruno, sit" immediately before pushing down on his hindquarters or scooping his hind legs under him, gently molding him into a sit position. Praise your puppy lavishly when he does sit, even though it is you who made it happen. Again, a food treat always seems to get the lesson across to the learning youngster.

Let your hand rest on the dog's rump to reinforce the idea that the dog must sit until you say otherwise. If your dog makes an attempt to get up, repeat the command while exerting pressure on the rear end until the correct position is assumed. Make your Rottie stay in this position for a few seconds, then *slowly* increase the time as the lessons progress over the next few weeks.

Word to the Wise

When your very young Rottie puppy learns you are the pack leader, it is going to be very dependent upon you. Your pup will want to stay as close to you as possible, especially in strange surroundings. When your puppy sees you moving away, its natural inclination will be to go right along with you. This is a perfect time to teach the "come" command.

When you do decide your puppy can get up, call its name, say "Bruno, okay" and make a big fuss. Praise and a food treat are in order every time your puppy responds correctly. Continue to help your puppy assume proper positions or respond to commands until he performs on his own. This way your puppy always gets it right every time. You are training with positive reinforcement.

The Long Sit

Once Bruno has mastered the "sit" lesson, you can start working on the "stay" command. With Bruno on

Word to the Wise

Your puppy should always be wearing a collar and leash for lessons. Young puppies are not beyond getting up and walking away when they have decided you and your lessons are boring.

Watch Out!

Do not test a very young puppy's patience to the limits. As brilliant as the Rottweiler is, remember you are dealing with a baby. The attention span of any youngster, canine or human, is relatively short.

leash and at your left side, give the "Bruno, sit" command. Put the palm of your right hand in front of his eyes and say "Bruno, stay." Take a small step forward.

Any attempt on Bruno's part to get up must be corrected at once, returning him to the sit position, holding your palm up and repeating "Bruno, stay!" Once Bruno begins to understand what you want, you can gradually increase the distance you step back. With a long leash attached to your dog's collar (here again, lightweight rope is fine), start with a few steps and extend that to several yards. Bruno and Gretchen must eventually learn the "sit, stay" command must be obeyed no matter how far away you are. Later on, with advanced training, your dog will learn the command is to be obeyed even when you move entirely out of sight.

Your Rottie should be able to sit still until you say it's okay to get up.

As your Rottie masters this lesson and is able to remain sitting for as long as you dictate, avoid calling your dog to you. This makes the dog overly anxious to get up and run to you. Instead, walk back to your dog and say "okay," which is a signal that the command is

Doering

Mt. Raven Rottweilers

Beth Fitzgerald

Armstrong

over. Later, when your Rottweiler becomes more reliable, you can call it to you.

It is best to keep the "stay" part of the lesson to a minimum until the puppy is at least five or six months old. Everything in a very young Rottie's makeup urges it to stay close to you wherever you go. The puppy has bonded to you, and forcing it to operate against its natural instincts can be bewildering. The important thing here is to teach the puppy that your command is to be obeyed until and unless you give a different command.

Get Down with Your Dog

Once your Rottie has mastered the "sit" and "stay" commands, you can begin work on "down." The down position is especially useful if you want your Rottie to remain in a particular place for an extended period of time. A dog is usually far more inclined to stay put when it is lying down than when it is sitting.

Teaching this command to some Rottweilers may take a little more time and patience than the previous lessons. That's because the down position is a submissive one for dogs. Therefore, the more forceful breeds and the dogs within those breeds that are inclined to be more dominant may take more time to develop any enthusiasm for this exercise.

With your Rottweiler sitting in front of and facing you, hold a treat in your right hand and gather up the slack in the leash in your left hand. Hold the treat under the dog's nose and slowly bring your hand down to the ground. Your dog will follow the treat with its head and neck. As it does, give the

Word to the Wise

Use the "down" command only when you want the dog to lie down. If you want your dog to get off your sofa or to stop jumping up on people, use the "off" command. Don't interchange the two commands. Doing so only serves to confuse the dog and will delay the response you want.

command "Gretchen, down!" and exert light pressure on the shoulders with your left hand. If your pup resists the pressure do not continue pushing down—doing so will only create more resistance.

An alternative method of getting your Rottie headed into the down position is to move around to the dog's right side as you draw its attention downward with your right hand. Then slide your left arm under the dog's front legs and gently slide them forward. In the case of a puppy, you will undoubtedly have to be on your knees next to the youngster.

As Gretchen's forelegs begin to slide out in front of her, keep moving the treat along the ground until her whole body is lying on the ground. Once she has assumed the position, give her the treat and a lot of praise. Continue assisting her into the down position until she does so on her own. Be firm and be patient.

The Long Down

In teaching your Rottie the long down you will follow the same basic procedure you used in working on the long sit. With your dog on leash and at your left side, give the "Gretchen, down" command. Put the palm of your right hand in front of her eyes and say "Gretchen, stay!" Take a small step forward. If she attempts to get up, firmly say, "Gretchen, down," and then "Gretchen, stay!" While you are saying this raise your hand, palm toward the dog, and again command, "Gretchen, stay!"

Once Gretchen begins to understand what you want, you can gradually increase the distance you step back. Use the same long leash you used for the "sit, stay" exercise, starting with a few steps back and gradually increasing the distance to several yards.

Walking on a Loose Leash

This lesson is important for two reasons. First, it is difficult enough to walk a Rottie puppy that is attempting to pull your arm out of its socket, but when Bruno reaches 110-plus pounds you are going to find yourself in a horizontal position hanging onto the leash as he races down the street with you streaming behind.

I have found the link-chain training collar very useful for leash lessons. It provides both quick pressure around the neck and a zipping sound, both of which get the dog's attention. Some people refer to this as a "choke collar," but fear not—the link-chain collar used properly does not choke a dog. The pet emporium from which you purchase the collar will be able to show you the proper way to put it on your dog.

Do not leave the link-chain collar on your puppy when training sessions are finished. Since the collar fits loosely, it can get hooked on protruding objects and cause injury or even death. Also, when the link-chain collar is used, your Rottie knows it's get down to business time and not just a casual saunter.

Word to the Wise

Remember, many people become frightened when they see a Rottweiler coming down the street. A Rottweiler lunging at the end of the leash, even if it is done out of friendliness and to greet the passerby, can be extremely intimidating.

As you train your puppy to walk along on the leash, you should insist the youngster walks on your left side. The leash should cross your body from the dog's collar to your right hand. The excess portion of the leash should be folded into your right hand and your left hand will then be free on the leash to make corrections. Keep the leash slack and only tighten it to give a quick jerk to get your dog back in position.

A quick, short jerk on the leash with your left hand will keep your dog from lunging to the side, pulling ahead or lagging behind. As you make a correction, say, "Bruno, heel." Keep the leash slack as long as your dog maintains the proper position at your side. Insisting that your Rottie walk quietly along with no pressure or strain on the leash will avoid giving the dog the urge to pull you along.

If your dog begins to drift away, give the leash a sharp jerk and guide the dog back to your left side. Do not pull on the lead with steady pressure. What is needed is a sharp jerking motion to get your dog's attention. I've heard Obedience trainers tell students that success in training will be in direct proportion to the jerk at the end of the lead. Everyone in the class usually doubles up with laughter at this point, but it is a point well made. Eventually, your pup will automatically go to your left side as you walk along.

Learning the "Heel" Command

In learning to heel, your Rottweiler will walk on your left side with its shoulder next to your leg no matter which direction you might go or how quickly you turn. Your fingers should be able to touch your dog's shoulder with your left arm hanging directly down at your left side. If you have to swing your arm out or bend your fingers, the dog is not in the right place.

The dog should not lag behind, move on ahead of you or drift away from your side. Insisting on heeling in a precise way is very important when the two of you are out walking in public places. A Rottie that obeys this command properly will make a far more tractable companion when the two of you are in crowded or confusing situations.

Bet You Didn't Know

If you plan to progress on to formal Obedience training, heeling is one of the lessons that all trainers will demand your dog follows to a T. Well, it's not really a T at all. In fact, in Obedience competition your dog will have to be able to maintain the precise position even if you walk in an X, Y or Z!

To teach your dog to heel, begin with your Rottie sitting at your left side with its shoulder next to your leg. Step forward on your right foot, and as you take your first step give the command "Bruno, heel!" The leash should be slack. When you start off, Bruno will probably move out with you. If he attempts to pull away in any direction, give the sharp jerk and command "Bruno, heel." Do not keep the leash taunt and attempt to pull the dog back into position. The well-trained Rottie will maintain the correct position no matter how fast or slow you go and no matter which direction you turn, including your doing an abrupt about-face.

Training Classes

As mentioned previously, there are few limits to what a patient, consistent owner can teach their Rottweiler. For the advanced basic obedience course, which all Rottweilers should have, and for work beyond that, it is wise to consider local professional assistance.

Qualified professional trainers have had long experience in avoiding the pitfalls of basic training and can help you to avoid these mistakes as well. Even Rottweiler owners who have never trained a dog before have found that with professional assistance, their dogs have become superstars.

Training classes are particularly important for your Rottie's socialization. The dog will learn that it must obey even when there are other dogs and people around. These classes also keep the Rottweiler ever mindful of the fact that it must get along with other people and other dogs. There are free classes at many parks and recreation facilities, group lessons at training schools and very formal, and sometimes very expensive, individual lessons with private trainers.

Word to the Wise

There is one exception to the sharp jerk correction. Occasionally a dog will be frightened or intimidated by the heel exercise. In this case, coax the dog into position and try to make obeying a fun game and worthy of a treat when done well. The well-trained Rottie will maintain the correct position no matter how fast or slow you go and no matter which direction you turn, including your doing an abrupt about-face.

There are also some obedience schools that will take your Rottweiler and train it for you. A Rottweiler can and will learn with any good professional. However, unless your schedule gives you no time at all to train your own dog, having someone else train the dog for you would be last on my list of recommendations. The rapport that develops between an owner who has trained their Rottie to be a pleasant companion and a good canine citizen is very special—well worth the time and patience it requires to achieve.

Finding a Good Dog Trainer

When you decide to seek the help of a dog trainer you will probably be overwhelmed by the number of them available. All will claim to have years of experience and use a training method known only to them but guaranteed to make your dog a canine *Jeopardy* winner and a shoo-in for a costarring role in the next Lassie film.

129

Take promises of overnight success with a grain of salt. Smart as our Rotties are, good trainers take as much time with each dog as is necessary, and no two dogs learn at the same rate. Good dog training is about training your dog well, not how fast the dog completes the course.

Don't misunderstand what a dog trainer's real purpose is. The ideal trainer is one who is experienced at teaching you to train your dog. The fact that an outsider is able to have Gretchen behave like a perfect lady will have no effect upon her behavior at home if you are not equipped to enforce the rules.

Here are some tips that will help you find a trainer who will be able to teach you and your Rottie what you both need to know and in a manner that is suitable for the breed:

➤ Always check to see how long the trainer has been in business and if he or she has references you can contact.

➤ The trainer should have a working knowledge of many breeds with a good understanding of their origin and purpose and differences. It is extremely important that the trainer have an awareness of the different instinctual behaviors found in the different breeds of dogs.

➤ The trainer should have had considerable prior experience in training Rottweilers.

➤ Be wary of a trainer who promises overnight perfection or makes claims that sound too good to be true.

➤ Good professional trainers always put what they intend to teach your dog in writing and will always offer post-training assistance if you experience problems.

➤ The trainer's methods or goals may be in conflict with yours. If there are specific things you

Word to the Wise

Although many trainers have proven to be extremely capable of training Rottweilers, there is no substitute for trainers who have bred and raised the breed themselves.

don't want your dog learn or if there are training methods you object to, make your wishes clear to the trainer.

➤ The trainer should be able to explain to you what is required in the various levels of obedience training.

➤ Professional trainers have a standard rate list so that you will know beforehand just how much your dog's education will cost.

Experienced professionals have no difficulty discussing any of the items in this list. They have the knowledge to back up their answers and do not feel threatened by your questions. I would be very wary of any trainer who is unable or reluctant to answer the questions you pose.

Emotional Conflicts—Yours or the Dog's?

It's well nigh impossible for two animals (human or otherwise) to have a relationship without occasional conflict. That's life. However, when emotions constantly run at a high pitch, that's a problem, both for us and our dogs.

Animal behaviorists who have been called in to deal with incorrigible dogs often report that the problems are environmental. When the dog is moved out of a hostile environment and into one that is serene and accommodating, what appeared to be hopeless behavior resolves itself.

Particularly sensitive breeds are highly susceptible to environmental conditions. When I say sensitive, I do not necessarily mean shy or fragile dogs. It is my belief that the more intelligent breeds are especially attuned to their owner's feelings and are at greatest risk in this area. I include the Rottweiler among these.

Watch Out!

Be very careful about your children roughhousing with their playmates in your home. Rotties attach themselves to the children in the family and do not want them to be hurt. It is difficult for them to tell when children are playing and when they are being harmed.

It may well be the human members of the family that are at the root of a dog's behavior problems, but unfortunately, it is more apt to be the dog who will suffer the consequences.

Sometimes It's the Dog

Those of us who admire the Rottweiler are fully aware that if left unchecked, the breed's determined character can be a distinct liability rather than the asset it was intended to be. Fearlessness, determination and a high energy level are the components that help create the free-spirited character that is another admirable trait of the breed. However, when Gretchen and Bruno are consistently allowed to do what they want to do, when they want to do it, they may have great difficulty following the rules when you find it is necessary to impose them.

Rotties who have convinced themselves their way is the only way can respond to having their reins tightened with some highly unacceptable behavior. An inability to focus, aggressiveness and often outright rebellion are not uncommon reactions. Behavior of this kind is undesirable in any dog, but inexcusable and dangerous in a Rottweiler.

Word to the Wise

Where should you go for help? A professional trainer can help you. So can a responsible breeder. This is yet another reason to keep in touch with the dog's breeder. If you haven't remained in touch with your pup's breeder, this is time to correct that situation. An experienced breeder will undoubtedly be able to suggest who would be most able to help you through your problem.

Although we can not be permissive in dealing with a Rottie, neither can we be overbearing. A dog with the strength of character a well-bred Rottie normally possesses must be given direction, but you can not constantly browbeat and harass a Rottweiler without ill effects. Hitting your Rottie or frenzied yelling at every minor infraction creates a dog who lives in constant confusion and fear.

If your Rottie is acting and reacting in any of these socially unacceptable ways, the cause may or may not be the manner in which you have been approaching the dog's training and discipline. Regardless of whether the mistake is yours, you must seek professional help to assist you and your dog to get back on track at once. Even initial indications of rebellion or retaliation out of fear are cause for immediate concern.

The proper solution might be a trainer experienced in dealing with problem Rotties, or your dog's behavior might warrant finding an animal behaviorist. You and you alone are responsible for the behavior of your Rottie, and it is up to you to find the most suitable solution to any behavior problems that develop.

The Least You Need to Know

➤ Set behavior goals for your Rottie and make sure you insist they are reached.

➤ Positive reinforcement is the best way to train an intelligent dog like the Rottweiler.

➤ There are basic training lessons that should begin the day your Rottie comes to live with you. Learning its name and the meaning of the "no!" command top the list.

➤ Going beyond basic training can be assisted to a great extent with the help of a professional trainer, but it is important to know the trainer's qualifications.

➤ Problem behavior can be environmental just as frequently as it is hereditary. Getting to the cause of the problem is the first step in correcting it.

Part 3

Keeping Your Rottweiler Healthy

Sex and the single Rottie? Think twice about this. There are more cons than there are pros to raising a gang of Rottweilers. If you are thinking about it, this section may help you make up your mind. Old wives tell us (or at least, I've been told they tell us) that all dogs should have sex at least once in their lives to "settle them down." Forget it! Sex will not settle your Rottie down. On the contrary, it may just drive your precious pooch up the wall looking for more.

In fact, there are a lot of old wives' tales that dog owners accept as fact when the tales are, in reality, pure fiction. Knowing what makes your Rottie tick and how to keep that well-functioning clock in perfect order are important if you want your pal to live a long and healthy life.

One tale the old wives tell is worth paying attention to, and that's that an ounce of prevention is worth a pound of cure. That ounce keeps all those internal and external parasites at bay. Good grooming, good food and a sufficient amount of exercise are bottom-line basics that can keep your pal out of the veterinary hospital. You'll learn about all three in this section.

Accidents and illnesses are not always avoidable, so it is wise to be fully prepared at home and be on good terms with your Rottie's veterinarian. A good vet who knows your dog well can help both of you through all kinds of problems, from minor to disabling and chronic. By the time you finish this section, you'll probably feel equipped to star as a medic in your own TV series.

Chapter 9

The Rottweiler at a Glance

You have already spent a good deal of time boning up on what a good Rottweiler is and what it looks like. You shopped 'till you dropped and managed to find the perfect breeder, and you were lucky enough to be able to get the first perfect (well, at least near perfect) pup. Now that you and your little gangbuster have begun life together, you no doubt want to make sure all that time invested in finding the little tyke was not for naught, and that little Gretchen or Bruno will remain happy and healthy.

Through experience, your breeder was able to supply you with a healthy, well-socialized puppy. Keeping the pup that way is more about preventive maintenance than it is about anything else. By this time what you've learned about Rotties has moved you out of "complete idiot" status. Congratulations, you are no longer complete! And I do mean that only in the most positive sense of the word.

However, just so your veterinarian, or anyone else for that matter, will not think you are still among the unlearned, it's time you began to learn what the different parts of your dog's anatomy are called. Yes, this is your course in Rottweiler anatomy. (Don't worry, the course is designed for idiots, so you're not going to have to dissect a whole Rottie to figure out what's what and where it belongs.) After this introductory course you'll be able to call up your vet and say your boy injured his hock, rather than saying he has a boo-boo on that bump that's just above his foot.

Anatomy of the Rottweiler

Since we all know which end of the dog the nose is on, let's start there. What the nose is set into is called the *muzzle*.

The muzzle fits right into the *skull*, which is what holds the eyes and ears in place. Right at the top back of the skull you'll feel a fairly prominent ridge of bone. It corresponds to the little ridge of bone that is at the top back of your own skull. In dogs it is called the *occiput*.

Dog Talk

Should anyone ever ask why a dog has an **occiput**, just say in an offhand way, "Why that's needed for neck muscle attachment, of course." Be sure to add "of course." It makes you sound even smarter.

Right behind the occiput is the *crest of the neck*. It's where the neck begins. The part that follows the crest is the neck (of course!), and that runs down into the *shoulders*.

If you run your hand from the crest and down the neck, your hand will come to a stop at the *withers*. Lots of people call that point the top of the shoulders, but you'll sound very hip if you say, "Oh, you mean here, right at my dog's withers?"

After that, much like you and I, your Rottie has a back (of course). The line of the back, all the way to the end of the dog, is called the *topline*. The back extends clear on to the *hips*. Anatomy experts say only part of that is really the back on a dog, but we're not anatomy experts, so calling it the back is perfectly fine.

The area on the dog's side, between where the rib cage ends and the pelvis begins, is called the *loin*. The *croup* (it has nothing to do with what little human babies get) is the part of the body above the hind legs, and it extends from the loin to the base of the tail at the *buttocks*. Buttocks are buttocks—no matter who they're on.

Moving down, we have the *upper thigh*. It's that place that corresponds to your own thighs. (You know, that place on your legs that Suzanne Somers sold you that useless machine for!) The next area down is called the *lower thigh*, and below it is the *hock* joint. Next down from the hock is the rear *pastern*. (We'll get back to what pasterns are when we return to the front of the Rottie.)

Heading back up the rear leg, on its bottom side and between the upper and lower thigh we have the *stifle* joint. The stifle corresponds to our knee. (Again, your response should be, "Why that's the stifle," and then you add—you got it—"of course!")

The tail bone's connected to the . . .

That little claw-like thing near the bottom inside edge of the Rottie's leg is called a *dewclaw*. What it's got to do with dew is beyond me. Actually, it's an undeveloped toe that harks back to before the time

139

Gretchen and Bruno's ancestors had even become wolves. And that, my friends, is far back! Dewclaws grow on the front legs as well, but don't panic if your dog doesn't have any dewclaws. Most breeders remove them just a few days after the puppies are born.

Now we're up in front of the Rottie again. You know what feet are (of course!), so let's look at what sits just above the Rottie's front feet. It's the area between the foot and the wrist, and is called the *pastern*.

The *forearm* is the area between the wrist and the elbow. It hooks up to the *upper arm*, which connects to the bottom edge of the *shoulder blade*. And lo and behold we've come full circle and you have passed your Rottweiler Anatomy 101 course with flying colors!

Inherited Health Problems and Diseases

Like all breeds of domesticated dogs, including the mixed breeds, the Rottweiler has its share of hereditary problems. Fortunately, the problems are relatively few. And any genetic problems I'll describe here are far less apt to be present in the Rottweiler you buy from reputable breeders, because their stock is tested and rigidly selected to avoid these problems. These are complications that exist in the breed, however, and you should discuss them with the breeder before you purchase your dog. If you ever suspect symptoms of any of these problems, make an appointment to see your veterinarian without delay.

As stated previously, the reputable Rottweiler breeder is aware of genetic breed problems. Even though breeders constantly test and do their utmost to breed around inheritable problems, they're not God, and occasionally one of the following problems can arise in even the best-planned litter.

Dog Talk

When all the parts hang together correctly so the dog moves like one collected unit, the doggy set refers to this as being **sound**. When you watch your Rottie move around with strength and ease and its legs move directly forward with purpose, you can then say, "My, my, isn't he a sound looking Rottweiler!"

Hip Dysplasia

This is an orthopedic problem that affects most large and many smaller breeds of dogs. It is a malformation of the hip joints. It usually occurs unilaterally, meaning in both hips. Hip dysplasia can vary in degree, from the mildest form that is undetectable other than by X-ray, on through to extremely serious and painful cases that require surgery.

The normal hip can best be described as a ball and socket arrangement. The upper bone of the rear leg (the femur) has a head that should fit neatly and firmly into the socket of the pelvis. A well-knit ball and socket allows the femur to rotate freely within the socket, but it is held firmly in place. In a dog with hip dysplasia, the socket is shallow, allowing the femur head to slip and slide. The shallower the socket, the more sliding and the more it impairs movement and causes pain.

Dog Talk

Hip dysplasia is considered to be **polygenetic**. This means it is caused by the interaction of several genes, making it extremely hard to predict. Although it can be detected in the individual adult dog, only the law of averages reduces the occurrence when breeding individual dogs X-rayed clear of the problem.

Osteochondritis Dissecans

OCD is a condition in which the cartilage lining the bone surfaces in the shoulder joint, elbow or stifle and hock joints thickens until it enlarges and cracks. When that happens, the bone beneath it becomes inflamed and deteriorates. This lameness varies from an occasional limp to a chronic condition, depending on how much cartilage is affected. In Rottweilers it can occur more frequently in males. The area most commonly affected is the elbow, and this is referred to as elbow dysplasia.

Eye Problems

Rottweilers can be affected by any of several eye conditions:

➤ **Entropion.** The eyelids are turned inward so that the eyelashes constantly rub against and irritate the eyeball. Untreated, it can severely damage vision. A simple veterinary procedure can fully correct the condition.

➤ **Ectropian.** A condition of the eyelid that causes the lid to roll out and hang down, exposing the eyeball. The sagging eyelid forms a pocket that traps debris that constantly irritates the eye. This condition can also be corrected with surgery.

➤ **Progressive Retinal Atrophy (PRA) and Cataracts.** Both of these conditions are degenerative diseases of the eye that can lead to total blindness. Though not rampant in Rottweilers, cases have been reported. Tests conducted by a registered ophthalmologist can assure Rottie owners that their dogs have no concerns in this area.

Bet You Didn't Know

There is a misconception that wild and feral dogs, or dogs of mixed breeds, have no hereditary diseases or infirmities. This is entirely untrue. There are documented cases of both canines and felines captured in the wild who have shown evidence of developing eye and bone abnormalities. Untreated, the afflicted animals would perish. This only goes to prove that domesticated animals are not alone in developing genetic dysfunctions. The difference is that affected wild animals often don't survive long enough to breed. Do understand, though, that this does not eliminate the carriers of the disease.

Demodectic Mange

Demodectic mange is a form of skin infection caused by a parasite that lives in the hair follicles. Susceptibility is believed to be hereditary in some lines of the breed. Damage to the coat and skin varies to the degree it affects an individual dog. It can be extremely severe in dogs whose immune systems are weakened at puberty or by some diseases.

Bet You Didn't Know

We who control the breeding of our domesticated dogs are intent upon saving all the puppies in a litter. In preserving life we also perpetuate health problems. Our humanitarian proclivities thus have a downside as well. This has made genetic testing and screening an important part of all modern breeding programs.

Healthy, Wealthy and Wise

A well-bred and well-socialized Rottie will not only make you the envy of most dog owners, but it will also keep you from going to the poorhouse. Sick dogs are not only an unhappy situation, but they also cost money. If you don't believe me, just ask your veterinarian. Vets know better than anyone just who is helping them make the payments on their new Mercedes and the condo at the edge of the golf course.

Lawsuits arising from your dog taking a chunk out of some passerby are not exactly cheap, either. In this day and age, we have a lot of folks roaming around out there just waiting for something to happen so that they, too, can wind up with a Mercedes and a condo on the golf course.

You and your well-bred Rottie will share a relatively carefree life together if you give your pal reasonable care and lots of training and affection. With that all-important preventive maintenance you won't have to worry about renting space at the vet's office.

Checkups Can Stop Check Writing

We humans have medical insurance because we know how staggering those hospital bills can be without it. Your Rottie's medical bills may not be quite as high as your own, but they won't be cheap. A good many of the causes for expensive treatment could be prevented by

143

regular checkups. The old adage "An ounce of prevention is worth a pound of cure" certainly applies here.

Just because your Rottie doesn't have long hair doesn't mean you have no grooming to do. Regular brushing keeps the coat clean and healthy and helps keep down doggy odor. It also gives you an opportunity to check out each part of your dog's anatomy so that you can catch any problems early on. Chapter 11, "An Ounce of Prevention," deals in depth with each of the items on the following list.

A Healthy Rottie Checklist

Make it a habit to check all of the points here regularly. You can do it as part of your grooming session, or when you're just hanging around with your dog and cuddling.

- ❏ Check skin for eruptions

- ❏ Coat should be thick, lustrous and clean

- ❏ Ears should be clean without offensive odor

- ❏ Teeth should be white without accumulated tartar

- ❏ Eyes should be clear and bright with no discharge or irritation

- ❏ Nails should be short, with no cracks or ragged edges

- ❏ Check the rectal temperature whenever your dog appears out of sorts; normal is between 101.5° and 102°F

Word to the Wise

It's easy to forget looking at and into certain parts of your Rottie's anatomy as you go along through your busy life. A smart idea is to create a checklist containing all the things you should be looking for as you groom your dog. Post that where you groom your dog so that you can glance at it while you are brushing away.

To Breed or Not to Breed?

Ah yes, that is the question. My answer: Don't! Believe me, there is a great deal more to consider than the fun you might have with a half dozen or more chubby little Gretchenettes or Bruno Juniors wagging their stubby little tails at you.

The first thing you should do before you think further about the possibility of adding to the world's Rottweiler population is pay a visit to your local humane society or animal shelter. I don't know about your town, but there are thousands of purebred dogs in need of rescue all over the country. Unfortunately, a good percentage of them are Rottweilers. The American Humane Society reports approximately 15 million healthy and friendly dogs and cats were euthanized in 1998 alone. Many of them were born into good homes but obviously fell into the hands of irresponsible buyers.

Something else you have to give serious thought to is the suitability of Gretchen or Bruno for breeding. Not all Rotties, even though well bred, are suitable as breeding stock. If you discussed your breeding plans with the person from whom you purchased your dog, a responsible breeder will have undoubtedly selected a pup for you that was worthy of being bred. The operative word here, of course, is "worthy." Your Rottie may be the smartest fellow that has hit the boards since Lassie came home, he could be the most courageous and protective Rottie in town and the dog may love you beyond all reason, but none of these are sound reasons for producing offspring.

Watch Out!

When those cute little puppies start growing by leaps and bounds (none of them old enough to house-break!), getting them off to their new homes is going to be your top priority. That priority may interfere with your making absolutely positive that the person relieving you of your burden is the right person to own a Rottie.

If your dog's breeder sold the dog to you specifically as a pet, the person obviously had no desire to have it bred. You should respect that experienced person's wishes. If you are unable to get in touch with the breeder, or if you doubt the credentials of the person from whom you purchased your dog, do some research and find a local breeder who has the reputation for producing show-quality Rotties. This is the best person to advise you on whether or not your male or female should be bred.

Breeding requires a lot more thought and effort than simply putting two dogs together and letting nature take its course. (D. Gallegos)

Even if your Rottie is of the quality that warrants breeding, there are consequences that must be considered. Gretchen's litter can easily bring your dog population to eight or ten overnight. This can be great fun for the entire family for the first couple of weeks when the puppies spend their lives nursing and sleeping. But do note, I said for the first couple of weeks. The day will come very quickly when Gretchen will look at you as if to say, "Well, you wanted puppies—now take care of them!"

Bet You Didn't Know

All too often I hear people who have purchased purebred pets say, "Gretchen needs to have a litter to complete her development" or "Bruno needs a girlfriend to relieve his frustration." Believe me when I say neither Gretchen nor Bruno needs a sexual liaison to make their life complete. Actually, especially in the case of Bruno or any other male, breeding will serve to increase his frustration rather than relieve it.

It won't be long before the puppies will not only outgrow the whelping box, they'll outgrow the whole room! Then, too, they will have transferred their dependence upon mom to you and they will want to be with you *all the time*! Think back on the patience and work involved in housebreaking and training your single Rottie puppy. Now multiply that by eight or ten. Fun? I wonder!

Realize the commitment you will have to make to be on hand when weaning time comes. Newly weaned puppies need four meals a day. Will you or a responsible member of the family be on hand to feed morning, noon, evening and night?

We've talked about the need for properly socializing Rottie puppies. Not only will they object to being shunted off into the garage or the backyard, but it will do nothing for their temperaments. Rottie puppies must have continuous human contact from birth on if they are to achieve their potential as companions. Ask yourself if you are willing to give them all the time they need and deserve until you have found a responsible home for each puppy in the litter. This may take weeks, sometimes months. And that's after you have already decided it is time for the puppies to be off to their new homes.

Parents who want to have their young children experience "the miracle of birth" can do so by renting videos of all kinds of animals involved in this miracle. Handling the experience this way saves adding to pet overpopulation. In addition, all too often the miracle of birth is accompanied by the miracle of death. You cannot control what your children will see.

There is constant lobbying throughout America to restrict the rights of all dog owners and dog breeders because of the pet overpopulation problem and the unending need to destroy unwanted animals. Thoughtful dog owners will leave the breeding process to experienced individuals who have the facilities to keep all resulting offspring on their premises until suitable and responsible homes can be found.

Watch Out!

All too often, people are willing to commit to all the hard work and time involved in raising a litter of Rotties in anticipation of financial gain. Think again! Consider the cost of a stud fee and prenatal veterinary expenses, then add the cost of possible whelping problems, tail docking, health checks and the necessary inoculation series and food for the puppies. These will all put a very large dent in any anticipated profits.

Spaying and Neutering

Spaying or *neutering* will not change the personality of your pet and will help Gretchen and Bruno avoid many health and behavior

147

problems. Males that have not been altered have the natural instinct to lift their legs and urinate on objects to mark the territory in which they live. It can be extremely difficult to teach some unaltered males not to do this in your home. Then, too, not only does the unaltered male Rottie have the ongoing need to prove he's the toughest guy on the block, he also has a greater tendency to roam if there is a female in heat in the area.

Unaltered females will have two estrus cycles each year that are accompanied by a bloody discharge. There will be extensive soiling of the area in which she is allowed and, much more disastrous, she could become pregnant. Unspayed females also have a much higher risk of developing pyometra (a potentially deadly uterine infection) or mammary cancer later in life.

Dog Talk

Female dogs are **spayed**, which means removing the uterus and ovaries. Male dogs are **neutered**, which means removing the testicles.

It is important to understand that spaying and neutering are not reversible procedures. If you are considering the possibility of showing your Rottie, altered animals are not allowed to compete in American Kennel Club or United Kennel Club conformation dog shows. Altered dogs may, however, compete in all performance events except Beagle trials. (And you wouldn't enter your Rottie in a Beagle trial anyway.)

Looking for Dr. Dream Vet

There is no one who knows more about the best veterinarian for your Rottie puppy than the breeder from whom you purchased the pup. If you are fortunate enough to live in the same area, your problems are solved. You can continue right on with the vet who has known your puppy since birth.

Unfortunately, that may not be possible because of distance. And I do recommend that you have a veterinarian that you can get to in a hurry. As good as a veterinarian might be, if he or she lives hours away and you have an emergency situation, it may cost your dog's life.

Still, your breeder may be able to help by asking friends or fellow dog breeders in your area to provide recommendations. Your neighbors may be able to help you in this respect as well. Do check ahead though. It is even a good idea to pay the recommended veterinary hospital a visit before you bring your puppy home. Inspect the premises and discuss Rottweiler care with the vet. Some veterinarians have had little or no experience with Rotties and may even be intimidated by the prospect.

If the facility and the person you speak to meet your approval, make an appointment to take your puppy there for its first checkup and insist that you see the same veterinarian each time your dog pays a visit. Some clinics have several veterinarians in attendance and it becomes the luck of the draw as to who will see your Rottie. Don't let that happen.

Hospital visits can be traumatic enough for some dogs, and being treated by a complete stranger each time can only add to a dog's anxiety. On the other hand, if your dog seems to take a dislike to a particular vet, ask if there might be value in having someone else look at your dog. Some Rotties will take an instant like or dislike to someone and are not about to change their minds.

If your Rottie doesn't approve of anyone at the hospital, it may well be Gretchen or Bruno needs a personality adjustment. That's up to you, as no veterinarian should have to face being eaten alive while trying to be helpful.

The Least You Need to Know

➤ Being able to name the parts of your Rottie's anatomy can be extremely helpful when discussing possible problems with your veterinarian or breeder.

➤ Be aware of the genetic strengths and weaknesses of the Rottweiler as a breed.

➤ Regular grooming and a Healthy Rottie Checklist can save many trips to the veterinarian and many dollars in vet bills.

➤ A litter of Rottweiler puppies may be more than you have bargained for, so it is important to look before you leap.

➤ Spaying or neutering helps a lot and harms not at all.

➤ You should be as satisfied with your veterinarian as you are with your own doctor.

Chapter 10

Nutrition and Exercise

In This Chapter

➤ Let's look at dog food

➤ Nutrition needs for puppies, adults and seniors

➤ Special diets for special dogs

➤ Why exercise is important at all ages

➤ All about couch potatoes

There is no one answer to the question of what the best food is for your Rottie. I have spoken to successful Rottweiler breeders in many parts of the world, and each person seems to have their own "tried and true, absolutely the best, under no circumstances would I ever change" method. Probably the best answer to the question is, feed your dog what works best—not necessarily what the dog *likes* best, but what is most apt to keep the dog looking and acting the way a Rottweiler should.

Who can tell you which food that is? I sincerely recommend you consult with the breeder from whom you purchased your Rottie. I can only assume you decided upon that breeder because the adult dogs at their kennel were in fine fettle and the puppies in the litter you selected yours from were equally healthy. That means whatever your breeder has been doing works for the dogs he or she is breeding.

151

How Much Is Enough?

The correct amount of food to maintain a Rottie's optimum condition varies as much from dog to dog as it does from human to human. It is impossible to state any specific amount of food your dog should be given. Much depends upon the amount of exercise your dog is getting, which uses up the calories consumed. A Rottie that spends the entire day pounding the pavement doing police work needs considerably more food than the house dog whose exercise is limited to a leisurely walk around the block once a day. If there is a rule of thumb, I would say the correct amount of food for a normally active Rottie is the amount it will eat readily in about 15 minutes. What your dog does not eat in that length of time should be taken up and discarded. Leaving food out for extended periods of time can lead to erratic and finicky eating habits.

But here again, you need to use your common sense. Remember that the Rottie was originally bred to be a working dog—herding cattle, pulling carts or putting in a hard day at the Colosseum. Meals were of questionable nutritious value back then, but the quantities were undoubtedly large and probably were not served until after a long, grueling day's work. Today's Rottie has inherited the appetite of its ancestors, but may not get the exercise necessary to use up the calories consumed.

Word to the Wise

Today's Rottie has inherited the constitution of a combat hero, and an appetite to go with it, but many Rotties only burn enough calories to accommodate an office clerk. Rotties can gain weight very easily if their food intake is not controlled and they are not given sufficient exercise.

A way to determine whether or not your Rottie is receiving the right amount of food is to closely monitor the dog's condition. You should be able to feel (but not see) the ribs and backbone through a slight layer of muscle and fat.

Fresh water and a properly prepared balanced diet, containing all the essential nutrients in correct proportions, are all a healthy dog needs to be offered. If your Rottie will not eat the food offered, it is because it is either not hungry or does not feel well. If the former is the case, your dog will eat when it is hungry. If you suspect your Rottie is not well, an appointment with your veterinarian is definitely in order.

The Balancing Act

Dogs, whether Rottweilers or Chihuahuas, are carnivorous (meat-eating) animals, and while the vegetable content of your dog's diet should not be overlooked, a dog's physiology and anatomy are based upon eating animal protein. Protein and fat are absolutely essential in a dog's diet. The animal protein and fat your dog needs can be replaced by some vegetable proteins, but the amounts and the kind required necessitate a diet with some meat in it. Please don't try to force your dog to go against its nature. If you prefer a pet that eats no meat, consider a rabbit.

A great deal of research is conducted by manufacturers of the leading brands of dog food to determine the exact ratio of vitamins and minerals necessary to maintain your dog's well-being. Research teams have determined the ideal balance of minerals, protein, carbohydrates and trace elements a dog needs. There are so many excellent commercial dog foods available today that it seems a waste of time, effort and money to try to duplicate the nutritional content of these carefully thought-out products by cooking food from scratch. It is important, though, that you read dog food labels carefully or consult with your veterinarian, who will assist you in selecting the best moist or dry food for your Rottie.

You Get What You Pay For

Dog food manufacturing has become so sophisticated that it is now possible to buy food for dogs living almost any lifestyle from sedentary to highly active. This applies to both canned and dry foods, but like most other things in life, you get what you pay for. It costs the manufacturer more to produce a nutritionally balanced, high-quality food that is easily digested by a dog than it does to produce a brand that provides only marginal nutrition.

Whether canned or dry, look for a food in which the main ingredient is derived from meat, poultry or fish. Remember, you cannot purchase a top-quality dog food for the same price as one that lacks the

Bet You Didn't Know

By law, all dog food must list all the ingredients in descending order by weight. As in food for human consumption, the food's main ingredient is listed first, the next most prominent follows and so on down the line. A food in which meat or poultry appears first on the ingredients list is going to provide more canine nutrition per pound of food than one that lists a grain product as the leading ingredient. The diet based on meat or poultry will also cost more than a food whose primary content is inexpensive fillers, but you will need to feed your dog less of the meat-based product. In the end, the cheaper grain-based product is not really much of a savings, and the meat-based product is a lot better for your dog.

nutritional value you are looking for. In many cases, you will find your Rottie not only needs less of the better food, but there will be fewer feces to clean up as well.

Appearance Isn't Everything

Dog foods advertised and packaged to look like a steak or a block of cheese are done up that way to appeal to the dog owner, not the dog. Chances are the manufacturer used a lot of chemicals to make the food look that way. The better dog foods are not manufactured to resemble products that appeal to humans. Your dog could care less that a food looks like a juicy steak or a wedge of Wisconsin Cheddar. All Bruno and Gretchen care about is how their food smells and tastes. The "looks like" dog foods are manufactured that way to tempt you. So unless you do, in fact, plan to join your dog for dinner, don't waste your money.

Be careful of those canned or moist products that are advertised as having the look of "rich red beef," or the dry foods that are red in color. In most cases, the color is put there to appeal to you. It looks that way through the use of red dye. Dyes and chemical preservatives are no better for your dog than they are for you.

Feeding Through the Ages

Most manufacturers of premium dog food now produce special diets for weaning puppies, growth, maintenance, and overweight, underweight and older dogs. The calorie and nutritional content in these foods is adjusted to suit the particular needs a dog has at each period in its life.

It is very important to use the correctly formulated food for each of these stages of your dog's life. A food that is too rich can cause your dog just as many problems as one that is not rich enough. Read the labels on the can or box, study the promotional literature that is published by the manufacturer of the dog food you are considering and seek the advice of those who are experienced in raising Rottweilers.

Word to the Wise

A good red dye test is to place a small amount of the canned or dry food that you have moistened on a piece of white paper towel. Check the food in half an hour or so to see if there is any red staining on the towel. If there is, you can rest assured the color is there to appeal to your eye and not your dog's.

Rottweilers need different food formulas at different times in their lives. (Casa Ramon Kennels)

Feeding Puppies

A good puppy diet will consist of at least 20 percent protein, but protein is not the only nutrient essential for growth. Puppies also need fat. Fat has the calories that a puppy's little energy-burning furnace needs to keep it stoked. Fat also produces healthy skin and helps build resistance to disease. Animal fats should make up approximately 10 percent of the puppy diet.

Carbohydrates also supply energy and provide the bulk that is also a necessity in the Rottie puppy's diet. Potatoes, rice and even pasta are good sources of carbohydrate. Just be sure they are well cooked, because a young puppy won't be able to process them if they are not.

Puppy foods must also be easily digestible and contain all the important vitamins and minerals, including calcium and phosphorous. Calcium and phosphorous are extremely important for bone growth. They work in tandem to do their job, but they must be present in the right proportions to be effective. Be careful here though: Too little calcium can subject a young dog to bone deformities such as rickets; too much calcium is suspected of causing many of the bone diseases dog breeders are dealing with today.

A great deal of controversy surrounds the use of vitamin supplements for dogs. Many breeders believe that hereditary conditions are not entirely to blame for the high incidence of orthopedic problems modern dogs face. They suspect these problems are exacerbated by overuse of vitamin supplements. Their suspicions are not without merit, because most high-quality commercial dog foods are well balanced and highly fortified. Supplementation could easily throw that balance off and lead to growth problems. Before adding any supplement to the food you give your dog, discuss the product with both your dog's breeder and your veterinarian. If you do decide to use a supplement, never exceed the prescribed dosage.

All this should make it quite clear that cooking your own properly balanced dog food from scratch is something that requires a good deal of knowledge about nutrition. I sincerely advise talking to your breeder or veterinarian if your are thinking about adopting a feeding plan that is not based on a prepared top-quality and scientifically balanced commercial dog food.

Maintenance Diets

As dogs mature, their energy requirements decrease—I said decrease, not stop! If the dog is extremely active, whether the activity is fun or work, the dog will burn more calories than the same dog napping around the house all day long. Again, a well-balanced maintenance diet eliminates any complicated guesswork as to supplying all nutritional needs.

Feeding the Old Codger

As Bruno and Gretchen age, getting out of bed in the morning is no less difficult for them than it is for their aging owners. There is less activity and a slower metabolism, but like their aging owners, the elderly Rottie will probably still feel entitled to the same size food portions. A senior food will enable you to reduce the dog's caloric intake without reducing its rations.

Activity should be reduced in its intensity but should not be stopped. The old folks need exercise, albeit for shorter periods, but a nice long walk every day will keep them healthier and you'll see just how much they look forward to it.

Special Nutritional Needs

The diets I've described so far are those fed under normal circumstances as your little pup progresses from puppyhood to adulthood and eventually to old age. There are exceptions to the everyday rules, however, and at those times, diets must be adjusted accordingly.

> **Word to the Wise**
>
> Unfortunately, it is you who are going to have to steel yourself and start cutting back on the amount of food the old timer is being given. Fatty foods and gas-producing vegetables are no-nos at this point in their lives. Solid food, especially meat, should be chopped or ground so it is not swallowed in large chunks.

Chicken Soup for the Ailing Pooch

When your Rottie is under the weather, diet becomes a very important part of the recuperative process. Sick dogs need a diet that is low in carbohydrates but high in vitamins, minerals and fat. Rather than attempting to mix food on your own to accomplish this end, you are much better off speaking to your vet about a prescription diet that is specially formulated for this purpose.

There are other dogs that may have chronic gastrointestinal problems of various kinds that require an entirely different approach to nutrition. Normally speaking, dogs with conditions of this nature will need food that is easily digestible but low in fat. Here again, prescription diets are advised. As a general rule, it is best to speak to your veterinarian about foods if your Rottie is experiencing anything but optimum health.

What to Do for the Tubby One

Watch your Rottie's midsection. Dogs, young or old, don't become obese overnight. The excess weight comes on gradually, and your eye may accustom itself to the gradual gains so that nothing seems out of the ordinary. Periodic hops onto the scale will be very helpful for monitoring your dog's weight.

Gretchen and Bruno may seem fit as a fiddle, but I still strongly suggest twice-a-year visits to the vet's office for weight control and preventive maintenance. Most vet's have scales made especially for weighing animals and will automatically have your Rottie hop on as part of their normal office procedure. If your dog tips the scales way over, your vet can advise you on how much Gretchen or Bruno needs to lose and how you should go about seeing to the loss.

Word to the Wise

If your Rottie is not overeating and is getting sufficient exercise, there may be some other cause for the weight gain. Your vet should look into this.

There are commercial reducing diets available through your veterinarian that will keep the dieter satisfied but are low in calories. Their use will enable the dog to lose weight without the chubby one feeling you are running a concentration camp.

Shake Your Booties

So far we've done nothing but talk about what you must do for your Rottie. Now here's something your Rottie can do for you. It may not be something that tops your Christmas wish list, but like elementary school math, cod liver oil and church on Sunday, you will be a better person because of it. What could that possibly be? It's EXERCISE!

Exercise is something your Rottie needs, and it is also something that will improve your own health and state of mind. Fortunately, you do not have to become a marathon runner to give your Rottie the exercise it needs. Walking at a pace that lets your body know you are doing something more than just slogging along is a good pace for both you and the dog.

If improving your health isn't incentive enough to get you out and moving, think about exercise this way: It's a nonprescription mood relaxer for your dog. Although Rotties aren't classed among the high-strung breeds, remember their heritage: herding, carting, taking on all comers in the arena—all pursuits that required a higher than average energy level. That energy doesn't just go away because you'd like it to. It will be used in some way, and if you would prefer that Bruno does so by eating the sofa or taking down the wall paper, so be it. Most Rottie owners would prefer to have their dog use up the energy taking a good brisk walk, playing catch or bringing back a Frisbee.

Watch Out!

Rottweilers are susceptible to bloat (see Chapter 12). Both veterinarians and Rottweiler breeders caution against feeding immediately before or after strenuous exercise, as they believe it definitely can bring on this life-threatening condition.

Don't expect Gretchen or Bruno to get exercise on their own unless there's another dog around, and even then they probably won't be all that active after they emerge from puppy-hood. As maturity and then old age set in, you'll find Rotties become less and less inclined to be self-starters in the exercise department. However, if their lord and master (that's you, in case you forgot!) is involved, a Rottie of any age is ready, willing and able to enjoy outdoor activities. It is always best to supervise your Rottie's exercise, anyway; that way you'll be sure the dog is getting enough of the right kind.

Puppy Exercise

If you watch puppies at play with their littermates, you will see frequent but brief bouts of high-level activity. This is nearly always followed by a good long nap. Puppies need exercise, but only as much as they themselves want to get, and then they should be given ample time to rest.

Just as soon as you and your puppy master the collar and leash, the two of you can be off to explore the neighborhood and perhaps the nearby park. That is, of course, after all inoculations are up to date. This gives you both the exercise you need, and when you're out and about you'll be working on your tyke's socialization process as well.

Word to the Wise

Don't expect a baby pup to take a 10-mile hike. The smart pup will plunk its little rear down and refuse to budge, and you will have to tote it all the way back home. However, your pup may try and please you by trying to keep up and exert itself beyond what is reasonable. Remember: brief periods of exercise with lots of rest periods.

Adolescents and Healthy Adults

Once they're out of puppyhood, Bruno and Gretchen will probably be able to outwalk you any day of the week and still be up for some aerobics afterward. They'll also be ready for every conceivable game you can think up and will probably want to continue far longer than is good for either one of you.

Just as you should do for yourself, whenever you start on a new form of exercise for your Rottie, do so gradually and increase the duration very slowly. I don't think it is a good idea to start jogging with a young Rottie—at least not before the dog is at least 18 months of age. By then the bones and muscles have formed and strengthened to the point where the jarring involved will not do permanent damage.

If you live near a lake, most Rotties love to swim and there couldn't be any better exercise. Any place that is safe for you to swim will be safe for your Rottie as well. Please don't let your Rottie swim in a place you think is too dirty or too dangerous for you. If it is ocean swimming for the two of you, make sure you understand the dangers involved and are aware of the areas in which riptides and undercurrents prevail. Rotties that love the water can be too adventurous for their own good. Make sure you don't send your pal into a dangerous situation.

You must also be extremely careful in hot weather. Confine exercise periods to the early morning hours before temperatures rise or to the evening after temperatures drop down.

Most Rotties love to swim. (Powderhorn/ Wencrest Rottweilers)

Regardless of the dog's age, be sensitive to bone or joint injuries sustained while exercise or playing games. Always inspect sore or tender areas, and if they seem particularly painful for the dog, see your vet at once. Concrete walkways and stony paths can be hard on the Rottie's feet. Inspect your dog's foot pads for cuts and abrasions often if exercise takes place on cement.

Sixty-Five and Counting—Exercise for Seniors

Just because the old-timers have reached the twilight of their years doesn't mean they have to stop living! The older fellow will still enjoy taking those walks with you every day. Maybe Bruno won't be thrilled about heading outdoors on cold or blustery days, but when the weather is fair there is absolutely no reason why the two of you can't be out there taking a nice leisurely walk around the block or down to the park.

Don't push it, and I wouldn't be too hasty about throwing balls and Frisbees even though the old codger might think he's still capable of doing the 100-yard dash. Be kind and be careful with the old folks (human and canine), and they'll be with you for a long, long time.

All About Potatoes (the Couch Variety)

Maybe having your wardrobe reduced to a patch quilt or watching your furniture being redesigned by a bored Rottie doesn't bother you. Perhaps the fact that neither you nor your Rottie can bend over to touch your toes doesn't make you depressed. Then the two of you

161

will not have to be concerned about becoming couch potatoes. Just remember that neither one of you will live as long or as well as you might have.

Nature did not intend your dog to be a couch potato. (D. Gallagos)

Eating properly and maintaining a sensible exercise program will keep you both happier and healthier for a lot longer, but it is you who will have to design the menus and implement the exercise program. Gretchen and Bruno will be happy to help, but they won't be able to get you into your jogging shorts, nor can they cook. If you aren't up to thinking about your own health, think about your dog's welfare.

The Least You Need to Know

➤ Rotties have different nutritional needs as they grow from puppyhood to old age. It is important that calorie and protein levels are adjusted to accommodate each level.

➤ When it comes to dog food, you get what you pay for. A top-quality commercial diet will provide your dog with excellent nutrition.

➤ Special situations like obesity or recuperation from illness or surgery require special diets. It is best to discuss coping with these special feeding problems with your vet.

➤ Exercise is important for Rotties of all ages. It is important to remember, however, that each level of maturity requires different amounts and different levels of exercise intensity.

Chapter 11

An Ounce of Prevention

In this day of high medical costs, for both humans and animals, an ounce of prevention is most certainly worth a pound of cure. Pay attention to your Rottweiler and deal with problems as soon as they arise—before they become serious.

Rottweilers are, by and large, a healthy breed. Compared to a good number of other breeds, they are what can be referred to as low maintenance. This does not mean one can be negligent. Rottweilers are living, breathing creatures subject to various accidents and ailments as they progress from puppyhood into adulthood.

Inoculations

Vaccines introduce a minute amount of a specific disease into your dog's system so that the dog can build up an immune response to the disease. Subsequently, the dog will be able to ward off the disease,

163

should it be exposed at a later date. The appropriate age of your dog and the timing of the inoculations vary from region to region. Therefore, it is critical that you discuss this schedule with your own veterinarian on your dog's first visit.

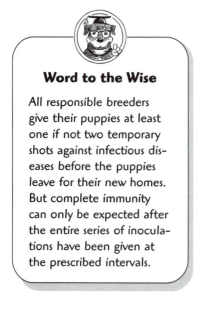

Word to the Wise

All responsible breeders give their puppies at least one if not two temporary shots against infectious diseases before the puppies leave for their new homes. But complete immunity can only be expected after the entire series of inoculations have been given at the prescribed intervals.

Diseases that once were fatal to many dogs are now very effectively dealt with through the use of vaccines. The danger of your Rottweiler being infected with distemper, hepatitis, hardpad, leptospirosis or the extremely virulent parvovirus is unlikely, just as long as the dog is properly inoculated and the recommended series of booster shots is given.

Cases of rabies among well-cared-for dogs are practically unheard of here in the United States. Still, dogs that come in contact with wild animals of any kind can be at risk if not properly immunized. Rats, squirrels, rabbits and many other small rodents can be encountered even by a city dog, and these pests have been known to carry rabies, so it is important to have your dog immunized no matter where you live.

On rare occasions, there are dogs that do not, for one reason or another, develop full immunity against infectious diseases. It is therefore important to be familiar with the signs of these illnesses, in case your Rottweiler is one of the few that are not completely immune and actually do develop the disease.

Canine Parvovirus

This is a particularly infectious gastrointestinal disease commonly called parvo. It can be contracted by direct contact or by being exposed to areas where infected dogs have been housed. Although dogs of all ages can be and are infected by parvo, this disease is particularly fatal to puppies.

Symptoms include acute diarrhea, often bloody, with yellow or gray colored stools. Soaring temperatures, sometimes as high as 106°, are not uncommon—particularly in puppies. Death can follow as quickly as one to three days after first symptoms appear. Early treatment is critical. If there is any suspicion of this disease, contact your veterinarian at once!

Canine Virus Distemper

An extremely high fever can be the first sign of this very serious and often fatal disease. Mortality among puppies and adults that have not been immunized is extremely high. Other signs may be loss of appetite, diarrhea and blood in the stools, followed by dehydration. Respiratory infections of all kinds are apt to accompany these conditions. Symptoms can appear as quickly as a week after exposure.

Hardpad

Considered to be a secondary infection, hardpad often accompanies distemper. A symptom is hardening of the pads of the dog's feet, but the virus eventually attacks the central nervous system, causing convulsions and encephalitis.

Infectious Canine Hepatitis

Infectious canine hepatitis is a liver infection of particularly extreme virulence. It is a different virus than the one that affects people, but it attacks some of the same organs. It eventually affects many other parts of the body with varying degrees of intensity, so that the infected dog can run the entire range of signs from watery eyes, listlessness and loss of appetite to violent trembling, labored breathing, vomiting and extreme thirst. Infection normally occurs through exposure to the urine of animals affected with the disease. Symptoms can appear within a week of exposure.

Word to the Wise

Most boarding kennels and training groups will not accept your dog if you cannot furnish copies of your dog's immunization record or if the inoculations are not up to date. This requirement is enforced to protect the kennel owner and the other dogs that are on their premises.

Leptospirosis

Leptospirosis is a bacterial disease contracted by direct exposure to the urine of an affected animal. Both wild and domestic animals can get leptospirosis, and it can be contracted by one animal simply sniffing a tree or bush on which an affected animal has urinated.

Lepto, as it is known, can be contagious to humans as well as animals and can be fatal to both. Rapidly fluctuating temperatures, total loss of maneuverability, bleeding gums and bloody diarrhea are all signs. The mortality rate is extremely high.

Leptospirosis is not prevalent in all sections of the country, so discuss this vaccination with your veterinarian—particularly if you intend to travel with your dog.

Rabies

Rabies infection normally occurs through a bite from an infected animal. All mammals are subject to infection. The rabies virus affects the central nervous system through inflammation of the spinal cord and central nervous system. Rabies symptoms may not be as quick to appear or as detectable as those of other diseases because they often resemble the symptoms of other, less virulent diseases. Withdrawal and personality change are common symptoms, as well as the myriad of symptoms associated with the other infectious diseases already described.

Watch Out!

Humans bitten by any animal suspected of being rabid should seek the advice of their personal physician at once. If your dog is bitten by a suspect animal, call your veterinarian without delay.

Kennel Cough

Kennel cough, or bordatella, while highly infectious is actually not a serious disease. It might be compared to a mild case of the flu in human beings. Infected dogs act and eat normally. The symptoms of the disease are far worse than the disease itself. Symptoms are particularly nerve-wracking because there is a persistent hacking cough that sounds as if the dog will surely bring up everything it has ever eaten!

The name of the disease is misleading in that suggests a dog must be exposed to a kennel environment in order to be infected. In reality, it can be easily passed on from one dog to another with even casual contact. In severe cases of kennel cough, antibiotics are sometimes prescribed in order to avoid secondary infections such as pneumonia.

An intranasal vaccine is available that provides immunity. This type of vaccination is advised for any dog that visits dog parks or is taken to a boarding kennel. In fact, most boarding kennels now insist upon proof of protection against kennel cough before they will accept a dog for boarding.

The Great Vaccination Debate

All over the world debates rage over whether a dog should or should not continue to receive annual inoculations against infectious diseases after the important first year. There are those who believe annual revaccinations are vital to a dog's health, and those who believe just as strongly that we are overvaccinating our dogs and doing them more harm than good. In the middle are those who think revaccination is a good idea, but it should be done less often—perhaps once every three years.

There appears strong evidence to substantiate all sides of the debate. Those opposed cite occurrences of chronic health problems, sterility and aborted litters as a result of over-administration of the vaccines. Those who oppose abolishing the annual shots argue that the number of negative reactions to annual vaccines is such a small percentage of the vaccinated population that the benefits far outweigh any small risks.

The problem is that nobody knows exactly how long immunity from a vaccine lasts in dogs. What we do know is that many of the infectious diseases (the distemper virus leading them all) ran rampant before these vaccines were developed. In many cases, contracting the diseases meant certain death.

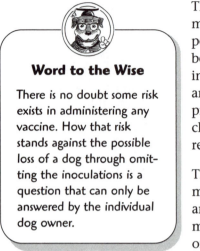

There does seem to be growing agreement that vaccines have a longer period of effectiveness than previously believed. It seems a two- or three-year interval between the first set of shots and revaccination is probably appropriate. Some cities and counties have changed their rabies vaccination requirements to reflect this trend.

There is also some debate about how many shots to give at once. Veterinarians have traditionally ganged up as many inoculations as possible into one shot. But this can be a big viral load for a dog to cope with all at once.

Most breeders recommend that the puppy owner wait as long as possible to give a rabies shot—up to one year of age if at all possible. Thereafter, give rabies inoculations as required, but never any less than two weeks before or after any other vaccine.

Many puppies are extremely sensitive to the five-, six- and seven-in-one vaccines using modified live virus. (This vaccine is known as DHLPP.) Some pups get very ill within two or three days of receiving the vaccines, or within a couple of weeks. In other cases, seizures and/or symptoms of hypothyroidism, liver and kidney problems and heart complications show up several years later. A good many breeders now recommend giving separate shots over a longer period of time. Discuss this with the breeder who sells you your puppy and insist your veterinarian follow those recommendations to the letter.

What Vaccinations Must You Give?

There are no legal requirements to vaccinate your dog against any of the communicable diseases other than rabies. The rabies vaccine is not without risk in isolated cases, but the possibility of a negative reaction is far outweighed by the consequences of contracting the disease. Rabies can be transmitted to humans and it can be fatal to us. It is always fatal to dogs.

It is extremely important that you keep your dog's rabies inoculations current and that you attach the tag issued by your veterinarian to your dog's collar. If your dog should ever bite someone, you must be able to offer proof of current rabies inoculation. If not, your dog may, by law, be held in quarantine for a considerable length of time. Again, rabies inoculations are not optional!

It is also extremely important to obtain a detailed record of the shots your puppy has been given and the dates upon which the shots were administered. Get this from the pup's breeder, or the shelter or rescue orga-

Watch Out!

If you know your dog is sensitive to the multi-vaccine shots, insist on seeing the vial containing the vaccine your veterinarian uses before the inoculation is given. Many owner's hearts have been broken and pocketbooks emptied because the veterinarian has cavalierly dismissed any concerns the dog's owner may have.

nization where you adopted your dog. This way, the veterinarian you choose will be able to continue with the appropriate inoculation series as needed.

Parasites

Potential parasitic invasions can take place both inside and outside your Rottweiler. As you will see, there is even at least one form of parasite that is both internal and external. Cleanliness, regular grooming and biannual stool examinations by your veterinarian can keep the infestations to a minimum, but do not be upset or surprised to find that even with your best efforts some of these nasty creatures will find their way into your home or inside your Rottie's skin or tummy.

The most common external parasites are fleas and ticks. The most common internal parasites are roundworms, tapeworms and heartworms. All three are best diagnosed and treated by your veterinarian. Great advances are constantly being made in dealing with all these parasites, and what used to be complicated, messy and time-consuming treatments have been replaced and/or simplified over the years.

Fleas

No matter how careful and fastidious you might be in the care of your Rottweiler, fleas can still be a problem. By just playing in the yard or even going on daily walks, your dog can bring fleas into your home. Once there, the little creatures multiply with amazing speed. Cats with outdoor access compound this already difficult problem by attracting fleas on their neighborhood patrols and bringing them back home on their fur.

Those of you who live in northern climates where there are heavy frosts and freezing temperatures have a winter respite from the flea problem, because fleas cannot survive these conditions. People who live in the warmer climates face the flea problem all year around.

Unfortunately, flea baths will not get rid of all the fleas. If you find even one flea on your dog, there are undoubtedly hundreds, perhaps thousands of them lurking in the carpeting and furniture throughout your home. The minute your Rottweiler completes its flea bath, the fleas are ready and able to return to their host.

Aside from the discomfort flea bites cause your dog, the severe scratching they induce can cause what are known as hot spots. Hot spots are created when a dog chews and scratches so hard that the skin is broken. If not attended to promptly, these sores can form moist, painful abscesses and all the hair surrounding the area falls out.

Bet You Didn't Know

Fleas also act as hosts for tapeworm eggs, carrying them wherever they go. When a dog swallows a flea (which happens often as the dog tries to get at the itching bite), the tapeworm eggs grow in the dog's intestines. Unfortunately, if your dog has fleas it will almost invariably have tapeworms.

After your home and dog have been infested, there is only one sure-fire way of eliminating the problem and keeping it in check. It takes a bit of planning, but is well worth the time:

1. Make an appointment for your Rottweiler to be given a flea bath by your veterinarian or a professional groomer. Most groomers use products that will completely rid your Rottie of fleas. Leave this bath to the professionals, who will make sure every part is washed safely and thoroughly.

2. While the dog is out being bathed, have a commercial pest-control service come to your home to get rid of all the fleas that are sitting around waiting for Gretchen and Bruno to return. If you bring your dog home before this is done, the fleas will be back on the dog within hours. The service will spray both the interior of your home and the surrounding property. Most of these companies guaranty the effectiveness of their work for several months.

3. The day *after* your Rottie comes home from its bath, apply an insect growth regulator. These new flea control products can be used monthly or year-round, and control fleas by stopping their reproduction cycle. The nice thing is that these products have no deadly effect on mammals at all. There are pills you can give your dog or liquids that are placed on the dog's skin between the shoulder blades. Administered regularly, these preventives are proving to be highly effective in keeping both fleas and ticks off of household pets.

Watch Out!

While home spraying is effective, there is a downside. Your home must be vacated and kept closed for at least a few hours after the spraying, and toxic chemicals are used for this operation. Some services are now using nontoxic sprays, and it is obviously to your advantage to seek them out.

Lice

Well-cared-for Rottweilers seldom have a problem with lice, because the parasites are spread by direct contact with other infested animals. A dog must spend time with another animal that has lice or be groomed with a contaminated brush or comb in order to be at risk.

If no fleas are present and you suspect lice, the dog must be bathed with an insecticide shampoo every week until the problem is taken care of. Lice live and breed exclusively on the dog itself, so it is not necessary to treat the dog's environment the way you must with fleas.

Ticks

If you live near a wooded area you are bound to run across at least the occasional tick. In fact, your Rottie can pick up these parasites just by running through grass or brush. Ticks are bloodsucking parasites that bury their heads firmly into a dog's skin. The ticks gorge themselves on the dog's blood and then find a dark little corner to raise a family. And family is an understatement—tick children arrive by the thousands!

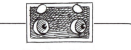

Watch Out!

Ticks represent a serious health hazard to both humans and other animals. In some areas they carry Lyme disease and Rocky Mountain spotted fever. The entire area where the dog lives must be aggressively treated against ticks with sprays and dips made especially for that purpose.

To remove a tick, first soak it with a tick removal solution that can be purchased at most larger pet supply shops. When the tick releases its grip, you can remove it with a pair of tweezers. It is important to make the tick loosen its grip before you attempt to remove it. Otherwise, the head may break off and remain lodged in the dog's skin, where it could cause a severe infection. After the tick is removed, swab the area with alcohol to avoid infection.

Do not flush the tick down the toilet, because it may survive the swim! Also do not crush it between your fingers, because that will expose you to whatever diseases the tick is carrying. The best way to get rid of a tick is to put it in a jar with a bit of alcohol and then screw the lid on tight. Dispose of it that way.

Always use latex gloves and tweezers to avoid the possibility of infecting yourself on the chance that the tick is a disease carrier. Wash your hands and any instruments you've used with alcohol as well. If you suspect your area to be infested with disease-carrying ticks, you can put the tick in a jar or plastic bag and take it to your vet to be tested.

Some of the same insect growth regulators that control fleas also do an excellent job of keeping ticks off your dog. I can attest to their effectiveness. We live at the edge of a huge forested track and my dog and I take hikes through the woods all the time. He comes home tick free, but more often than not I end up picking the little varmints off myself.

Mange

There are two kinds of mange—demodectic and sarcoptic. Both are caused by mites and must be treated by your veterinarian.

Demodectic mange (*Demonex canis*) is believed to be present on practically all dogs, and it generally does no harm. However, some dogs just seem to be sensitive to the little creatures, and this sensitivity may be inherited. About 1 percent of all dogs have problems with demodectic mange.

There are two forms of demodectic mange: local and general. Dogs affected locally may lose the hair around their eyes and in small patches on the chest and forelegs. This form of demodectic mange can be easily treated by a veterinarian. It must not be neglected, even if it seems very mild, because it can be uncomfortable for the dog and because on rare occasions the local form can develop into the more severe generalized form.

Word to the Wise

Although the word mange may strike a note of terror in the hearts of most people, there are several types of mange and only sarcoptic mange is communicable to humans. And sarcoptic mange responds well to treatment.

Sarcoptic mange (*Sarcoptes scabiei var canis*), also known as scabies, can be present over the entire dog. Symptoms include loss of hair on the legs and ears and often in patches over the entire body. Your veterinarian must do a skin scraping to identify the type of mange and prescribe treatment. Weekly bathing with medications especially formulated for this parasite can usually eliminate the problem. This type of mange is passed on by direct contact and is highly contagious.

Tapeworms

As I mentioned, tapeworms get into your dog when it swallows a flea. On an infested dog, you'll often see small rice-like segments of the worm crawling around the dog's anus or in the stool just after the dog has relieved itself. Periodic stool examinations done by your veterinarian can detect tapeworms even though you may not observe the segments yourself. There is an inoculation your vet can administer that quickly and completely eliminates the problem.

Heartworms

Heartworms are parasitic worms that take up residence in dogs' hearts, where they can do fatal damage. The worm is transmitted by mosquitoes that carry the worm larvae. Dogs are the mammals most commonly affected, and the condition is far more prevalent in warmer climates and areas with standing water. Blood tests can detect the presence of this worm, but it is difficult to treat.

Your veterinarian will know if heartworm is prevalent in your area. If it is, there are preventive medications you can give your dog that are safe and effective.

Whipworms and Hookworms

These two types of worms are shed in a dog's stool and can live for long periods in the soil. Both can attach themselves to the skin of humans as well as animals and eventually find their way to the lining of the intestines, where they burrow in. They are then seldom passed or seen. These two types of worms are only detected by microscopic examination of the stool, and each worm requires specific medication to ensure eradication.

Word to the Wise

Regular stool examinations by your veterinarian will keep your Rottie free of most worms. Testing for heartworms, however, requires a blood test.

Roundworms

Not an unusual condition, roundworms are seldom harmful to adult dogs. However, these parasites can be hazardous to the health of puppies if allowed to progress unchecked.

Roundworms are transmitted from mother to puppies, so responsible breeders make sure their females are free of worms before they are ever bred. Roundworms can sometimes be visible in a dog's stool, but are easily detected in a microscopic examination of a fresh stool sample. The coats of puppies affected by roundworms are usually dull looking, and the puppy itself is thin but has a potbelly.

Good Grooming for Health and Beauty

Now your Rottie is going to do you another favor: You're going to become a beautician! (Who would have thought?) Although you will never be as adept at the beautician's art as your Poodle-owning friends, there is enough to do to keep the average Rottie owner more than content.

Frequent grooming also gives you a chance to inspect the coat for the onset of any possible problems. Remember that Healthy Rottie Checklist I had you make back in Chapter 9, "The Rottweiler at a Glance"? Well, now you are going to have the opportunity to use it!

Bet You Didn't Know

The Rottweiler sheds its coat just like the longhaired breeds do. The fallen hair is just far less noticeable. Allow your Rottweiler to sleep on a white or light-colored sofa or chair regularly and you will be amazed at the amount of hair that leaves the Rottweiler's body in just a few day's time.

Brushing

Frequent brushing removes the old dead hair, cleans and massages the skin and allows the new hair to come in easily. A rubber curry comb is the ideal grooming aid for this project, and your Rottweiler will quickly learn to look forward to this regular "massage." A chamois cloth, which can be purchased at most hardware stores, can be used to finish off your brushing job and remove any stray loose hairs. This final touch will produce a high luster on your dog's coat.

Bet You Didn't Know

A grooming table that puts your dog at a comfortable working level will save your back and keep your dog still while you attend to it. These tables can be purchased from any pet supply dealer or can be built at home. Trying to groom your dog while it is standing on the ground is difficult at best, because the dog will be inclined to pull away from what it doesn't like and you will have to hang on with one hand while you work with the other. Sometimes you need to use both hands, particularly when clipping nails or cleaning teeth. Having the dog on a grooming table will help.

Brushing should always be done in the same direction as the hair grows. You should begin at the dog's head, brushing toward the tail and down the sides and legs. This procedure will loosen the dead hair and brush it off the dog.

Check the skin inside the thighs and armpits to see if those areas are dry or red. Artificial heat during winter months can dry out the skin and cause it to become chapped. Place a small amount of Vaseline or baby oil on the palms of your hands and rub your hands over the dry areas.

With regular grooming, your Rottweiler won't need a bath too often. (Beth Fitzgerald)

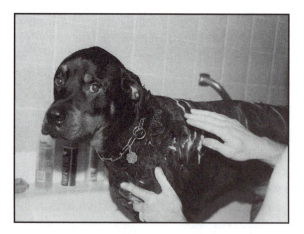

If brushing is attended to regularly, bathing will seldom be necessary unless Bruno or Gretchen have been off on a treasure hunt and found their way into something that leaves their coat with a nasty odor. Even then, there are many products, both dry and liquid, available at your local pet supply store that eliminate odors and leave the coat shiny and clean.

A damp wash cloth will put even the Rottweiler that has given itself a mud bath back in shape very quickly. Should your Rottie's coat become wet in cold weather, be sure to towel dry the dog thoroughly.

Ears

The Rottweiler's ears are very sensitive, and a sore ear can make an otherwise happy fellow cross and cranky. Keeping your dog's ears clean is a simple job, as long as you remember never to prod into the ear any further than you can see. Dampen a cotton swab with warm water, squeeze out any excess liquid, and clean out all the areas inside the ear that you can see. Be careful when you do this that you do not injure any of the delicate ear tissue. If you ever smell a foul odor emanating from the ear, schedule an appointment with your vet without delay.

Rottweilers have sensitive ears. Make sure you keep your dog's ears clean and dry.

Teeth

If your Rottie has regularly been given those big hard dog biscuits or large knuckle bones to chew on, chances are its teeth are in great

177

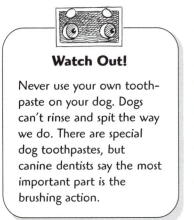

Watch Out!

Never use your own tooth-paste on your dog. Dogs can't rinse and spit the way we do. There are special dog toothpastes, but canine dentists say the most important part is the brushing action.

shape. Chewing helps keep tartar and plaque from forming. Buildup of either of these problems can cause extensive and permanent damage to the teeth and gums.

Don't laugh when I tell you to brush your Rottie's teeth. Doing so regularly can prevent tooth decay and the necessity of having your veterinarian take care of advanced cases under anesthesia.

How do you brush a Rottie's teeth? Just like you would your own. It's quite simple. Will your dog allow you to do so? But of course! Your dog is well trained, and you started this in puppyhood.

Eyes

If the eyes appear red and inflamed, check for foreign bodies such as dirt or seeds. Flushing the eyes using a bit of cotton with cool water or a sterile saline solution will usually eliminate foreign matter.

Should irritation persist and your dog's eyes remain red, or if off-colored mucous or a watery discharge is present, it could be a sign of entropion (described in Chapter 9) or conjunctivitis (an eye disease that is highly contagious). Both problems should be dealt with by your veterinarian.

Feet and Nails

Always inspect your Rottie's feet for cracked pads. Check between the toes for splinters and thorns. Pay particular attention to any swollen or tender areas. In many sections of the country there is a weed called a fishtail that has a barbed, hook-like end that carries its seed. This hook easily finds its way into a Rottie's foot or between its toes, and very quickly works its way deep into the dog's flesh. This quickly causes soreness and infection. It is best removed by your veterinarian before serious problems result.

To keep your Rottie's feet compact and well arched, it is necessary to trim the nails regularly. Long nails can cause your Rottie's feet to become flat and spread. This is unattractive, and the long nails can become deformed and cause a great deal of pain to the dog as well.

Do not allow the nails to become overgrown and then expect to easily cut them back. Each nail has a blood vessel running through the center called the quick. The quick grows close to the end of the nail and contains very sensitive nerve endings. If the nail is allowed to grow too long, it will be impossible to cut it back to a proper length without cutting into the quick. This causes sharp pain to the dog, and can result in a great deal of bleeding that can be very difficult to stop.

If your Rottweiler is getting plenty of exercise on cement or rough hard pavement, the nails may be sufficiently worn down. However, if the dog spends most of its time indoors or on grass when outdoors, the nails can grow long very quickly. They must then be trimmed with canine nail clippers, an electric nail grinder (also called a drumel) or a coarse file made expressly for that purpose. All three of these items can be purchased at major pet emporiums.

I prefer the electric nail grinder because it is so easy to control and completely avoids cutting into the quick. If you want to use a drumel, you must introduce your puppy to it at an early age. The instrument has a whining sound not unlike a dentist's drill. The noise, combined with the vibration of the sanding head on the nail, can take some getting used to, but most dogs I have used it on eventually accept it as one of life's trials. My dogs have never liked having their nails trimmed, no matter what device I used.

Word to the Wise

The Rottweiler's dark nails make it practically impossible to see where the quick ends, so regardless of which nail trimming device you use, you must proceed with caution and remove only a small portion of the nail at time.

Should the quick be nipped in the trimming process, there are any number of blood clotting products available at pet supply shops that will almost immediately stem the flow of blood. It is wise to have one of these products on hand in case there is a nail trimming accident or the dog breaks a nail on its own. In a pinch, a bit of cornstarch will do.

Anal Glands

The anal glands are located on each side of the anus. The scent they secrete identifies the individual dog. These glands can become blocked, causing extreme irritation and even abscesses in the more advanced cases.

While not a particularly pleasant part of grooming your dog, if regularly attended to, the glands will remain clear and relatively easy to deal with. Performing this function as part of the bath can be less awkward, for obvious reasons.

Word to the Wise

If you notice your Rottweiler pulling itself along the ground in a sitting position, you should check the anal glands. Contrary to popular belief, this habit is more apt to be the result of anal gland problems than of worms.

With one hand, place your thumb and forefinger on either side of the anal passage. Hold an absorbent cloth or a large wad of cotton over the anus with your other hand. Exert pressure to both sides of the anus with your thumb and forefinger and allow the fluid to eject into the cloth you are holding. The glands will empty quickly, so be prepared.

Should you be unsure of how to perform this procedure, or if your Rottweiler seems unusually sensitive in this area, it is best to seek the assistance of your veterinarian or a professional groomer.

Don't Forget!

It is not a bad idea to keep a record book alongside your grooming table to note any problems you observe. Just as soon as you note anything different in your Rottie's behavior or appearance, jot it down. If the situation develops into one that needs your vet's attention, record what the vet did. Should veterinary care be necessary again at a later date, you may be able assist in the diagnosis with the notes you have made in your dog's medical book.

Your Rottie should definitely have an annual checkup at the vet's office, and taking your book along to scan while you're waiting could prove invaluable in avoiding any problems. This book is a good place to keep your dog's veterinary health and inoculation records, as well. It will remind you which inoculations are due and the dates they should be given.

Most veterinarians keep computer records of their patients and automatically notify owners of necessary follow-up treatment, but computers are computers, and there are occasional glitches with the best of them. You should have your own record of when your dog needs heartworm and stool checks, or when booster inoculations are required.

The Least You Need to Know

➤ Although controversy surrounds the number of inoculations your Rottie should have, there is no doubt they are necessary to ward off disease.

➤ Rabies inoculations are required by law.

➤ Careful and thorough grooming will keep your Rottie healthy and out of the veterinary hospital.

➤ Record changes in your dog's behavior or condition, and if they continue, bring the symptoms to your vet's attention.

Chapter 12

When an Emergency Strikes

> **In This Chapter**
>
> ➤ Your emergency first-aid kit
>
> ➤ When to call the vet
>
> ➤ What to do in many common emergencies
>
> ➤ Getting your dog to take its medicine

No matter how careful you might be about keeping Gretchen or Bruno safe, dogs, like children, have an uncanny ability to get themselves into scrapes it would take a huge stretch of imagination to anticipate.

Then, too, accidents happen. We can be as careful as the day is long, but we can't protect our dogs from the world at large. Although veterinarians are there to help us when there is an emergency, there are times when immediate care is critical and you need to know what to do *before* you can get your dog to the vet. I hope you will never have to use home emergency care, but if it is needed, your dog's life could depend on whether or not you are prepared.

Your Own E.R.

In the table that follows, I've listed what I think are the basics for a well stocked home first-aid kit—for both you and your dog. Ask your vet for any additional recommendations about what should be a part of your home E.R. kit, because he or she may have a special device or product you (or I) may not have thought of. Do check the kit regularly to make sure that any liquids have not evaporated, medications have not expired and materials that may have been used are replaced.

Your Rottie's First-Aid Kit

Activated charcoal tablets

Adhesive tape (one- and two-inch widths)

Antibacterial ointment (for skin and eyes)

Antihistamine (approved by your vet for allergic reactions)

Bandages and dressing pads (gauze rolls, one- and two-inch widths)

Blanket (for moving an injured dog or warming)

Cotton balls

Diarrhea medicine

Dosing syringe

Eyewash

Emergency phone numbers (taped on the cover of the first-aid kit)

Hydrogen peroxide (3 percent solution)

Ipecac syrup (to induce vomiting)

Nylon stocking (to use as a muzzle)

Petroleum jelly

Pliers or tweezers (for removing of stings, barbs, quills)

Rectal thermometer

Rubber gloves

Rubbing alcohol

Scissors (preferably with rounded tips)

Tourniquet kit

Syringe (without needle, for administering oral medications)

Towel

Tweezers

White sock (to slip over an injured paw)

If there's an accident, your Rottweiler is relying on you to know what to do. (King)

If you have children, there is probably a list of emergency phone numbers already posted next to your telephone. Bruno or Gretchen are also your children, and if you haven't already done so, sit down and make out this important list today. You should include your regular veterinarian's phone number, along with that of the nearest 24-hour emergency veterinary hospital. The number of your local poison control center should be a part of this list as well. There is also a National Animal Poison Control Center. The phone number is inside the back cover of this book.

When to Call the Vet

There is one bit of advice that always applies in any case of your dog's illness or accident: If you are in doubt as to how to handle any health problem, do not hesitate to pick up the phone and consult your veterinarian. In most cases, your vet knows which questions to ask and will be able to determine whether or not it is necessary to see your dog.

If any of the following symptoms occur, get on the phone at once:

➤ Blood in the stool

➤ Limping, trembling or shaking

➤ Abscesses, lumps or swellings

185

➤ Dark or cloudy urine

➤ Difficult urination

➤ Loss of bowel or bladder control

➤ Gums appear deep red or white

➤ Persistent coughing or sneezing

➤ Loss or impairment of motor control

➤ Gasping for breath

➤ Chronic vomiting

➤ Chronic diarrhea

➤ Continued listlessness

➤ Loss of appetite

➤ Excessive thirst

➤ Runny nose

➤ Discharge from eyes or ears

Your veterinarian will be able to tell you what to watch for and whether or not you should bring the dog in. Sometimes these symptoms represent nothing more than minor ailments, but at other times they can mean your dog is at risk.

Word to the Wise

When in doubt, *always* call your vet. Waiting to see if symptoms get worse can be a very dangerous practice.

It seems all dogs ingest something at one time or another that can cause vomiting or diarrhea. This does not necessarily mean your dog is seriously ill. Dogs often purge their digestive tracts by eating grass to induce vomiting. Puppies will often vomit when they have eaten too much or too fast. Mother dogs that are attempting to wean their puppies will often eat and then regurgitate their food for the puppies. These are all common and harmless. But should either symptom persist, never hesitate to call your veterinarian.

Nervousness or fright can cause vomiting in some dogs and diarrhea in others. None of this is cause for alarm unless it occurs repeatedly. Occasional diarrhea is best treated by switching your dog's regular diet to thoroughly cooked rice with a very small amount of boiled chicken. Keep your dog on this diet until the condition improves, and then gradually add back your dog's regular food over a period of several days.

What to Do When You Need to Do It

You aren't a veterinarian, and what follows here is not meant to be a substitute for the knowledge and experience your own vet has spent a lifetime accumulating. There will be times, though, when know-how on your part can help prevent serious complications. There are also situations in which your intervention will keep your dog alive until you can get to your veterinary hospital.

These are basic lifesaving techniques every dog owner should know. Always exercise extreme care in dealing with very ill or injured animals. Don't forget where you and I use our hands in an automatic response to pain, a dog will use its mouth. That's why I'll start by telling you how to muzzle your dog.

Muzzling

Of course your Rottie loves you beyond all reason and would never think of biting you (on purpose!), but any animal can snap in reaction to pain. It's a smart idea to muzzle your dog when administering medical treatment. Get your Rottie accustomed to being muzzled now. You both could use the practice, and it will not make your dog think you are trying to kill it when and if the time comes that a muzzle is really needed.

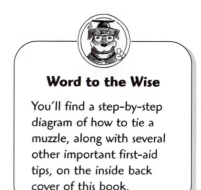

Word to the Wise

You'll find a step-by-step diagram of how to tie a muzzle, along with several other important first-aid tips, on the inside back cover of this book.

187

I use a discarded women's nylon stocking because it is strong and will not cut or irritate the dog's muzzle. Snugly wrap the center section of the stocking twice around the dog's muzzle. Do not wrap it so tight that you make the dog uncomfortable, but make it firm enough so that the dog cannot use its jaws to bite. Tie the two ends under the jaw, then draw them back behind the dog's ears and tie them there.

Moving an Injured Dog

Moving an injured dog the size of an adult Rottweiler can be a challenge, especially if you are alone. So start by trying to get someone to assist you. Lay the injured dog on a large bath towel or blanket. Then go open the car doors; you and your helper can then lift the blanket by the edges and transport the dog to the car.

If you are alone and cannot lift your dog by yourself, move the dog onto the blanket and drag the blanket along the ground until the dog is out of harm's way or until you reach your waiting vehicle. Hopefully, once you're out of the house you will be able to attract someone's attention to assist you when it comes to lifting the dog into the car. If not, do your best to move the dog into the car with as little disturbance as possible.

Burns

Minor burns can be treated by applying cold water or a cold compress. Use gauze pads to apply an antibiotic cream. Cover the burn with a gauze pad that can be held in place with an elastic bandage.

Serious burns or scalding need your veterinarian's attention at once. Cool down the burned area with very cool water or cover it with water-soaked towels.

Shock

Your dog may go into shock as a result of a burn or injury. If the dog is unconscious, check to be sure the airway is open. Clear secretions from the mouth with your fingers and a piece of cloth. Pull the tip of the tongue foreword beyond the front teeth to make it easier for the dog to breathe. Keep the dog's head lower than its body by placing a blanket beneath its hindquarters, and use another blanket to keep the dog warm on the way to the vet's office.

If the dog is not breathing, begin artificial respiration at once. To give a Rottweiler artificial respiration:

1. Place the dog on its side with its head low.

2. Close the mouth by clasping your hand around the muzzle (be careful that you do not cause the teeth to close over the tongue).

3. Place your mouth over the dog's nose, and blow into the dog's nostrils. The chest should expand.

4. Release your mouth to let the dog exhale.

5. Repeat so the dog gets 20 breaths per minute (one breath every three seconds).

6. Continue until the dog breathes on its own, or as long as the heart beats.

Watch Out!

Never practice artificial respiration on a dog that is breathing. You can hurt the dog.

Bites and Bleeding Wounds

If your Rottie is bleeding, you must attend to the wounds at once. If the flow of blood is not stemmed, your dog could bleed to death. Apply pressure directly to the bleeding point with a cotton pad or compress soaked in cold water. If bleeding continues, you must seek your veterinarian's advice by phone before transporting the dog.

Should your Rottweiler be bitten by another dog, get your dog to the vet without delay. Even the most minor bite wounds can get infected and should receive antibiotic treatment without delay.

Poisons

Always keep the telephone numbers of your local or national poison control center and the local 24-hour emergency veterinary hospital current and easily available. If you know or suspect what kind of poison your dog has ingested, give this information to the poison control center—they may be able to prescribe an immediate antidote.

Word to the Wise

Many apparently harmless substances can be extremely toxic to dogs. Chocolate, coffee and many decorative plants could easily take your dog's life. Read labels and discuss potentially harmful household items with your veterinarian.

When you speak to your vet, pass on any information the poison control center gives you.

If you are not sure if your dog has been poisoned or do not know which poison it ingested, be prepared to describe the symptoms you are observing to the poison control center or your veterinarian. Common symptoms of poisoning include paralysis, convulsions, tremors, diarrhea, vomiting and stomach cramps accompanied by howling, heavy breathing and whimpering.

Some Harmful Houseplants

Airplane plant	Mistletoe
Azalea	Mother in law's tongue
Caladium	Philodendron
Cyclamen	Poinsettia
Diffenbachia	Rhododendron
Foxglove	Spider plant
Holly	Yew
Jerusalem cherry	

Broken Bones

If you suspect your dog has broken a bone, it is extremely important that you remain calm. If not handled correctly and immediately, broken bones can cause fatal injuries. Panic on your part can upset your Rottweiler even further and cause it to thrash about, making matters even worse.

If your Rottie is unable to stand or if one of its legs is held at an unnatural angle, or if it reacts painfully to being touched, try to obtain assistance in moving the dog. This is particularly important if the dog was injured on the road. Make every effort to support the dog's body as much as possible. If a blanket or coat is available, slip this under the dog and move the injured animal the way I described on page 188.

Do not attempt to determine how serious the injuries may be. Often there is internal bleeding and damage that you are unable to detect. Get your dog to the veterinarian's office at once. If there is someone available to drive you and your dog to the veterinary hospital, all the better. That way you will then be able to devote your attention to keeping the dog calm and as immobile as possible.

Word to the Wise

You can create a temporary cast by forming a tube around the injured Rottie's leg with a magazine or a substantial section of the newspaper. Then wrap the tube with gauze bandage or adhesive tape.

Foreign Objects and Choking

All puppies and even adult dogs have a need to vacuum up every little object they find on the floor or out in the yard and get it into their mouths. It isn't the least bit unusual for all kinds of objects to get lodged or trapped across a dog's teeth, usually halfway back in the mouth or even where the two jaws hinge. If you see your Rottweiler pawing at its mouth or rubbing its jaws along the ground, check to see if there is something lodged in the dog's mouth.

If something is stuck there, grasp the object securely between your fingers and push firmly toward the back of the mouth where the teeth are wider apart. This normally dislodges the object. *Be sure to have a firm grip on the object so the dog does not swallow it!* If the object does not come loose immediately, get your Rottweiler to the veterinarian at once.

Word to the Wise

Whenever any small object is missing in the home and you suspect your Rottweiler has swallowed it, do not hesitate to consult your veterinarian. X-rays can normally reveal the "treasure" and save your dog's life.

If the object is not visible in the mouth, it may have already been swallowed. If it is still present in the dog's throat, the dog may be choking.

Wedge something like a screwdriver handle or similar object in the dog's mouth to keep the jaws open.

Pulling the tongue out should reveal any objects lodged at the back of the throat. If you see something, grasp the object firmly and pull it out (needle-nose pliers may be of use here). If the dog seems to be having trouble breathing, the object could be lodged in the windpipe. Sharp blows to the rib cage can help make the dog expel air from the lungs and expel the object as well.

Bloat

Gastric torsion or bloat can be fatal if it's not treated quickly. Drooling, pacing, panting and abdominal swelling are all signs of bloat. Do not attempt any home remedy without your veterinarian's immediate advice. In this situation, minutes count. Get on the phone at once. If you get a busy signal, call the operator and tell her you have an emergency call to put through.

Heatstroke

The temperature of a dog in heatstroke soars above the normal 100° to 102.5° and breathing is very rapid but shallow. It is critical to cool the dog down at once, either in a tub of cool water or with a garden hose. Place ice packs on the abdomen, head, neck and body. Cover the body with water cooled towels. Call your vet at once.

Watch Out!

The easiest way for a Rottie to get heatstroke is for the dog to be left in a car in hot weather. Anyone who is guilty of this should not have a dog!

Hypothermia

In northern climates a Rottweiler may be in danger of hypothermia, in which the dog's body temperature drops below normal. Even a few degrees could spell danger. With hypothermia, a dog's heart rate increases significantly and shivering sets in. Immersion in warm water or wrapping the dog in warmed blankets or heating pads will bring the dog's temperature back up to normal.

If the dog's mouth and tongue begin to turn blue, this is a sign that circulation is closing down. Warm the dog as much as possible and call your vet!

Stings and Bites

Rottweilers are forever curious and will give crawling and flying insects more attention than is wise. This often results in potentially very harmful stings and bites around the feet or, even worse, around the mouth and nose.

Visible stingers can be removed with a pair of tweezers. Once removed, apply a saline solution or mild antiseptic. If the swelling is severe, particularly inside the mouth, or if the dog appears to be in shock, consult your veterinarian at once.

Snake bites from poisonous snakes necessitate immediate action, as snake venom travels to the nerve centers very quickly. *Keep the dog quiet.* Venom spreads rapidly if the dog is active. Excitement, exercise and struggling increase the rate of absorption. If possible, carry the dog. Do not wash the wound, as this increases venom absorption. Do not apply ice, as this does not slow absorption and can damage tissue.

Since different snake venom requires different anti-venom, try to get a very good look at the snake and describe it to your vet in as much detail as you can.

Porcupine Quills

If your Rottie's nose has come up against the porcupine's defense system and you are unable to get your dog to a veterinarian, do your best to muzzle the dog before attempting to do anything else. Then cut the quills back to an inch or two and remove them with pliers, pulling them out with a straight outward motion. A vet's attention is important, even after you've removed the quills.

Skunks

If your suburban or country Rottweiler fashions itself a "great black hunter," it can easily come in contact with skunks. Your dog may not particularly enjoy its encounter with a skunk, but you will hate it! The odor is not exactly Calvin Klein's Obsession.

193

Bet You Didn't Know

Canine health insurance is offered to help owners with the cost of the new and expensive advances in veterinary procedures. The policies range from excellent to practically useless. As the Romans used to say, *caveat emptor*—let the buyer beware. Read the policies carefully and find out if the veterinarian you will be using honors such policies.

Even though a skunk encounter is not exactly a *medical* emergency, it is a situation that requires immediate action. There are many commercial products sold by pet emporiums that will eliminate the odor quickly and thoroughly. If you are unable to obtain one of these products when you need it, tomato juice is a handy and effective remedy. Spray the dog thoroughly with the juice, allowing it to remain on the coat for about 20 minutes. Then rinse it off and, if possible, allow the dog to dry in the sun.

Odor is not the only problem resulting from an encounter with a skunk. Reports of rabid skunks are alarmingly high, and skunks are not the least bit timid about defending themselves. If skunks are present in your area, or if you plan to take your dog to an area where skunks may be found, be sure your Rottie's rabies shots are up to date.

Take Your Medicine

Follow-up care often requires giving your dog some sort of medicine. If you think it's hard to get your 60-pound child to take his medicine, wait until you try it with your 100-pound Rottweiler! There are a few tricks that are handy to know.

Applying Medications and Ointments

If you can, ask for medications and ointments in tubes with nozzle applicators. These help aim the medication exactly where you want it to go, so you can make sure it finds its way into the eye or down the ear canal. This type of tube also helps get ointments into punctures or cuts. It is wise to muzzle your Rottweiler if you're applying an ointment that might sting or burn. The inside of a Rottweiler's ear is particularly sensitive, and applying medication there can sometimes be startling to the dog.

Time for Your Pill

While there are a number of ways to get a pill down your dog's throat, I have found the fine art of deception works best. I disguise the pill in a bit of the dog's favorite food or snack. While I certainly do not recommend sweets as a mainstay in your Rottie's diet, Mary Poppins' advice that "a spoonful of sugar makes the medicine go down" can be taken literally here: Rolling the pill up in a bit of soft candy or peanut butter can get the pill over the tongue and down the throat in a second and certainly beats trying to wrestle your friend into submission.

Cheese or tuna will work equally well if they are on your Rottweiler's top 10 treats list. I usually give my dogs a pill-free sample of the snack first to whet their appetite; this ensures the second treat containing the pill will be wolfed down in a second.

If trickery doesn't work, you may have to resort to manual insertion. Do this gently and whisper sweet nothings to your dog while you do so. Simply open your dog's mouth and place the pill at the back of the tongue. Close the mouth and tilt the dog's head upward until the pill is swallowed. To encourage swallowing, gently stroke your Rottie's throat. Once you see a gulp, you will know the pill is on its way to doing some good. Again, some dogs are very clever about this and have a way of swallowing without the pill going down. So watch your patient for a few minutes afterward to make sure the pill doesn't wind up on the floor.

Watch Out!

Putting medication in a dog's food dish and assuming it has been eaten is not a good idea. Many dogs have built-in detectors that can find a pill the size of a pin head. These same clever detectives also know just where to hide the pill so you won't find it for at least a week or two!

Liquid Medicines

Trying to put a spoonful of medicine into your Rottie's mouth can be a bigger chore than you might imagine, especially if the medicine has a taste your dog dislikes. A turkey baster (or a syringe minus the needle if there is only a small amount of liquid) can help you solve the problem easily.

It is best to shoot the medication into the side of the dog's mouth or under the tongue. Don't shoot any liquids directly into the throat, as the dog could easily choke. And if you are giving a large dose, administer it slowly and make sure you give your dog time to swallow.

The Least You Need to Know

➤ A fully stocked emergency first-aid kit can save your dog's life.

➤ All emergency numbers should be posted on your first-aid kit and should be clearly visible near the telephone.

➤ Knowing what to do and how to do it ahead of time will free you of becoming useless through panic if a real emergency occurs.

➤ Minor emergencies need your know-how and attention, too. Be prepared.

Chapter 13

Dealing with Chronic Health Problems

In This Chapter

➤ Managing chronic conditions

➤ Hip dysplasia and other bone disorders and skin conditions

➤ Eye problems

➤ The power of diet and exercise

➤ Alternative methods for pets

Responsible breeders do everything in their power to purge their breeding stock of genetic disorders. Concerned buyers seek out these breeders to avoid problems, and yet, through no one's fault, dogs from the very best of bloodlines can develop chronic health problems.

When that happens, finding someone to blame is not the point. You must find a way to either correct the problem or learn how to deal with it so that the dog can enjoy a long life that is as pain-free as you can possibly make it.

Living with Chronic Conditions

Many dogs with chronic health problems can still live long, happy lives. A little bit of work and a lot of patience on your part will go a long way toward making sure your dog has the best life possible. Sometimes it's just a matter of adjusting the dog's diet or exercise regime, or finding the dog a softer or warmer spot to be comfortable. Sometimes you'll be called upon to do some medical management as well, but this is often simple stuff: using a cream or ointment, or making sure your dog takes medication regularly.

Watch Out!

Although we want our pup-pies to be suitably plump, they should never be sloppy fat. You are not being cruel by controlling the amount of food you give your Rottie. Excess poundage weighs heavily on the mus-cles and skeleton of your dog and can lead to serious chronic conditions.

Hip Dysplasia

As I mentioned in Chapter 9, hip dys-plasia is of such a complicated genetic nature that even the most dis-criminating breeder will have to deal with it on occasion. The problem cannot be detected in very young puppies, but as a puppy grows, partic-ularly during the accelerated growth period that takes place between three and nine months of age, the condi-tion begins to manifest itself.

Symptoms can be so minor as to be undetectable without an X-ray exami-nation. On the other hand, hip dys-plasia can affect movement from a mild degree on through to crippling the dog. If any problem is sus-pected, the dog should be X-rayed and the results interpreted by a veterinarian who is trained in identifying this problem.

In some cases, symptoms seem more apparent while the dog is grow-ing and may diminish upon maturity. The degree of dysplasia and how much it affects the dog will determine what must be done to keep the dog from unnecessary discomfort. Mild cases may only require rest, restricting high-intensity exercise and weight control. Serious and debilitating cases may require surgery. Only your veteri-narian can make this determination, but rest assured, there are ways of coping with hip dysplasia.

Bone Disorders

Many large and giant breeds, including Rottweilers, are susceptible to bone and joint diseases that can be traced to nutritional, environmental or hereditary factors. Still others are brought about by physical stress or accident.

Because these bone and joint disorders can stem from such a wide range of causes, limping or painful areas should be observed closely. If they persist for more than a day, confine your dog and consult your veterinarian at once. A veterinarian's diagnosis is critical, because treatment—ranging from prescribed medication to physical therapy—could prevent permanent damage.

Eye Problems

Entropion and ectropion are best dealt with by corrective eye surgery. Veterinarians experienced in dealing surgically with these problems can entirely eliminate the conditions. It should be understood that surgery to correct these problems means the dog cannot be shown in AKC conformation dog shows—the rules bar any dog that has had surgery that alters its appearance. However, these are painful eye conditions, and there should be no question that a humane owner would choose corrective surgery over a show career. The AKC's stipulation applies only to conformation show events and does not restrict the dog from competing in any AKC performance events.

Word to the Wise

It's always important to have a good relationship with a veterinarian you know and trust. But that's especially true when you have a dog with a chronic health problem.

Conjunctivitis occurs when airborne debris such as pollen and dust, and even smoke and bacteria, create an inflammation of the membrane that covers the inner surface of the eyelid—the conjunctiva. The condition causes inflammation and tearing, and in advanced cases a sensitivity to light. Conjunctivitis can normally be cleared up by removing the airborne cause of the infection and medicating the eye. There is one particular type called follicular conjunctivitis that can be resistant to medication and may require surgery.

Cataracts are a degenerative condition of the part of the eye directly behind the pupil. The pupil then becomes either fully or partially opaque, giving it a milky white or blue color. The condition is not at all uncommon among older dogs, and it can also be caused by an injury to the eye. In advanced cases, cataracts can cause blindness.

Cataracts normally progress very slowly, so if they first appear in an elderly dog the dog may live out its entire life with only a minimal loss of vision. There is a form called juvenile cataracts that is hereditary, but it is seldom found in Rottweilers. When juvenile cataracts are present, the problem can be observed in puppies often immediately after the eyes first open. There is little that can be done for cataracts other than highly skilled and expensive surgery.

Skin Disorders

As with bone disorders, the causes of skin disorders can run the gamut, from hereditary allergies to infections, parasites and hormonal imbalances. Veterinarians have done extensive research into all of these areas, and while control can be involved and expensive, advances are made each year that can relieve you and your suffering Rottie from having a skin disorder run rampant with no hope of cure.

Usually the first time you will suspect a skin disorder is when Bruno or Gretchen starts scratching. Within days the dog may be scratching so often and so severely that parts of the coat will be scratched away. Check the skin in the area that is being scratched and in the areas that are harder for the dog to get at as well.

If your Rottie has this extreme sensitivity, it is absolutely essential to be especially diligent about keeping your home and property flea free. Your veterinarian will be able to recommend the products best suited to the flea-sensitive Rottie.

Lice and mange were what you were cautioned to look for back in Chapter 11. Actually, lice infestation is far easier to deal with than is

Word to the Wise

Any signs of skin eruptions, puffiness or irritation should be cause for concern. Some dogs are extremely sensitive to fleas, and at the first flea bite the dog will begin scratching so furiously that the skin will be damaged, bringing about the onset of chronic flea dermatitis.

commonly believed. Since lice only exist on your dog, you don't have the problem of reinfestation from insects in the environment unless there is actual contact with another host animal.

Bet You Didn't Know

Aging changes the quality and texture of the geriatric dog's skin. The skin of an older dog is far more sensitive to attacks from fleas, lice and ticks. It is important to be even more judicious about keeping your veteran Rottie's coat clean and well brushed. Your veterinarian may recommend a change in diet or adding diet supplements to help keep the aging Rottie's skin and coat healthy.

Mange, on the other hand, is not quite so easily dealt with. Demodectic mange is usually relatively mild, with minor hair loss only in isolated spots. There is a slightly rarer and more severe form of demodectic mange, but only your vet can determine the difference through microscopic examination of a skin scraping.

Sarcoptic mange is easier to recognize because it is extremely irritating to the dog and usually causes severe scratching. In some cases the scratching is so extreme that bloody lesions appear. These lesions form scabs and large areas of the dog's coat are shed. In extreme cases of this nature the skin can be permanently damaged. Sarcoptic mange is highly contagious and can infect both humans and other dogs. Like demodectic mange, it can only be diagnosed by microscopic examination of a skin scraping. Medicated baths, orally administered medications or injections may be prescribed.

Bloat

Most large dog breeds are susceptible to bloat. This is the condition in which the stomach twists and closes off, filling with gas. If not treated by a veterinarian at once, it is nearly always fatal. In many cases, surgery can save the dog's life. Surgeons can also reduce the possibility of the condition reoccurring by securing the stomach in a safe position.

Watch Out!

Signs of bloat vary, but any rapid distension of the stomach should be looked on with suspicion. If your Rottie appears extremely restless and unable to settle down and get comfortable, or attempts to vomit and cannot, call your vet at once! Bloat gets very serious quickly.

Dogs that have had bloat once are susceptible to it again. While the causes of bloat are poorly understood, it is generally accepted that feeding a dog more frequent, smaller meals helps. Avoid feeding right after the dog has exercised, and avoid strenuous exercise after eating as well. The dog should not be allowed to drink water after eating a large meal of dry kibble, either.

An Ounce of Prevention

What you've been learning and doing with your Rottie thus far is exactly what will help stave off infectious diseases and parasitic conditions that drain your pal's immune system. Regular visits to your vet from the first days your pup became a member of your family can help preclude the possibility of minor ailments becoming major illnesses.

Word to the Wise

Even though your Rottie appears to be fit as a fiddle, don't neglect those semi-annual health checks by your vet. It may seem like an unnecessary expense when there doesn't appear to be any problem, but rest assured that preventing the onset of problems is incredibly less expensive than curing them.

Vaccinations in their proper doses and frequency will protect your Rottie against canine distemper, parvovirus, hepatitis, leptospirosis and rabies. There are medications and products that will help your dog ward off kennel cough and parasitic complications.

Spaying and neutering will also help keep your Rottie healthy. A spayed female has a much lower risk of tumors and vaginal infections, and no risk of uterine infection. Male dogs benefit by a reduction of prostate problems as they grow older.

The Power of Diet and Exercise

In the 1990s the fitness craze attacked America with a vengeance. Bruno and Gretchen's owners ran here, jogged there, leaped and soared to the disco beat at aerobics classes and worked themselves into a lather at health clubs and spas. Vegetarian, or at least low-fat diets, became the rage. Then, too, Generation X discovered water, or at least discovered that water is necessary to keep the system flushed and healthy. Fortunes have been spent on drinking water that was reputed to have been ladled and bottled by native women from springs tumbling down the mountainsides of the Third World.

All this was done in hopes of capturing eternal youth, or at least staving off some of the ravages of time. One would think this new-found obsession would have given us all a clue that our canine friends would benefit from nutritional food and sufficient exercise, as well.

A good diet and plenty of exercise will go a long way toward keeping your Rottie healthy. (Rick Beauchamp)

Unfortunately, the message about dogs took a bit of time to sink in. But once it did, it was embraced with a typical American passion. Dog owners scurried off to health food stores and pet specialty shops to find the foods and supplements that duplicated their own health regimes.

Bet You Didn't Know

Exercise for you and your Rottie does not have to be restricted to endless (and boring!) gallops around the block. There are all kinds of activities a Rottie is suitable for and that the both of you could actually enjoy. Rotties are great swimmers, and many have demonstrated outstanding hunting ability. Any Rottie is capable and willing to hike as far as its owner cares to go. Every child in the neighborhood will be a ready volunteer to sit in a cart pulled by your Rottie, and when it comes to games, there aren't many breeds that do a better job at agility, flyball and Frisbee. Exercise can and should be fun for the both of you.

Poor Gretchen and Bruno got yanked off their favorite sofa and hauled off on a dead run up and down city streets. Good? Well, to a point. Some of the things that apply to humans apply to dogs as well, but only some.

Yes, dogs need a nutritional diet. It is important to remember, however, that dogs need a diet based on animal protein. And as I discussed in Chapter 10, "Nutrition and Exercise," commercial dog food manufacturers have given serious consideration to the other nutritional needs of the canine population as well. Good commercially produced pet foods are highly fortified and do not require additional supplements unless recommended by a veterinarian.

As we've already learned, your Rottie's genetic makeup provides the dog with a great capacity to work. Along with that capacity comes a corresponding appetite for work. Sufficient exercise satisfies both of these inherited predispositions. Exercise helps a Rottie use up that energy, and this in turn enables the dog to eat more than the dog who lounges on the sofa all day, without gaining weight.

Like you, your Rottie will benefit from exercise. And like you, a sedentary Rottie can not plunge headlong into an intense exercise program without danger of serious injury. Any exercise program, regardless of how beneficial, must be entered into gradually, extending the length and intensity in small increments.

204

Gretchen and Bruno can be your jogging partner, but not until they've reached maturity. Before 18 months, their bones and joints are not fully developed and the skeletal pounding their young bodies receive in an extended jogging regime can result in permanent damage.

This is not to say growing Rotties need no exercise. On the contrary, exercise for the youngsters is extremely important. But exercise periods should be brief and always followed by the opportunity for the young Rottie to rest.

Dogs in general, and particularly Rottweilers, are not cursed by heart attacks the way humans are. Still, no dog needs a sluggish heart. Hearts, human and canine, are the body's life-sustaining pumps, and keeping those pumps strong and active can only serve to keep all bodily functions operating successfully.

Proper nutrition and sufficient exercise help keep your Rottie's immune system in tune as well. Not everyone takes care of their dog as well as you do, so there are infectious diseases out there that your dog must ward off. Staying fit and trim will help Gretchen and Bruno do so.

Bet You Didn't Know

Most dogs are obese simply because they are given too much food and not enough exercise. There are, however, disorders that can be contributing factors. It is always best to work closely with your veterinarian when it comes to reducing the weight of an obese dog. Tests can be conducted to determine if the problem is simply based on an unhealthy lifestyle, or if it has been complicated by thyroid problems or diabetes.

Herbs and Homeopathy

It only makes sense that America's interest in a natural way to maintain health through diet and exercise would be accompanied by a fascination with nature's own way to restore fading health with natural remedies. A realization that many of modern science's drugs are derivatives or chemical simulations of plants and herbs found in nature created interest in the fields known as herbal and homeopathic medicine.

It has become quite clear that conventional medicine is not the only way to ward off chronic problems. Natural medication, as practiced by people all over the world for many centuries, and in many cases by our own grandparents, was found to have many of the healing properties and in a good many fewer of the side effects of artificially created medications.

Word to the Wise

Medicinal herbal teas are excellent for dogs because they are quickly and easily assimilated into the system and they can be added to your dog's food or, in some cases, to the dog's drinking water.

Watch Out!

With herbal remedies, do not assume what works for humans will also work for dogs. This is not always the case. Even though your Rottie may weigh as much as you do and may be suffering from the same or a similar malady as you are, the canine system operates much differently than that of a human.

Herbs have been used effectively for centuries and are now the basis for what is popularly referred to as herbal therapy. Scientific research has revealed there is certainly no mystery involved in their effectiveness and, when properly prescribed and administered, there is no risk involved. The operative words here, of course, are "properly prescribed and administered."

If you have found herbal remedies effective for yourself and wish to consider this alternative approach for your dog, it is very important that you consult a trained and experienced herbalist. Be careful here, however. This person is probably not a veterinarian. More and more veterinarians are using herbal remedies in their practices, but if you cannot find a veterinarian who does, I strongly suggest that you consider working with an herbalist and a veterinarian in tandem. Most vets are willing to work along with a herbalist. If, on the other hand, your Rottie has been under treatment with a veterinarian who does not feel comfortable with the use of herbs, it will be up to you to decide what the next step should be.

At the very least, only work with an herbalist who has extensive experience treating dogs. A human-trained herbalist will be able to suggest what works best for the problem at hand, but only a practitioner who knows dogs can ascertain whether the herb is canine safe. Then, too, your Rottie may already be on a prescription medication, and a veterinarian's scientific knowledge can assist you in deciding if the herbal recommendation and the prescription medication are safe to be used together. If they're not, it is up to you to decide which approach to use.

More and more reports are being published of successful use of herbal therapy in treating chronic skin conditions that were totally resistant to all other approaches. Owners whose dogs were suffering from rheumatoid arthritis report significant results through herbal therapy, as well. Holistic veterinarians are rapidly dispelling the belief that canine arthritis is only treatable and not curable. Changes in diet and the use of natural nutritional supplements are proving safe and effective and are allowing dogs to return to the natural flexibility and athleticism of their younger days.

Watch Out!

Because there are no regulatory controls placed on herbs and herbal remedies, strengths and required dosages will vary from product to product. Be extremely careful in this respect and never administer any herbal treatment that does not have the product's strength clearly printed on the container.

Recent studies have also revealed there are herbs that offer marked improvement in a dog's memory, in scent work and in reducing stress. Herbs are also being credited with improving general health and well-being.

Homeopathy

Although homeopathy may appear to be a product of New Age thought, it is far from being news. The basic principles can be traced to the ancient Greeks, but it is Dr. Samuel Hahnemann (1755–1843) who is credited as the father of the modern homeopathic approach to health care. Medical practices in his day were undoubtedly the reason why the old saw, "If this doesn't kill you it will surely cure you" was coined. Treatment was absolutely barbaric, using cutting, hacking, bloodletting and violent poisons, even when the patient was doing all he or she could to cling to life.

Bet You Didn't Know

There are now several organizations devoted to holistic veterinary medicine. If you call, they will be happy to help you find a practitioner in your area.

Academy of Veterinary Homeopathy, (305) 652-1590

American Holistic Veterinary Medical Association, (410) 569-0795

American Veterinary Chiropractic Association, (309) 658-2920

International Association for Veterinary Homeopathy, (770) 516-5954

International Veterinary Acupuncture Society, (303) 682-1167

Medicine in those days dealt solely with the symptoms of a disease. Even if the patient survived the often savage treatment of those symptoms, the cause remained untreated and reoccurrence was almost assured. Hahnemann believed symptoms are simply a sign that something is not working properly within the person's system. He set about trying to find a more sensible approach to dealing with the symptoms by seeking the source of the problem.

Hahnemann also felt that the best healer is the person's own system. It was his belief that if he could encourage the body to heal itself, permanent cures were possible.

To better understand how homeopathic medicine differs from conventional medicine (called allopathic medicine), let's use Bruno's skin rash as an example. The homeopathic approach would consider Bruno's skin rash as a manifestation of a much deeper problem. Thus, finding the internal cause and treating it would be the homeopathic practitioner's approach. Perhaps the underlying cause is an unhealthy immune system (allergies, for example). Then the homeopath would seek to help the body heal its inappropriate immune response. The allopathic or conventional practitioner would determine what kind of rash Bruno was suffering from and prescribe treatment to eliminate the rash. If the prescribed ointment or pill did not eliminate the rash, tests would be conducted to determine what external substances were causing the rash. Attempts would then be made to eliminate the substance from Bruno's environment.

Believe me, this is about as simplistic a comparison of the two approaches as one could possibly offer, but since this tome is by and for those of us with little or no medical background, I have made every effort to keep the explanation as simple as possible.

The two approaches do not necessarily conflict. In fact, the two move closer together as the years pass and as modern medicine more fully understands the value of the holistic approach. There is little doubt that in the future both views will be able to modify and assist each other in bringing about what is referred to as complementary medicine, and thereby bring about even greater medical advances.

Word to the Wise

It is important to be very careful in seeking out a homeopathic practitioner. Anyone can call themselves a homeopath, but not everyone call themselves a homeopathic veterinarian. To call oneself a veterinarian of any kind, the person must have a proper degree: Doctor of Veterinary Medicine (D.V.M.) or Veterinary Medical Doctor (V.M.D.).

Work That Body!

Acupuncture, acupressure, chiropractic, meridian therapy and massage—am I serious? For dogs? You betcha! These bodywork therapies are becoming increasingly popular with pet owners, and more and more practitioners are becoming available across the country. In fact, therapies like acupuncture work especially well for chronic conditions—conditions where conventional medicine works less well.

If old Doc Hahnemann was correct and our systems are regulated by a Vital Force, it would follow that we have to keep that Force flowing to all parts of the body. Right? Of course, right! That is exactly what bodywork therapies are all about: keeping the channels open so the Force can indeed be with us in every little nook and cranny of our bodies.

Acupuncture and Acupressure

The ancient Chinese practices of acupuncture and acupressure are proven methods of relieving pain and eliminating chronic conditions by using very thin needles or the fingers to stimulate specific points of the body. Weird, spooky? Not so. Modern science has found that needles or pressure applied help release corrective biochemicals within the system and also help realign the body's natural energy flows. When the channels are open the corrective substances are able to reach the injured or ailing points.

Chiropractic

This alternative approach to injury relief has been effectively used on human patients for many years, but only recently has it been found to be an effective and valuable tool in veterinary medicine. In this therapy, the careful manipulation of joints, bones and the surrounding tissues realigns the body and releases energy flows through the nerves and spinal cord to the affected areas.

Massage

Massage therapy is aimed at relieving tension in your dog's muscles and soft tissues. It is believed that our dogs take on a great deal of their owners' tension, creating stress that leads to abnormal tightness and makes a dog prone to injury.

Where There's a Will, There's a Way

I hope I haven't been too biased in recommending either conventional or homeopathic treatment for your Rottie. I've tried not to favor either approach, because I firmly believe it is cooperative combination of the two that provides the most avenues by which we can ensure our pets' health and welfare.

Today, many veterinarians offer their animal patients the benefit of both these approaches. I have found nearly every veterinarian I have dealt with has been very open minded, and most are anxious for any new and valuable information that might prove beneficial to his or her patients.

The Least You Need to Know

➤ Many chronic conditions, as aggravating as they can be, can be dealt with effectively.

➤ Even serious bone disorders like hip and elbow dysplasia can be relieved through surgery or managed with proper exercise, diet and alternative treatment.

➤ Proper diet and sufficient exercise are among the most important tools in keeping your dog fit.

➤ Herbs are rapidly becoming a part of animal health care, as is the homeopathic veterinarian.

➤ Acupuncture, acupressure and numerous other techniques that work with a dog's energy flow are producing excellent results in curing chronic ailments.

Part 4

One Life to Live

If you and your Rottie have just one life to live together, why not make it as enjoyable as possible? There are a good many fun things you and your Rottie can do, even in the heart of a major city. City dwellers, however, have to get along with their neighbors, so it's important that you keep abreast of the rules and regulations that govern your city parks and beaches. This section will help you decide the best places to go and how your dog must learn to behave when the two of you get there.

This doesn't mean city folk have to stay where they are. There are those long weekends and vacations when you and the whole gang, including the Rottie, can head for the hills and have one heck of a time doing so. Taking pleasant trips with your dog requires lots of planning and a good number of safety precautions. In fact, some people find there are too many details to take care of and opt to leave their dogs safely at home when they travel.

Pet sitters who come to your home while you are gone and boarding kennels are alternatives to taking your dog along on a trip. Here again, though, referrals and lots of advance work are important. When all checks out to your liking, you can leave on your trip without having to suffer guilt pangs for abandoning your best buddy.

Chapter 14

Rotties at Leisure

In This Chapter

➤ Girls (and boys) just want to have fun

➤ A few of our favorite games

➤ Finding dog-friendly parks and beaches

➤ The rules about dogs in public places

➤ Cleanliness is next to dogginess

There's no two ways about it: Getting through puppyhood is really the hardest part. At that stage, Bruno and Gretchen know nothing, so it's up to you to show them the ropes. But that's only the beginning. Just because you've carefully explained, or even demonstrated, the basics to your Rottie, don't expect a puppy to follow through unfailingly. There's all that practice the two of you need and all those occasions on which your patience reservoir will be drained to the bottom because your pup has developed a serious case of selective amnesia.

Ah, but take heart, the day will come when Bruno and Gretchen will drop right into the routine without a moment's hesitation. Those are the days that you can pat your Rottie and yourself on the back. The dog gets an A for performance and you get one for endurance.

One thing a lot of dog owners don't seem to understand is that training has to take place both at home and "out there"—out there being wherever you are and whatever you do when you aren't home. For some it will mean the shopping mall, for others it could be the park or a beach. Many Rotties perform like clockwork at home, but the picture changes rapidly when they're out on the town. When they get out to the dog park and see the gang, or if they're off leash on a hike and a bunny bounces by, your perfectly trained dog suddenly becomes stone deaf. However, if you train your dog in all sorts of situations, your dog will act trained wherever the two of you happen to go.

Get Out There

When you are sharing your life with a Rottie, you should spend a lot of time "out there" because your well-trained pal can accompany you to pretty much anywhere dogs are allowed. Many Rotties go to work with their owners and have learned all the office rules, so that they become a welcomed member of the staff.

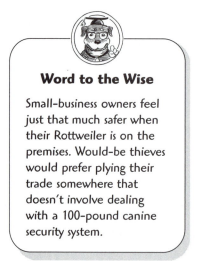

Word to the Wise

Small-business owners feel just that much safer when their Rottweiler is on the premises. Would-be thieves would prefer plying their trade somewhere that doesn't involve dealing with a 100-pound canine security system.

It is important that you realize the kind of Rottweiler that is welcomed out in public is the one that has been properly trained and is accustomed to regularly interacting with people. If your dog lives with you at home and only gets out into the real world once in a blue moon (whenever that is), it's only natural that the dog will be extremely curious, distracted and perhaps even leery of its surroundings. Strangers, strange voices and strange hands could be very intimidating and set your Rottie on edge. Think about a person who has been confined indoors for many, many years. Their excursions out into the big wide world are not going to be as much fun as they would be for someone who has interacted with strangers and strange situations every day.

There are many activities you enjoy that your Rottie can share and will enjoy simply because it means spending time with you. There are also a good many things the two of you can do that are all kinds of fun for the dog—and the exercise certainly won't hurt you either.

Games Are Us!

Just because Bruno has the stoic countenance of his German ancestry, don't think for a moment he doesn't enjoy having fun. Although Rottweilers can thoroughly enjoy the more formal pursuits of obedience trials and tracking, what the two of you can enjoy certainly doesn't stop with activities that have rules. Rotties are great at soccer, whizzes at fetching and masters at hide-and-seek.

If there are kids in the family, all the better. Kids and dogs create games they seem able to play for hours on end, day after day, without ever seeming the least bit bored. Whether or not kids and Rotties make compatible playmates, however, depends upon three things:

1. How well socialized your Rottie is.

2. How effective those early lessons were on what is permissible and what is not when playing with children. Don't forget, in many cases your Rottie will far outweigh the child it is playing with, so the dog must understand that roughhousing is taboo with toddlers.

3. The age of the children. Kids have to be old enough to understand what might injure a puppy or even a grown dog. What might seem great fun to the kid could be harmful to the dog or cause a defense reaction on the dog's part.

As I explained earlier, dogs have ways of communicating with us that take some time and patience to learn and understand. It is interesting that

Watch Out!

Small children always seem fascinated by what is in a dog's food dish. And, like all dogs, Rottweilers have a natural instinct to protect their food and will often react with a snap or real bite before they even realize what they have done. When there are toddlers present, it is always best to feed your Rottie in its crate. At the same time, it is important to teach children they should never put their hands in a dog's food dish.

while dogs and very young children have no language with which to communicate, they still seem to do quite well by using gestures and facial expressions. We can only wonder who taught our Rotties to respond to a child's giggles or outright laughter with a wagging tail. Who informed our dogs they should show outward signs of agitation or sound the alarm when the baby starts to cry?

Rottweilers and kids seem to have a secret language. Just make sure everybody understands the ground rules before you let them play together. (Regina Traxler)

The patience of a Rottie who has grown up with children is astounding at times. A dog, even a very young puppy, can spend an entire morning or afternoon with a child and never get bored or run out of things to do. I have seen huge male Rotties sit poker-faced while their young mistresses dress them up as everything from Arab sheiks to Paris street walkers.

Although kids seem to come by the following games naturally, there is certainly no reason in the world you can't play, too. After a long week in the office or studying for exams, a few let's-forget-everything-and-go-for-it hours can do everyone some good.

Follow the Bouncing Ball

Balls and Rottweilers go together. Old, beat-up footballs, basketballs and soccer balls can usually be picked up at garage sales and flea markets for next to nothing. The balls can provide more fun for your Rottie, your kids and yourself than the most expensive dog toy the pet emporiums could possibly offer.

Kicking that soccer ball around with your Rottie playing guard can go on for hours. A good many Rotties become so expert at guarding the ball that their human opponents have to be right on their toes to even think of getting past them.

Basketballs are too big for Rotties to grasp, so they very quickly learn to manipulate the ball with their noses. A Rottie can become so engrossed in nudging the ball back and forth that it can forget about time or possible danger. Make sure you only allow your Rottie to play ball on its own in a safe area. Your own fenced yard is fine (if the posies don't mind being trampled on!). Never allow your Rottie to play ball in an area where there is traffic. Chasing the ball will be far more important to your dog than watching for careless drivers.

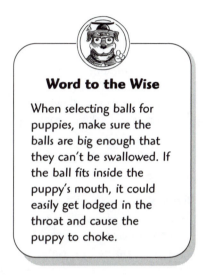

Word to the Wise

When selecting balls for puppies, make sure the balls are big enough that they can't be swallowed. If the ball fits inside the puppy's mouth, it could easily get lodged in the throat and cause the puppy to choke.

Bruno, Fetch!

Most Rottie puppies will chase after just about anything that rolls along the ground or flies through the air. Getting the pup to bring it back to you may prove to be a different story. The easiest way is to start off with two balls or toss toys. Throw one a few feet away. When the puppy picks it up there is usually a lot of proud prancing and dancing around. Encourage the pup to come back with praise and by waving the second toy. Getting the pup interested in the second toy will bring the youngster back to you, and if you indicate you are going to throw the second item, the first toy or ball will probably be dropped in front of you. When the pup does drop the toy, give lots of praise.

The pup will soon get the idea that you will not be throwing something again until the object is brought back to you. When the puppy returns with the object but does not want to relinquish its hold, you can gently remove the toy from the dog's mouth and say "drop!" as you place the toy on the ground.

Bet You Didn't Know

While most Rottweilers love to bring back things you've thrown, there is an occasional dog that looks at what you've tossed, then back at you with an expression of, "Well, she mustn't want it if she threw it away." This is very unusual for a Rottie, but it does happen. Even the disinterested dog can eventually be taught to fetch, but this becomes another lesson to be learned and will never fall under the dog's heading of favorite games.

Hide-and-Seek

This is a game that can be played two different ways. The first way, it is you who hides. This can best be accomplished by having someone hold your Rottie on leash while you find a nearby place to hide. Call the dog's name and have the other person unsnap the leash and say, "find!" You should keep calling until the dog finds you, and then give lots of praise. Eventually, you will be able to stop calling out and the person holding the dog will only have to say "find."

Another variation of hide-and-seek is done with one of your dog's favorite toys. Rub the toy briskly between the palms of your hands. Let your dog see the toy but then have the holder distract the dog while you go off and conceal the object in a place that is, at first, close by. Have the holder release the dog and give the "find!" command. You can stand near but not right at the hidden object and also repeat the "find" command. If the toy is one the dog knows by name, use a command like "find the squeaky" or "find the ball." You may have to lead the dog to the toy a time or two, but most Rotties get the idea very quickly. Once your Rottie gets the idea, you won't have to stand near the object at all.

Dog-Friendly Parks

Unfortunately, because of neglectful dog owners, it is becoming increasingly difficult to find parks and recreational areas that allow dogs, and even fewer that permit dogs ever to be off leash. This is understandable, because not all people love dogs as much as you and

I do. Even those who like dogs don't appreciate being harassed or threatened by someone else's dog or stepping in a pile of dog poop.

Although your well-trained Rottie would never think to threaten anyone, many people are thoroughly convinced that all Rottweilers are dangerous and become terrified at the sight of one, particularly if it is off leash. My best advice is to keep your Rottie on leash at all times when you are in a public recreation area. The popular Flexi-leads can extend themselves up to 25 feet if there is no one around to bother, but the retractable leads give you constant control over your dog at all times.

Woof.

Dog Talk

If you don't have anyone to help you with these hide–and–seek games you can give your Rottie the "sit and stay" command while you hide the toy or yourself out of the dog's sight. When this is done, give the "okay" command to let your dog know the sit-stay is done, and then follow with "find."

If you wish to use a nearby park, check with the local Department of Parks and Recreation to see what the rules are that apply to dogs. Some parks allow dogs only during certain low-use hours, and some even allow dogs to be off leash during specified time periods.

Many communities are creating special dog parks or are fencing in certain portions of public parks in which dogs are allowed to be off leash. The value of these dedicated areas is that they give a dog plenty of opportunity for some serious exercise and help improve socialization by letting the dog run with other canine pals.

Even when you are in a dog park where off leash is perfectly acceptable, make sure your Rottie has been properly socialized to accept other dogs. Is your Rottie of a nature to withstand being threatened or challenged by another dog without flying into a rage?

This brings us to the downside of the dog parks: Even though your dog, and nine out of ten of the others at the park, may be well socialized, the tenth dog may be the culprit. You know, like the kid who can't seem to get through a single school recess without antagonizing someone. The additional problem with dogs in groups is that even though a troublemaker may pick just a single dog to fight with, fighting ignites a pack reaction and soon every dog with a single aggressive bone in its body has to dive into the fray.

When trying out an off leash dog park, remember that you and your dog are the new kids on the block. Proceed with care and make sure there are no bullies present. If there is a dog that seems determined to rule the pack through aggression, my advice is take your Rottie home and try the park at another time. Most Rotties will not tolerate being pushed around for no good reason, and even though they may not start a fight, your average Rottweiler is more than capable of finishing one.

Water, Water Everywhere

Although there is nothing in the breed's history to indicate the Rottie has ever served as a water dog, they love the water. Retrieving from a pond, a lake or even the ocean is the Rottweiler's idea of good clean fun.

Rotties do like water, but don't make the mistake of throwing your puppy, or even grown dog, into the water on your first visit to the beach. Allow the dog to become accustomed to the water gradually and there is little doubt that you will wind up with an excellent swimmer on your hands.

Watch Out!

Ocean and river swimming can be dangerous. Consider currents, rip tides and the size of the surf. If you wouldn't let your child swim there, don't allow your Rottie to. Talk to lifeguards or people familiar with the beaches and tides in your area so that you don't make the fatal mistake of sending your Rottie off into a hazardous situation.

I usually take puppies that haven't been introduced to the ocean down to the beach on a calm day when the surf is relatively gentle. The sound and ominous look of huge crashing waves can be very frightening to a pup. On puppy days we also take along the older dogs that like the ocean. This gives the pup or new dog confidence that it will not be eaten alive by this huge wet beast.

If you don't have a seasoned dog for your dog to follow, attach a long leash to your dog's collar and walk through the shallows at a leisurely pace, allowing your dog to trail along and very gradually get its feet wet. If you walk too rapidly, the pup will begin to splash itself, and cold water on the tummy can be a little intimidating for the first timer.

Once your Rottie decides water sports are the next best thing to a steak dinner, it is up to you to sure the dog doesn't become totally exhausted. Some dogs will retrieve sticks or balls out of the water for as long as there is someone around to throw for them. Dogs are like children in that regard, so it is up to you to set some sensible limits.

Everybody into the Pool

Swimming pools have no tides or surf to contend with, but make sure your Rottie is completely familiar with how and where to get out. Begin by taking your dog down to the far end of the pool, and then allow the dog to follow you to the exit that will be easiest for the dog to use. Do this several times and your Rottie will quickly learn how to get out on its own. Never leave a dog in or near a pool on its own unless you are *absolutely certain* that the dog is able to get out of the pool.

Your Rottie will love a dip in the pool, as long as it knows how to get out. (Martha Kay Turner)

Responsible Beach-Going

Ocean and lake ecology is at an extremely fragile state at present, and quite frankly, most conservationists would like to keep dogs off our beaches entirely. They are not being unfair if you stop to look at the consequences. There are many additives contained in today's commercial dog foods that are not environmentally friendly. When dogs

223

eliminate along beaches, the harmful materials eventually wash down into the water and are capable of killing marine life.

You may think your dog's feces once a day or once a week could not possibly do any great harm to vast bodies of water, but multiply what your dog is responsible for by the hundreds of dogs that live in your area and the number of days and weeks in a year and you can see where the difficulty lies. If you take your Rottie to the beach, plan to pick up any droppings. Commercial concerns do enough damage to our waters. We who profess to be nature lovers and lovers of all animals need not contribute to the problem.

When you are on the beach, keep your dog on leash unless you are in a really remote area where it is practical and legal for the dog to run free. Do consider the fact that many people go to the beach to relax and read, and do not enjoy having someone's massive Rottie leaping over them or kicking sand on them.

Hit the Trail

It's wonderful to be able to hike through the beautiful trails cut through some of our state and national parks, and who better to share the beauty of it all with you than your Rottie pal? Bruno or Gretchen may not relate to the esthetics of it all on the same level as you do, but rest assured they are able to enjoy the day in their own way. The camaraderie and the opportunities for your dog to enjoy all the wondrous sights and smells of nature make for a perfect day.

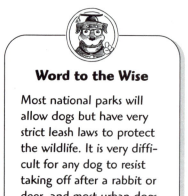

Word to the Wise

Most national parks will allow dogs but have very strict leash laws to protect the wildlife. It is very difficult for any dog to resist taking off after a rabbit or deer, and most urban dogs can chase an animal for miles before they realize they are lost.

Do be properly equipped on your hikes. Stash any emergency and first-aid materials that might be appropriate to the time of the year and the terrain in your backpack. Park rangers and the Department of Parks and Recreation can advise you on what might be worthwhile to carry along with you in case of emergency.

Hiking supplies for both dogs and dog owners are available at specialty shops and through pet supply catalogs. In fact, hiking with one's dog has become so popular that there is a wide range of equipment geared to the canine set alone: collapsible food and drink containers, booties to protect your dog's feet from sharp rocks or freezing terrain, rainwear and even doggie sun shades and sunglasses. And just so all of your Rottie's camping and hiking equipment doesn't become an additional burden for you, there are doggie backpacks designed to help your dog carry whatever it might need along the trail.

Do remember, dog lovers or not, no one wants to step in dog droppings along the trail. Carry your own disposable baggies to pick up the waste and a larger plastic bag to carry it in until you come upon the proper place to deposit trash.

Bet You Didn't Know

If Little League games are part of your youngster's life, why not make them a family affair and bring the family Rottweiler along? The crowds, the noise and the activity are wonderful socializing opportunities you can take advantage of. Once your Rottie becomes accustomed to all the hubbub, the games will be as much fun for the dog as they are for the doting parents. And your youngster will beam with pride over how much attention the dog gets.

Make Sure Each Step Is a Clean Step

The well-trained Rottie can go pretty much anywhere you can go, unless dogs are specifically prohibited. Always check on that ahead of time. But no matter where you go, make sure you clean up after your dog. It doesn't take more than a minute to place your hand inside a baggie, pick up the droppings and turn the bag inside out. Or you may prefer to carry a poop scooper and plastic zip-close bag. Whatever works best for you is what you should use, but use something. If you and your neighbors are diligent about picking up after your pooches, you will be allowed to continue using the parks and outdoor recreation areas. If you're not, you'll spoil it for everyone.

The Least You Need to Know

➤ All work and no play make a dull dog. There are all kinds of ways for you and your Rottie to have fun.

➤ Most fun games for dogs also provide an opportunity for you to stretch those limbs and get some exercise.

➤ City parks and beaches provide great opportunities for you and your dog to spend pleasant days. These facilities have strict rules about dogs, and it is up to you to be aware of them.

➤ Hiking and camping with your dog in our state and national parks can't be surpassed as a way to spend some of those vacation days. And there are ways that your dog can help you share the load while you hike.

➤ Wherever you go with your dog, make sure you always scoop the poop and dispose of it properly.

Chapter 15

On the Road with Your Rottweiler

To be or not to be . . . alone, that is. Long road trips, back and forth to the office, to and from vacations—all those trips can be extremely boring after a while, and you can only listen to the Top 50 from the 1980s just so many times before you start thinking about pulling the sound system out by its roots!

Why not take Gretchen or Bruno along with you for company? They're all grown up, completely house trained, car savvy and love to be with you regardless of where you're going. Another thing you can rely on is that they will never, ever ask, "Are we there yet?" In fact, they won't ask you anything. No backseat drivers, no needing to stop a million times to look at this, that and the other thing. Dogs somehow manage to be great company without saying a word. Nor do they complain if you choose to talk your head off, or even if you sing your head off!

But it's not simply a question of whether or not your pal should hop in the backseat. Taking your dog along when you shop, go out of town on a business trip or on vacation involves some forethought, and the longer you are gone the more considerable the preparation. If there's an airplane flight involved in your plan, there are a number of legal requirements that must be met as well.

Even if you decide the answer must be no this time and your precious pooch will have to stay behind, there are questions to be answered if there isn't someone at home to take over. Where will your buddy stay while you are gone?

Sooner or later, every dog owner I've known, married or single, family person or not, has had to answer all these questions. And since you didn't buy this guide just to occupy space on your bookshelf, I'm going to do everything I can to point you in the right direction for the best answers.

Custom Cars for Rotties?

Well, not really, but if you have a new Rottweiler and it's also time to shop for a new car, there are a few things to think about. Although you might look like you've just driven off the cover of *GQ*. with your Rottie pup sitting in the passenger seat of your Ferrari, it won't work for very long. Large Rottweilers from little Rottie pups grow, and the two of you will soon be wedging yourselves into a space that wasn't made to accommodate all that mass. (Not your mass of course, your Rottie's!)

Do think about space and what you will be transporting. Consider the safety of both your dog and your valuables. The larger the car, the easier it will be to safely accommodate your pal. Station wagons and mini-vans are extremely popular and are actually far more useful to you and your Rottie than a passenger car.

Who would have thunk you would one day be buying a car for your Rottweiler? But didn't I tell you in the beginning that there was no such thing as a cheap Rottweiler? See what I mean? (The only thing I would put up close to the high cost of Rottweiler ownership is the cost of owning a free cat. But that's a subject for an entirely different book.)

Bet You Didn't Know

Another thing to think about is that on a warm day your Rottie will use up the available oxygen in a closed sports car at a rate that might surprise you. And who in this day and age is going to leave their nifty little sports car sitting there open to the world? Bruno will guard the car with his life, you think. Sure! Unless someone is clever enough to waltz a sweet young bitch in heat by the car or a cat goes racing by. Then who's to prevent that nasty car thief from streaking down the highway with your prized possession? There you will be—sans car, sans Rottweiler.

Keeping Safe and Sound on the Road

Before you embark on any kind of trip, whether it's down to the shopping mall or across the state, there are a number of things you must think seriously about. Two of the most important are temperature and the length of time required for the stops you will be making. It can be very warm outdoors, but if you and your dog are traveling in an air-conditioned car or van, it won't make a whole lot of difference; that is, if you don't plan to stop.

Time and Temperature

If there are stops planned in hot weather, will your Rottie be able to accompany you indoors or to a shaded spot? Once you stop, the car's air-conditioning is turned off, and on a sunny day the temperature inside the car can soar to a dangerous level in minutes. You may find that those gourmet restaurants you are accustomed to dining in along the way will have to be relinquished for

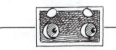

Watch Out!

Although most people don't think of temperatures in the 80s as unbearable, on a sunny day the temperature inside a car, even one with windows partially rolled down, can soar up over 120° in just a few minutes. No dog is able to sustain these temperatures without suffering permanent brain damage or death. Do not take chances with your dog in a car on warm days!

drive-thrus so that you can keep the air-conditioning going or sit out-side on the grass with your dog.

Leaving windows open really doesn't help much on a hot day, either. The sun shining through the front and rear windows sends tempera-tures up at an alarming rate, and the metal of the vehicle seems to trap the heat inside. When it's just 80° outside, it can reach 120° in 20 minutes inside your car—even with the windows partially rolled down. The safest rule on a hot day is never leave your pet in a vehi-cle unless the vehicle can be parked in a completely shaded area and you can leave the windows rolled down all the way.

If you do leave the windows down, you must be able to keep the vehicle in view at all times. Regardless of how well trained your Rottie is, if it gets too hot inside the car, good sense is going to make the dog try to escape. My advice: If it's very hot and you know you will have to make prolonged stops and are not sure of available shade, leave your dog at home in a cool room!

Word to the Wise

Although it might be nice to have Gretchen loose right next to you so she can get the full impact of your words of wisdom, she can be injured or killed by being thrown against the windshield in a sudden stop or collision. Then, too, if she were to spot the dog of her dreams through the driver's side window, she could interfere with your sight or controls and be the cause of an accident.

Buckle Up for Safety

All the reasons we are given for buck-ling up with seatbelts when we drive apply to our pets, as well. Canine seatbelts are now available that can be adapted to just about any make of car and size of dog. They provide both the safety and restraint that can ensure both you and your pet have a comfortable and safe trip.

A dog is safest confined to the rear seat of a passenger car or behind a barrier in a van. Whether with seat-belts or in a crate, all dogs should be restrained for safety's sake. Even though riding in a solid crate may rob your dog of the opportunity to see all the sights as you travel, that's better than being hurled out of the backseat or along the full length of a van. This problem can be solved by purchasing one of the wire collapsible crates that can be firmly secured in the back of your wagon or van.

A travel crate will give you a little peace of mind if you do have an accident. Aside from the physical protection it affords your dog, imagine being in a wreck where your car is damaged badly enough that the doors pop open. Gretchen or Bruno may jump out to go find help for you (or simply out of fear), run across a busy highway and never be seen again. If your dog is in a crate, you know this cannot happen.

Watch Out!

Once you hit country roads, you will probably see ranch and farm dogs in the back of pick-up trucks. Nothing could be more dangerous! A sudden stop could send your dog catapulting through the air, and if the dog is tethered in the truck, the sudden stop could easily break the dog's neck.

Another reason for a travel crate exists if the hosts at your destination also have a dog. Most dogs are not particularly happy about another pooch invading their home territory, and some can be downright hostile about it. Thinking they'll work it out between themselves might be just fine for a couple of Chihuahuas, but when you are talking about dogs the size of Rottweilers, working it out is not really an option.

I.D. and Medication

Most states throughout the country, as well as the governments of Canada and Mexico, require up-to-date vaccination against rabies. Be sure your rabies inoculations are current and that your Rottie is wearing the tag your veterinarian will issue when you have that taken care of. Crossing the border to Canada and Mexico will also require health certificates validated by your veterinarian.

Your vet will also be able to advise you of any special precautions you might have to take, depending upon the area you are traveling to. Certain sections of the country present increased risk of tick-borne diseases such as Lyme disease, and heartworm, which is spread by mosquitoes.

Travel Musts

If you plan ahead, even the longest trip with your Rottie can be a totally pleasant experience. Think about your doggie musts at home, and that will help create your list for on the road.

Professional dog show handlers are on the road a good part of every week, and experience has taught them to carry everything their dogs might need both for their daily routine and in case of an emergency. Your traveling companion probably has no need for all the cosmetic equipment that a show dog requires, but there are a number of doggie items that you should definitely be stowed in your Rottie's steamer trunk:

➤ Enough food for the length of trip, plus a bit more. Changing food suddenly can cause diarrhea.

➤ Regular drinking water in gallon plastic containers. Changing water suddenly can cause stomach upset.

➤ Food and water dishes

➤ Leash and collar, with clearly marked I.D. and rabies tags

➤ First-aid kit (see Chapter 12 for what you need to put in it)

➤ Current medications, if any, including flea and tick controls and heartworm preventives

➤ Solid or collapsible crate

➤ List of parks and rest stops along the way that welcome dogs

➤ Poop scooper and plastic bags for disposal

➤ Paper and terry towels for cleanup and drying

➤ Appropriate bedding for the season of the year

➤ Favorite toys

➤ Brush and comb

➤ Grooming tools, including nail clippers and toothbrush

Vacations for the Whole Family

There is no doubt about it: Your Rottie is just as much a part of the family as you and the kids. Why shouldn't Bruno share in the fun you will be having on that vacation? You've done your job well, and Bruno is well trained and well socialized. Why not reap some of the rewards of all your effort and have this well-behaved family member join you?

Granted, you might not find New York City or the Paris Boulevards an entirely appropriate place for your Rottie, but there are all kinds of vacation plans that can easily accommodate you and your pal. Take a tip from the singles crowd and think of your Rottie as an ice-breaker. You will be amazed at how many people find it much easier to strike up a conversation with you when they can start with comments on your pooch. (I know several young men who borrow friends' dogs to take to the dog park, with nothing but their own socialization in mind!)

On the other hand, those with less than honorable intentions are inclined to shy away from a child or family being watched over by a Rottweiler. You can always feel confident that you and yours are relatively safe with your Rottie standing by.

Again, it's simply a matter of planning and knowing what destinations offer the most pleasure and convenience for all of you. Lakeside cottages and mountain cabins provide a degree of privacy yet plenty of opportunity for family fun and social events in nearby towns. Look into beach houses, as well, because Rotties love to swim. A good friend of ours spends a couple of weeks each year on a houseboat with wife, daughter and the family pooch. A hiking-camping trip provides lots of fun and adventure, to say nothing of the excellent exercise in the great outdoors.

Finding Dog-Friendly Lodgings

It is important to understand that not all the hotels and motels accept dogs. Even though you may not be the type of person who likes to have your travel plans so structured that every stop is reserved ahead of time, do give this some serious thought. Driving until you are totally exhausted and then starting a search for dog-friendly accommodations will not be a very attractive option.

You'll find your traveling more relaxed when you know for sure that you have accommodations waiting at a specific location. It's best to speak directly to the hotel or motel beforehand. Even though some establishments advertise the fact that they accept dogs, this may mean only small dogs or that all dogs must be confined to their travel crates.

If you will be spending time in a specific city or town, the local Chamber of Commerce can be very helpful, as well. Chambers of Commerce can usually provide a list of hotels and motels that accept dogs and may also be able to provide a list of local veterinarians. Vet's offices are usually aware of which local accommodations will accept dogs, and it certainly isn't a bad idea to have quick reference to a veterinarian anyway.

Bet You Didn't Know

The Automobile Club of America publishes catalogs listing accommodations throughout the nation, and most indicate whether they accept dogs. Travel agents are also able to make reserved bookings and will be able to find accommodations that will accept your Rottie. Dawbert Press also publishes a series of dog-friendly travel guides written by Dawn and Robert Habgood called *On the Road Again with Man's Best Friend*.

Up, Up and Away

If your plans include traveling by air, the whole picture becomes a bit more complicated. Not impossible mind you, but certainly not as easy as having your Rottie safely secured in the back of your station wagon. The fact that our Rottweilers will not fit under the seat in front of us on an airplane means we don't have the option of carrying them on board.

If your Rottie is going to travel with you by air, the dog must fly as excess baggage in the cargo hold of the plane at a cost of about $50 each way. Air travel for dogs is no longer unusual—hundreds of dogs accompany their owners back and forth across the country each day.

The Department of Agriculture estimates that approximately 600,000 animals travel by air every year. A good percentage of them are dogs and cats.

It is possible to have your Rottie travel on the same plane as you are on with more than reasonable expectations that the two of you will reach your destination safely. However, since dogs travel in the cargo area of the plane, it should be understood that while this area is pressurized, there are no air-conditioning or heat controls. Because of this, federal regulations require that no animal be shipped by air if the ground temperature at either end of the flight is above 85° or below 45°.

Obviously, air travel for pets is not entirely risk-free. Whenever travel by air is necessary, there are a good number of safety measures that will help increase your dog's odds of a safe arrival:

➤ **Check out the airlines.** Call the airlines you prefer and ask about their policies regarding shipping dogs. Select the airline that offers the greatest safety assurances.

➤ **Make sure you understand the rules.** Airlines have all kinds of rules about what kind of crate they'll accept, what identification needs to be on it, where and when you drop off and pick up your dog and everything else related to your trip. Each airline has different rules. Make sure you understand exactly what you must do, well in advance of your trip.

➤ **Make an advance reservation.** Most airlines will only accept a limited number of dogs per flight. Your travel agent is able to do this for you when making your own reservation. However, reconfirm (and then reconfirm again) before flight time.

➤ **Schedule a direct, nonstop flight.** Making connections, changing planes and long

Watch Out!

The Air Transport Association reports that 99 percent of all animals shipped in the U.S. reach their destination without incident. Of course, that remaining 1 percent includes everything from minor complaints to the death of the animal.

stopovers are just some of the ways you increase the risk of loss and fatalities. Red-eye (overnight) and very early morning flights are least crowded and offer better temperatures.

➤ **Talk to your vet.** Many states require a health certificate signed by a veterinarian, and nearly all airlines will require one whether your destination does or not. Discuss your travel plans with your vet. He or she will probably advise against shipping geriatric dogs, pregnant females and any puppy less than eight weeks old. Trust me, take this advice! Should your vet give you the okay, discuss whether you should tranquilize your dog before shipping. When it comes to sedatives, my advice is always: Don't if you don't have to.

➤ **Take a last-minute potty break.** Exercise your Rottie at the last minute possible to make sure it has relieved itself before the journey begins.

➤ **Use an airline-approved shipping crate.** The crate you ship your dog in must be airline-approved or purchased directly from the airline. It must be large enough for your dog to stand up and turn around in. This does not mean the crate should be the size of the Taj Mahal. Just enough room protects your dog from being jostled about.

Word to the Wise

Fill one of the water bowls from the shipping crate and put it in your freezer the night before you ship your Rottie. Just before you leave home, take out the frozen bowl and place it in the crate. The ice will melt gradually and provide water for your Rottie for a longer period of time and with less spillage.

➤ **Prepare the crate well.** Federal law requires absorbent bedding on the bottom of the crate. You must also supply food and water in dishes that are attached to the inside of the crate's wire door. Tape a small bag of food to the top of the crate along with food and water instructions for the next 24 hours, in case of delays. You are not allowed to put a lock on the crate door. However, you can offer double security with bungee cords or tape.

➤ **Mark the crate.** You must include a "Live Animal" sticker on the crate. Airlines have these stickers available at the point of departure. Tape a sign giving full information regarding contact persons at the points of departure and destination, with phone numbers and addresses.

➤ **Make sure your dog has a collar and I.D. tags.** Regardless of how careful everyone might be, accidents do happen and a dog can manage to escape from its crate. If your Rottie should elude officials and get beyond the airport, there will be no way for anyone to contact you unless the dog carries identification. There are even cases of owners opening the crate at arrival and their dog bolting out in panic. Include a telephone number on the tag where someone can be reached 24 hours a day. And remember, buckle collars only *whenever* your dog is in a crate. Training collars (the ones known as chain collars or choke collars) can get caught on crate wires and hang your dog.

➤ **Arrive at the airport early.** Make it a practice to get to the airport a minimum of an hour and a half before flight time (two hours ahead is even better), and go directly to the passenger check-in counter. Make sure the dog is fully checked in and insist that you stay where you can see the dog until it is time to transport the crate to the loading area. At that point make a headlong dash for the gate and watch to see if your dog is loaded on the plane. When you get on board, have the flight attendant check to make sure the dog actually is on board. Will this make you seem like a bit of a nuisance? Perhaps, but better that than you ending up in one city and your Rottie in another.

What If Your Pal Can't Go?

Although it might be great fun to have your Rottie along, it just may not be practical. What then? Cancel

Word to the Wise

When you do arrive at your destination, your Rottie will be ecstatic to see you again after all those hours away from you. However, do leave your dog in the crate until you get to a place that is less frantic and a bit safer than the airline terminal. Have a good, sturdy leash with you in your carry-on bag and snap the leash on while your pal is still in the crate.

the trip? Well, you could. Or as an alternative, you could find a good boarding kennel that will take super care of your pal while you're gone.

Impossible to find anyone who will care for Bruno the way you do? That's true, but there just might be a kennel somewhere out there that can do a very adequate job. In fact, they might do such a bang-up job your dog will love it! My spoiled-rotten buddy is mad for the kennel at which he vacations while I'm away. All I need to say is "doggie dude ranch?" and he's at the door!

I was extremely fortunate to have the nearest boarding kennel also turn out be one of the best in the state. That was just pure luck. I definitely do not recommend simply dropping your dog off at the closest kennel. The only way you can find a great kennel is by doing a lot of checking. To help steer you in the right direction, your vet can offer local recommendations, and there is an American Boarding Kennel Association that can do likewise. Your dog's breeder may also have recommendations, and so may your neighbors.

Even with recommendations, no kennel is adequate for your Rottie unless it meets your approval. When you have several kennels that sound interesting, drop by during business hours and ask if you can have a tour. Understand that few kennels are going to be as neat and spiffy as your kitchen or living room. Imagine your own home with a couple of dozen dogs in it. At the same time, this doesn't mean the kennel should give you a sense of unsanitary conditions and neglect. It's hard to keep any kennel smelling as sweet as a meadow in springtime, but bad smells and smells that hang through the air no matter where you go don't offer much promise of sanitary conditions.

Watch Out!

Any kennel that will not allow you to look around definitely should *not* get your business! Accept no excuses.

Are food and water containers kept clean? Do the runs show signs of regular care and cleaning? Look at what the surface of the runs is made of. Do the surfaces provide good footing and easy cleanup and sanitizing? Is the run your dog will be kept in big enough? If not, what provisions are made for exercise? What about security: Are the runs escape-proof?

Even though your practically perfect Rottie may not be a fighter, the dog in the next run at a boarding kennel just might be, and could encourage your pacifist to do battle. Not a good idea. Look at the fencing and make sure it provides safety without making the dog feel totally cut off from the world. Metal mesh between runs keeps ears and paws attached to the proper owner, but the dogs are still able to see each other.

Discuss your dog's attitude toward strangers and ask the kennel employees what their views of Rottweilers are. Understanding the breed is very important, and Rotties seem to sense those who can relate to them. The owner of the kennel I use thoroughly understands the Rottie psyche and gets on famously with even the toughest visitors.

If your Rottie wants and needs attention, make sure the kennel attendants will be able to provide this. Many kennels provide what they call playtime, where there is time in a large paddock and someone to play catch with. They may charge a few dollars per day more for this service, but it can mean a big difference in your pal's stay.

Ask the manager what inoculations and health precautions boarders are required to have when they check in. Every kennel I have ever used demands proof of current rabies inoculations and protection against kennel cough. Are incoming dogs screened for fleas, ticks and other parasites? If there are no requirements regarding health safeguards, I would strongly suggest looking elsewhere.

When you check your pal in, be sure to leave your veterinarian's name, address and phone number in case of emergency, and do leave a contact number where you can be reached while you're gone. Bring Gretchen's blanket and plenty of her favorite toys. Check on the food the kennel feeds before you arrive, and if you do not feel that it is suitable for your dog you must bring enough of the food your Rottie is accustomed to for the duration of your absence.

Fear not, Bruno will probably have just as good a time as you do on your vacation. Well-run kennels are managed by people who love dogs, and they do their best to return Bruno to you in as good shape (or better) as when he checked in.

Pet Sitters

Even with all my praise of well-run boarding kennels, you still might feel there is absolutely no way you would even consider abandoning your buddy to the kennel life. In that case, think about a pet sitter. That's someone who will come to your home at regular intervals during the day to feed your dog and provide time for exercise and those calls of nature. Although you won't be home to hold Gretchen or Bruno's paw, with a pet sitter everything else remains the same. If your Rottie isn't happier about this, at least you will be.

If you think your dogs can't live anywhere except on their own couch, a pet sitter who comes in while you're away might be your best option.

No doubt you have a friend or relative who gets along well with your Rottie (important!) who will happy to do this for a day, or perhaps even two days. But if your absence is going to extend beyond that, do consider paying someone to come in to take care of everything. Here again, your vet may be able to recommend someone, and there are national organizations dedicated to making recommendations for qualified pet sitters. Two of them are the National Association of Professional Pet Sitters and Pet Sitters International.

It is best to hire a professional pet sitter for many reasons. Most professionals provide credentials and written agreements as to what they will and will not do, and what they agree to be responsible for. Of course, in your case, you want a sitter who knows and understands the Rottweiler and who your Rottie agrees to get along with.

A professional pet sitter who is a member of a national pet sitting organization is usually bonded and insured. This is very important, because any dog lover can advertise that they are a professional. You don't want to come home to find your Rottie is sitting there waiting for you in a home stripped of every valuable possession you ever had.

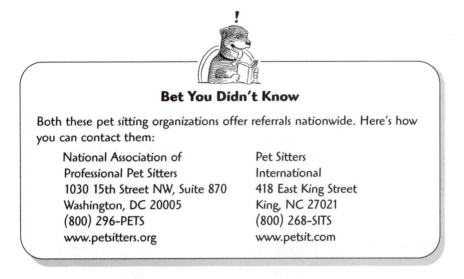

Bet You Didn't Know

Both these pet sitting organizations offer referrals nationwide. Here's how you can contact them:

National Association of Professional Pet Sitters 1030 15th Street NW, Suite 870 Washington, DC 20005 (800) 296-PETS www.petsitters.org	Pet Sitters International 418 East King Street King, NC 27021 (800) 268-SITS www.petsit.com

So, while a pet sitter might seem like a simple alternative to a boarding kennel, it gets a bit more complicated as you look into the situation. Just because the sitter and Bruno hit it off like long-lost friends doesn't mean the sitter is honest, nor does the bonded and insured sitter guarantee he or she knows what to do with your canine treasure in case of emergency.

Entrusting your pal and your entire household to someone that may well be a perfect stranger is a serious step. There are a number of items that you should consider bottom-line requirements:

➤ Is the person a member of a bona fide professional pet sitter organization?

➤ Have you spoken directly to an official of the organization about the individual you are considering and determined that the person is bonded and insured?

➤ Have you checked a realistic number of the person's references?

➤ What kind of experience has the person had with Rottweilers?

➤ Does what is included in the sitter's agreement cover everything you feel is important?

➤ Has the sitter provided you with a complete list of questions concerning what he or she needs to know about your dog and your home?

➤ Does the sitter have a 24-hour pager or cell phone?

➤ Is the sitter familiar with the local laws and regulations that govern animal care?

➤ Is there an alternate who can step in for the sitter in case of illness or accident?

➤ Have you and the sitter completely agreed upon the charges for everything you wish to have taken care of?

These items are listed to start you off in the right direction. There are undoubtedly other items specifically relevant to your situation that should be included.

The Least You Need to Know

➤ Traveling can be a lot more enjoyable for you if your Rottie pal can go along.

➤ Traveling with your Rottie requires advance consideration and planning.

➤ When traveling by car, always keep your dog in a crate and never leave your dog locked up in the car.

➤ Not all hotels and motels accept dogs, and the ones that do might have special requirements you should be aware of.

➤ Finding the right boarding kennel for your Rottie requires personal inspection on your part.

➤ Pet sitters can take care of your Rottie in your home, but it is important to check out experience and references.

Part 5

Tapping the Rottie's Resources

That little pup you brought home in a basket awhile back now weighs practically as much you do. All those lessons you spent time on have paid off, and your whiz kid minds like a Marine cadet. So what now? The two of you have earned some fun time, and Rottie owners are twice blessed in that their dogs are not only capable of learning, they thrive on it.

This section lets you in on all kinds of things you and your Rottie can do together—some just for the heck of it and others that can equip your dog to take a very serious role in life. It really depends upon your capacity to learn and to teach. A Rottie is always raring to go. Do you think you will be able to keep up?

Chapter 16

It's in the Blood

In This Chapter

➤ Testing a Rottie's herding instincts

➤ The three phases of schutzhund

➤ A formidable guard dog

➤ Carting for a living

➤ Rotties in search and rescue work

A Rottweiler's genetics give this clever and talented breed the ability to perform well on so many levels that it is highly unlikely any owner is ever able to really exhaust his or her dog's full capacity to perform.

The introductory chapters of this guide highlighted the many duties that have been assigned to the Rottweiler through the ages. Even though science has developed a myriad of ways to replace the need for our Rottie's services, that doesn't eliminate the breed's ability to perform them. In this chapter we will look at just a few of the many ways in which this ingenious breed can serve its owners.

Herding Tests and Trials

Bruno a herding dog? Yup. Remember when his great, great (multiplied a couple of hundred times) granddad was hard at work in that little town in Germany? Well, old Bruno hasn't forgotten how to work as a herder, even though a lot of time has elapsed in the interim.

Herding trials are sponsored by many organizations—the American Kennel Club is just one of them. The American Kennel Club's trials are limited to all dogs over nine months of age that are registered with the organization as a herding breed (Rotties are!). There are three levels of competition in the program.

Herding Tested

This is a very simple test that is designed to see if the dog is willing to respond to the handler. The test also shows if the dog is able to control the movement of the livestock—which can be sheep, goats, cattle or ducks.

To pass the test a dog has to be able to:

➤ Stay on command.

➤ Obey two commands to change the direction of the livestock.

➤ Halt the livestock on command.

➤ Come on recall.

Bet You Didn't Know

Even though Rottweilers have been flexing their herding muscles since the days of ancient Rome, it wasn't until 1994 that the American Kennel Club admitted the breed to the list of those eligible to compete for herding titles. Since that time, the Rottie has proven capable of herding just about anything herdable: sheep, cattle, horses and even ducks and geese.

Rotties can herd anything that is herdable. It's in the genes. (Judy Butler)

Ten minutes are allowed for the exercises. The Rottie must pass two of these basic tests with two different judges presiding. There is no score—the dog simply passes or fails. If the dog is successful on both attempts, the official Herding Tested degree (HT) is awarded.

Pre-Trial Testing

With an HT degree under its belt, a Rottie becomes eligible for the pre-trial test. The challenges here are:

➤ Guide the livestock through obstacles.

➤ Stop the livestock.

➤ Turn the livestock in a different direction.

➤ Reverse the direction in which the livestock is moving.

➤ Pen the livestock within 10 minutes.

Here again, this is simply a pass or fail event with no scores. Two successful tests under two different judges are required to earn the Pre-Trial Tested (PT) title.

Herding Trials

Here the Rottie is given the option of competing in three different designated courses. Each course demonstrates different areas of working ability, and each of these options has three levels of accomplishment: Herding Started (HS), Herding Intermediate (HI) and Advanced. Success in the Advanced level earns the dog a Herding Excellent (HX) title, the loftiest degree attainable by a herding dog.

In herding trials, a dog must score a minimum of 60 out of a possible 100 points. The points are divided into six categories of proficiency, and the competing dog must earn at least half of the points allotted to each category in order to qualify. The courses are complex, and many of them require a dog to respond to hand signals with no verbal commands given by the handler.

The requirements for all of the AKC's herding program can be obtained directly from the organization's office in Raleigh, North Carolina.

Schutzhund

Remember what I told you about a Rottweiler needing work to do in order to achieve that incredible potential the breed has? Well, schutzhund is the way to accomplish that. This program isn't just busy work for a Rottie, it is a program that in the end will provide you with a dog who is not only your friend and companion, but who can protect you if the need arises.

Dog Talk

Schutzhund is a German word meaning "protection dog." But actually, schutzhund competition has three phases: protection, tracking and obedience.

The sport began in Germany about 100 years ago as a means of testing and maintaining the character and usefulness of working dogs. It sprang from the peasant farmers' need to train their herding dogs to also protect the livestock from predators and poachers. Though born of the aristocracy, Captain Max von Stephanitz admired the impressive capabilities of the peasants' herding dogs. Having always been an animal lover, he decided to try his hand at dog breeding—but not just random dog breeding or breeding of dogs purely for entertainment or exhibition. He had a definite plan in mind. His goal was to breed the ultimate shepherd dog. The dogs he observed in the shepherds' fields were, in his mind, the finest and most intelligent working dogs of his day.

Von Stephanitz became actively involved in the *Verein fur Deutsche Schaferhunde* (SV), the national German Shepherd Dog club, and helped shift the direction of the organization toward carefully recording and registering the dogs that would be produced to develop the breed he had in mind. Captain von Stephanitz installed himself as president of the organization and dictated the rules, regulations and criteria by which dogs would be deemed worthy to be included in the stud book of the SV. The captain's goals were the goals of the organization, and fortunately for his breed and the many other German breeds that would eventually follow suit, von Stephanitz's unswerving dedication was to the preservation of intelligence and trainability—beauty he cared nothing about.

The SV also organized training contests for dogs, configured to include tests measuring excellence in obedience, tracking and protection. Those tests were the foundation for the schutzhund trials of today.

Schutzhund trials test on three distinct areas. The first two, obedience and tracking, are very similar to the obedience and tracking trials offered by the AKC. The third area is ability and courage in protection work. Schutzhund devotees value all three areas equally, and believe they are interdependent in creating a top all-around working dog. There are three levels of proficiency—Schutzhund I, II and III—with increasingly difficult skills and demands for each. Before any dog can even begin to compete for one of these titles, it must successfully pass a preliminary test for steadiness.

Schutzhund Tracking

This phase tests a dog's trainability as well as its tracking ability and endurance. As in the other two phases of schutzhund work, temperament plays an important role in the tracking test. It begins with a temperament test given by the presiding judge. The dog must be neither shy nor independently aggressive. To be successful in this aspect of the trial, a dog must be completely reliable, and neither shyness nor uncontrollable aggressiveness lend themselves to the prerequisite stability.

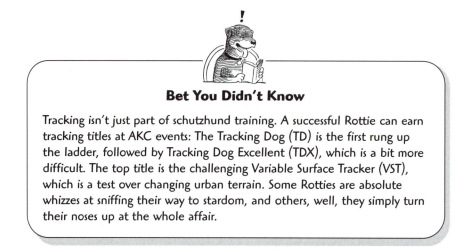

Bet You Didn't Know

Tracking isn't just part of schutzhund training. A successful Rottie can earn tracking titles at AKC events: The Tracking Dog (TD) is the first rung up the ladder, followed by Tracking Dog Excellent (TDX), which is a bit more difficult. The top title is the challenging Variable Surface Tracker (VST), which is a test over changing urban terrain. Some Rotties are absolute whizzes at sniffing their way to stardom, and others, well, they simply turn their noses up at the whole affair.

In the test, a track is laid on a natural surface of either grass or dirt. The track includes some turns. The person making the trail drops objects along the way directly on the track. While on leash, the dog is expected to follow the track and locate and indicate the objects.

Schutzhund Obedience

Here again, the dog's temperament is tested along with its physical soundness and willingness to work for humans. The dog is given a sequence of heeling exercises, during the course of which groups of strangers must be negotiated and a gun is fired. All this is to observe emotional stability. The standard sit, stay and lie down commands are given while the handler continues to move along, and the dog is required to remain in position until the handler indicates the dog should catch up or change positions.

Other exercises test a dog's ability to continue to follow through on the handler's instruction whether or not the handler is in sight. And finally, the dog is required to retrieve objects over both flat and elevated surfaces.

Schutzhund Protection Work

This phase tests the dog's courage and puts its agility and strength to the test, as well. The protecting phase includes finding and apprehending a person under the direction of the handler. The dog is expected to perform these exercises with sufficient aggression, but only under the strict command and control of its handler. While all this does, in fact, test the dog's courage, it also measures the dog's ability to refrain from becoming aggressive without the handler's instruction to do so.

Please don't think a schutzhund-trained dog is a fighting machine. Schutzhund relies heavily upon the complete cooperation of both dog and handler, and no properly trained schutzhund dog would ever act aggressively toward a human or other animal without the explicit instruction of its handler. Schutzhund training is by and for the dog and handler team.

Guard Work

Although many different names are given to dogs who do this work—attack dogs, guard dogs, protection dogs and patrol dogs—all dogs trained for it are highly specialized dogs that should remain in the hands of skilled, professional trainers. They are not household pets. These dogs are trained specifically to be spontaneously aggressive in performing their duties, even without commands from a handler. Their job is normally to protect property or individuals.

Generally speaking, guard dogs have been trained to protect a given area or person with any and all force necessary. If what they have been trained to protect is invaded, they will attack and, if necessary, bite intruders without waiting for a command to do so. It should be obvious what a lethal

Watch Out!

A Rottie owner should never attempt to train his dog for guard work without the supervision of a highly qualified and experienced trainer. Guard work taught by an amateur can unleash aggressive tendencies in a Rottie that may be difficult, if not impossible, to redirect.

weapon this would be to have in a residential neighborhood or any area into which an unsuspecting person could inadvertently trespass.

Whenever there is need for this kind of dog, it is best obtained from trained professionals who are experienced in providing services of this kind. Posted signs, fencing and a myriad of other requirements are usually required when you keep a trained guard dog.

Carting

All carting requires is one Rottie, something that needs to be hauled and one cart. The cart can either be professionally manufactured or homemade. Rottweilers just love carting (remember the butcher's dogs of Rottweil?), and if there are children around to be carted, most Rotties are in seventh heaven.

We have friends whose young son was born with a handicap that makes it extremely difficult for the boy to walk any great distance. The family has a Rottweiler who absolutely adores the boy, and the dog somehow seems to understand that he brings great joy into his young master's life. The Rottie transports his young master around the neighborhood and on outings the family takes together into the desert or on hiking trails.

The lads go out on the town. (Armstrong)

A good many Rotties are still used to haul goods in the more remote and less affluent villages throughout Europe. On a recent winter trip to Russia, we found it not the least unusual to find several children on a sled attached to the family Rottweiler's harness as they trucked down the icy streets of both downtown St. Petersburg and Moscow.

Bet You Didn't Know

The South African Kennel Union provides highly regimented competitions for excellence in carting, with specific degrees and qualifications that apply to both individual and team competitors. It is an extremely popular event and has been attracting more and more interest here in the United States as well.

Search and Rescue

Search and rescue teams have proven their worth beyond a shadow of a doubt in assisting local law enforcement in countless ways. Searching for and finding lost children and adults are just a few of the many ways these canines have proven themselves heroes and lifesavers. Search and rescue teams are also invaluable at disaster sites, where they can find trapped victims faster than any human-made equipment can.

Search and rescue work requires a dog that has a good sense of smell, a great sense of urgency and the physical strength and stamina required to perform long, sometimes exhausting searches. There are water, land and snow specialists that have been able to perform incredible rescues. In fact, many say search and rescue dogs are more useful in some rescue operations than a human ever could be.

Many volunteer organizations assist in training both dog and handler for search and rescue work. The handler is given instructions in first aid, map reading and even water rescue. The dogs are highly trained in tracking, hauling and alerting when a person is located.

Word to the Wise

Search and rescue is a team effort. That means you must be in as good shape as your dog. It also means you have to train just as often and just as hard.

The Least You Need to Know

➤ When you're looking for fun things to do with your Rottie, you can choose activities that tap into its innate working abilities. Remember, your pal is capable of learning just about anything you are capable of teaching.

➤ Even if you aren't from down on the farm, getting involved in herding trials can be a great way to establish a communication system with your dog that exceeds anything that you might have imagined possible.

➤ The degrees of excellence that can be achieved in schutzhund will not only make your dog smarter and better behaved, but also what the dog learns could save your life.

➤ Rotties can be trained for guard dog work, but the training should never be attempted by anyone other than an experienced professional.

➤ Carting with your Rottie can be put to use around home and garden, as well as offering your kids a mode of transportation they will probably prefer over even the fanciest sports car.

➤ Search and rescue teams serve the world over, performing lifesaving and sometimes dangerous work.

Chapter 17

Just for the Fun of It

In This Chapter

➤ Showing your Rottie in dog shows

➤ Why obedience work is just what you need

➤ Flipping out for flyball, freestyle, agility and Frisbee fun

➤ Canine Good Citizen—your Rottie's B.A. degree

➤ Therapy work—fun for the soul

There's not a whole lot you've read about the Rottweiler so far that somehow doesn't work its way back to the same basic truth—this is a breed whose entire history revolves around serving humanity: guarding, fighting, herding, hauling and tracking—the list goes on and on. It all sounds terribly serious, doesn't it? But those of you who have been living with a Rottie, even if it's been just a few weeks, know there's another side to this breed—an energetic, fun-loving, enthusiastic side.

When all that energy and enthusiasm is harnessed and channeled constructively, there are few heights a Rottie cannot reach in the canine world. Rotties are natural athletes and they can run, jump, sniff or strut with the best. Some of their abilities provide unquestionable service to people and others, well, just to prove that Bruno is not all work and no play; there are some fun pursuits that both your Rottie and you will enjoy so much that you just might get addicted.

There's No Biz Like Show Biz

Have you ever considered going into show business? Dog show business, that is. The Rottweiler is a very popular show dog. Many owners who had thought of their Rottweiler only as a friend and companion have entered the dog show world and found it to be an exciting and fascinating hobby. The dog show fraternity extends around the entire world and affords competitors an opportunity to create new friendships from all walks of life. It is an activity in which one person or an entire family can participate.

The dog show fraternity is like a big family, and it extends all over the world. (Rich Bergman)

In the United States, the American Kennel Club sponsors many kinds of competitive events in which all registered purebred dogs may compete. They run the gamut from very formal events like the Westminster Kennel Club Show (the one you watch on TV from New York every February) to local match shows.

Conformation shows are currently the most popular and well-attended dog events. The original purpose of conformation shows was to give breeders a means of comparing their stock to that of other fanciers and thereby improve their breeding programs.

Today, not all people who participate in conformation shows intend to become breeders. Many simply find enjoyment in the competitive aspect of these events. Conformation dog shows take place nearly every weekend of the year in one part of the country or another, and are open to all unneutered, AKC-registered dogs.

Generally speaking, conformation shows fall into two major categories: match shows and championship events.

Dog Talk

Dog shows are called **con-formation events**, because dogs are judged by how well they conform to the breed standard.

Match Shows

Match shows are primarily staged for young or inexperienced dogs that are not ready to compete for champion-ship points. In most cases, classes are offered for dogs from about three months of age and older.

Matches are great places for beginners to learn how to show their own dogs. These matches are far more informal than championship events. Since they are more laid-back, there is plenty of time for the novice handler to make mistakes along with everyone else and to ask questions and seek assistance from more experienced exhibitors or from the show judges.

Match shows can be held for all breeds of dogs recognized by the AKC, or they can be specialty matches—matches for just one particu-lar breed of dog. When there is a club devoted to a specific breed in an area, that club will often hold these match shows so that the newer club members and the young puppies will have an opportu-nity to gain some experience. Rottie breeders are usually aware of local Rotties-only specialty matches, and if you have any interest at all, you can check with the breeder that your pal came from. Information regarding these matches can usually also be found in the classified sections of Sunday newspapers under "Dogs for Sale."

Word to the Wise

You can contact the AKC at 5580 Centerview Drive, Raleigh, NC 27606-3390, (919) 233-9767. Their Web site, a very useful resource, is www.akc.org.

Matches can be entered on the day of the show. Most clubs accept entries on the grounds of the show site on the morning of the event. The person taking your entry will be able to help you fill out the form and give you the preliminary instructions you will need. All the information required is on your Rottie's registration certificate, so you might want to take a Xerox copy of that and bring it along with you.

Championship Shows

Championship shows are a lot more formal, and my suggestion would be to consider entering them after you've gained some experience by showing in a few match shows. The championship shows are sponsored by various all-breed kennel clubs or, in some instances, by a club specializing in one particular breed of dog. The AKC can provide you with information about an all-breed kennel club in your area and the American Rottweiler Club can let you know if a local Rottweiler club has been organized in your area.

Bet You Didn't Know

For a dog to become an AKC champion, it must be awarded a total of 15 championship points. Points at a show are awarded to the best male and best female non-champions in each breed. Only one male and one female in each breed win points at a dog show. The number of championship points that can be won at a particular show is based on the number of entries in the dog's breed and sex, but it's never 15. That means the dog must win the points at several shows to become a champion. Of the 15 points required, two of the wins must be what are called majors (that is, a show at which three or more points are offered). These two majors have to be won under two different judges.

How do you enter a championship show? All clubs sponsoring an AKC championship show must issue what is called a premium list. A premium list contains all the information you will need to enter that club's show. These premium lists are sent out by a professional show superintendent several weeks before the date you must enter the show. (Unlike match shows, which can be entered the same day, championship shows must be entered in advance.)

If you want to get on the mailing list for these premium lists, you must advise the show superintendent in your area. A list of show superintendents can be obtained from the AKC. Once your name is on a show superintendent's list, you will continue to receive premium lists for all shows staged by that organization as long as you continue to show your dog.

The premium list gives you the date, location and closing date for entries for a particular show. It will also list the entry fee, the judges for each of the breeds eligible to compete at the show and the prizes that will be awarded in each breed.

Also included in the premium list is the entry form, which you must complete to enter the show. All of the information you need to complete the entry form appears on your dog's AKC registration certificate. The information that you enter on this form will appear in the catalog on the day of the show.

Word to the Wise

Generally, dog shows in the United States do not offer cash prizes. The prizes are trophies, ribbons and similar mementos.

Pick a Class

When you enter your dog in a show, there are several classes you can choose from. Read the information contained in the premium list carefully. Often there are lower rates for puppy classes, as well as other exceptions that you should be aware of.

Listed here are the classes in which you can enter your Rottweiler at AKC shows. As you read the requirements for the different classes, it will become apparent that the classes are organized according to a dog's age and prior accomplishments. If you are a beginner, I strongly advise entering your Rottweiler in the Puppy class if it is young enough. If your Rottweiler is over 12 months old, enter it in the 12-to-18 Month class. Those Rottweilers that will have passed the 18-month cutoff can be entered in the Novice class. Judges are far more forgiving of immaturity and lack of experience in these classes than they would be in some of the other classes that normally accommodate more seasoned dogs and handlers.

Each of the following classes is divided by sex, and all dogs must be six months or older on the day of the show to be eligible.

Dog Show Classes	
Puppy class	Pups under 12 months of age on the day of show that are not champions.
12-to-18 Month class	Dogs at least 12 months old but under 18 months on the day of the show that are not champions.
Novice class	Dogs born in the United States, Canada, Mexico or Bermuda that have not earned three first-place ribbons in the Novice class or one first-place ribbon in the Bred-by-Exhibitor, American-Bred or Open class. Dogs in this class may not have won any points toward their championships.
Bred-by-Exhibitor class	Dogs being shown by any one of the breeders of record who is also an owner or co-owner. The dog may also be shown by a member of the immediate family of any one of the breeders of record. No champions of record are eligible for this class.
American-Bred class	For any dog whelped in the United States as the result of a mating that took place in the United States that is not yet a champion.
Open class	Any dog six months or older.
Best of Breed	This class is for champions only, so you probably won't have to worry about this one for a while.

You must include the dog's sex on the entry blank so that your Rottweiler is not put into the wrong class.

Showing Your Own

Getting ready for a dog show begins long before you actually walk into the ring at a championship show. Beginners have a great deal to learn. At first it seems totally overwhelming, but keep in mind that everyone was a novice at one time. No matter how the pros may whirl and twirl around you, remember they did not know how to do all that when they entered their first show.

Much of what you need to know is contained in books and magazine articles. Read everything you can. Attend dog shows and observe the people in the ring who are winning with their Rottweilers. You will quickly see how much skilled handling enhances a dog's looks and its chances of winning.

Woof.

Dog Talk

In dog show terminology, males are referred to as **dogs** and females as **bitches**. It is also important to remember that while at the show, only the males are dogs, and your beloved and adored Gretchen will have to suffer being referred to as a bitch.

The next step is to begin to master the art of handling your own Rottweiler. This can start just as soon as you bring your puppy home. Teaching your puppy to stand still while it is being brushed is the first phase of learning the proper stance in the show ring.

Rottweilers are examined by the judge while the dog is stacked (standing evenly on its four legs). It is bottom-line important that your Rottweiler not be apprehensive when the judge attempts to examine it. You can practice this at home whenever strangers stop by. If your Rottie is going to be a show dog, the more strangers who are allowed to put their hands on your dog, the better. The dog must be completely at ease when the judge does his or her examination. Any attempt to snap at the judge will be result in your being dismissed from the ring immediately.

There are many all-breed clubs that sponsor handling classes for people who wish to show their own dog. These classes are usually taught by professional dog handlers, who will be able to offer you worthwhile tips both on handling in general and showing your Rottweiler specifically.

In these classes you will learn a great deal about general ring procedures. At the same time, your Rottweiler will become accustomed to being handled by strangers. As you attend more classes you will observe your Rottweiler growing confident and less distracted. This makes good presentation easier for both you and your dog.

While showing dogs is an enjoyable hobby, it takes hard work and a lot of study to master the art of handling your dog well. Patience and practice will help make you proficient. You will not become an expert overnight.

Bet You Didn't Know

Professional handlers offer their services to those who do not wish to handle their own dog at a show or who are unable to do so. These professionals can be contacted at most dog shows. When they have completed their work for the day, they are happy to discuss the possibility and the practicality of having your Rottweiler professionally handled.

Obedience

Obedience trials are held at both championship shows and at matches, along with the conformation events. The same informal entry procedures that apply to conformation matches apply here, as well. And the same formal rules apply when you are entering an obedience competition held in conjunction with a championship show.

Obedience classes are definitely a prerequisite here. Obedience competition work is based entirely on how well your dog performs a set series of exercises, and the requirements are very precise. The exercises range from the basics like heel, sit and lie down in the Novice class, on through to scent discrimination and directed jumping in the Utility class.

Rottweilers have proven to be excellent candidates for obedience work. Many have earned advanced titles through the years, and the breed is proud to claim title-holders in even the most demanding of the categories.

Don't let the rules, regulations and titles intimidate you. Actually, obedience competition follows in a very logical order that makes it easy to learn and easy to follow. Instructional classes must come first, and even if you decide you don't want to enter shows, what you and your dog learn in obedience training is priceless. From there on, it is step-by-step up the ladder, and by the time you complete a step you will already know how to go on to the next level.

Flyball

Flyball is certainly one of the most exciting activities you and your Rottie can choose from the breed's never-ending list of fun things to do. The degree to which Gretchen and Bruno are obsessed with their tennis balls will determine, in a good part, how successful they might be at flyball.

In flyball the dogs are organized into two teams, with four dogs on each team. The team races relay-style. At the signal, each dog must clear four hurdles, release a ball from the flyball box, catch it in the air and return with the ball to the starting point so that the next team member can start off. The team that races the fastest wins, and the speed and excitement make for a very enthusiastic ringside.

Word to the Wise

Information regarding rules, training and where events are held can be obtained directly from the North American Flyball Association, 1002 E. Samuel Avenue, Peoria Heights, IL 61614.

Freestyle

Canine freestyle is a relatively new canine sport with one paw in obedience and the other in dance. Many of the basic obedience exercises are called upon, but in freestyle, dog and handler set a complicated routine to music.

There are two main approaches to the sport here in the United States: The Canine Freestyle Federation puts the spotlight primarily on the dogs and their movements, with the handlers being as inconspicuous as

Word to the Wise

Musical Canine Sports International, c/o Val Culpin, 3466 Creston Drive, Abbotsford, British Columbia, Canada V2T 5B9.

Canine Freestyle Federation, c/o Alison Jaskiewicz, 576 Jackson Road, Mason, NH 03048.

possible; the Musical Canine Sports International is a bit more flamboyant, with more emphasis on the handler's costuming and movement. Both approaches seem to attract staunch followers, and both are growing rapidly in popularity.

Teamwork and coordination are prime factors in this event. Scoring is based on the performance of both dog and handler. Execution of some of the standard obedience movements is required, but non-standard movements that the dogs are called upon to perform also weigh heavily. Enthusiasm, degree of difficulty of the movements and appropriateness of the music and its interpretation are additional scoring factors.

Frisbee

Not all dogs are mad about playing Frisbee. However, if Gretchen or Bruno decide catching that plastic disc while it flies through the air is a jolly good time, it could well become an obsession. Some Rotties will take to catching and retrieving a Frisbee at their first try and get better and better with each catch. Other Rotties need to develop a liking for the object first, and one of the easiest ways to do this is to initially use the Frisbee as a food dish.

Word to the Wise

For more information about Frisbee contests, call Alpo Frisbee Contest at (888) 444-ALPO or Friskies Canine Frisbee Championships at (800) 423-3268.

Whether your Rottie's interest is mild or extreme, Frisbee is excellent exercise and can help keep your pal in great shape. If you find your Rottie is a Frisbee fanatic, there's no limit to the heights to which the two of you can soar. There are local, regional, national and international Frisbee competitions, and prizes range anywhere from a couple of hundred dollars into the thousands. There are even international Frisbee teams that meet annually for the World Cup!

If this seems like something you and your canine athlete might be interested in, there are countless books, Web sites and videos that can help launch you on your way to stardom.

Agility

Agility competition is simply an obstacle course for dogs. Everyone involved (and everyone who watches) appears to be having the time of their lives, and the sport has become outrageously popular at dog shows and fairs throughout the world. There are tunnels, cat walks, seesaws and numerous other obstacles that the canine contestants have to master off leash while they are being timed.

The idea began in England and caught the public's attention when it was first presented at the world famed Crufts Dog Show in London in 1978. By 1986 it was already a major event in Great Britain and had caught on so well here that the United States Dog Agility Association (USDAA) was organized.

The enthusiasm of the dogs, the supportive roar of the crowd at ringside as their favorite dog jumps over, under, around and through the obstacles gives an electric feeling to the event, and the canine participants seem to thrive on it all. It does take teamwork, because the handler has to act as navigator. Although the dogs do all the maneuvering, it is the handler who directs the dog, because the

Word to the Wise

United States Dog Agility Association, P.O. Box 850955, Richardson, TX 75085-0955.

sequence of the individual obstacles is different at every event. Both the AKC and the USDAA can provide additional information, as well as names and addresses of the organizations sponsoring events nearest to your home.

Canine Good Citizen

The purpose of the Canine Good Citizen program (CGC) is to demonstrate that a dog is a well-mannered asset to the canine community. This really isn't a competition of any kind, because a dog is scored completely on its ability to master the basic requirements for a well-behaved dog. There are 10 parts to the CGC test, and the dog must pass all 10 in order to be awarded the CGC certificate. They are:

1. Appearance and grooming. The dog must be clean and appear to be free of parasites.

2. Accepting a friendly stranger. The dog is required to allow a friendly stranger to approach and speak to the handler.

3. Walking on a loose leash. The dog has to walk along attentively next to the handler.

4. Walking through a crowd. The dog is required to walk along, paying attention to the handler, without interfering with other people or dogs.

5. Sitting and down on command and staying in place. The dog has to respond to each of the handler's commands.

6. Come when called. After being put in a sit or down position 10 feet away, the dog must return to the handler when called.

7. Sit while touched by a stranger. A friendly stranger must be able to pet the dog.

8. Positive reaction to another dog. The dog has to keep its attention on the handler even in the presence of another dog.

9. Calm reaction to distracting sights or noises. These distractions can be an unusual or loud noise, a bicycle going by or an unusual object.

10. Supervised separation. The dog must wait calmly while tied with leash, while the owner is out of sight for three minutes.

Anyone interested in this program can obtain information regarding the rules, and when and where testing is held, directly from the AKC.

Therapy Dogs

I can just hear you now: "You think working with the sick, the handicapped and the aged is fun?" Actually, yes. You and your Rottie may not be rolling in the aisles after a therapy visit, but you'll be amazed at the warm and cozy feeling you'll come away with when you've spent the day bringing a little sunshine into some lives that otherwise can be quite dreary. Children and elderly people especially seem to light up when they are visited by dogs, and they are amazed how sweet and attentive those big dogs can be.

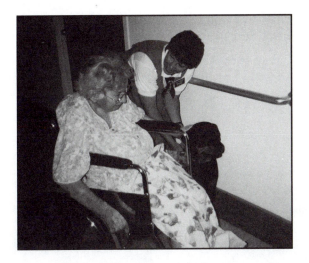

Liberty brings a lot of joy to the people she visits. (Beth Fitzgerald)

It has been found that there is great therapeutic value to the patients who come in contact with these dogs. Medical journals have substantiated stress reduction and lowered blood pressure as a result of these human-to-animal associations. And what you'll get out of it is beyond measure; trust me.

Two organizations—the Delta Society and Therapy Dogs International—test and register Rottweilers and other breeds that are temperamentally suitable to visit hospitals and homes for the aged. Rottweilers can also be trained in a wide range of assistance roles. Their keen awareness makes them ideal companions for the hard of hearing and the sight-impaired.

Word to the Wise

Therapy Dogs International, 88 Bartley Road, Flandres, NJ 07836.

Delta Society, 289 Perimeter Road East, Renton, VA 98055-1329.

The Least You Need to Know

➤ Showing your dog at conformation shows is not only fun and challenging for you both, but it can create a whole new world of friendships.

➤ Obedience training is a challenge, a reward and a gift you'll thank yourself for years later.

➤ If your Rottie loves a tennis ball, flyball could soon become your favorite sport.

➤ Guiding a Rottie through an agility maze of obstacles can be more fun than a barrel of monkeys.

➤ Chasing down a Frisbee can keep both Rottie and owner in tiptop shape.

➤ A Canine Good Citizen degree means your Rottie is a respected member of the community.

➤ Therapy visits remind you of the wonder and magic dogs can work.

Glossary

American Kennel Club (AKC)   Organization that registers pure-bred dogs and sanctions dog shows and other competitions.

angulation   The angles formed by the meeting of the dog's bones. The term is usually used in respect to the bones of the forequarters and rear quarters.

balanced   A term used to signify a dog is symmetrically and proportionally correct.

bitch   A female dog (even the well-behaved ones!).

Best in Show (BIS)   Designation for best dog at an all-breed show.

Best in Specialty Show (BISS)   Designation for best dog at a Rottweiler-only show.

Best of Breed (BOB)   Designation for best Rottweiler at an all-breed show.

Best of Opposite Sex (BOS)   Once Best of Breed (BOB) is awarded, the best individual of the opposite sex receives this award.

Best of Winners (BOW)   Winners Dog (WD) and Winners Bitch (WB) compete to see which is the best of the two.

Bitter Apple   A commercially available liquid used to discourage dogs from licking or chewing on themselves or household objects.

body language   A dog's method of communicating its feelings and reactions.

Canine Eye Registration Foundation (CERF)   Tests and certifies eyes against genetic diseases.

Canine Good Citizen   Basic test of a dog's good manners and stability. Passing the test earns an official CGC designation, which can be added to the dog's name.

castration   Surgical removal of the testicles of the male dog. Also known as neutering.

Champion (CH)   Winner of 15 American Kennel Club (AKC) championship points under three different judges. Two of the wins must be "majors" (three or more points).

character   The general appearance and/or expression that is considered typical of the breed.

condition   A dog's overall appearance of health or lack thereof.

conformation   Form and structure of a dog, as required by the breed standard.

cryptorchid   Male dog whose testicles have not properly descended.

dentition   Arrangement of the teeth.

down   The command used to instruct a dog to lie down.

estrus   Stage of the reproductive cycle in which the female will stand willing for mating.

Federacion Cynologique Internationale (FCI)   Controlling body of pedigreed dogs in most of the European and Latin American countries.

heartworm   A parasitic worm that invades the heart and lungs of a dog and can so affect those organs as to become fatal. Veterinary treatment is required.

heel   The command given to a dog so that it will walk along at the handler's left side with its shoulder in line with the handler's knee.

herding trials   Trials designed to test a dog's ability to control livestock.

hip dysplasia   Abnormal development of the hip affecting dogs in varying degrees of intensity.

hookworm   An internal parasite of the dog that can create an anemic condition.

incisors   The teeth located between the fangs in the front of the upper and lower jaws.

Int.Ch.   International Championship, which can only be awarded by the FCI.

level bite   When the front or incisor teeth meet exactly top to bottom.

Lyme disease   A disease transported by ticks that can create joint and neurological problems in both dogs and humans.

molars   Rear teeth that are used for chewing.

monorchid   A male dog that has only one testicle descended.

neuter   Surgical removal of the testicles of the male dog. Also known as castration.

Orthopedic Foundation for Animals (OFA)   Certifies X-rays of hips and elbows.

overshot   When the front or incisor teeth of the top jaw overlap the front or incisor teeth of the lower jaw.

schutzhund   German dog sport that tests a dog's excellence in obedience, protection and tracking.

scissors bite   A bite in which the front upper teeth or incisors just barely overlap the lower front or incisor teeth of the lower jaw.

Sieger   Best male in a German Rottweiler show.

Siegerin   Best female in a German Rottweiler show.

sound   Overall good construction and health of a dog.

spay   Surgically removing the ovaries of the female dog.

specialty show   A show restricted to only one breed of dog.

standard   A written description of the ideal specimen of a breed.

stay   Command given to a dog that requires remaining in one place until a release command is given.

stop   The juncture at which there is a step-up from muzzle to skull.

therapy dogs   Well-trained dogs that bring comfort and companionship to hospitalized and elderly people.

tracking   Trials that test a dog's ability to track humans or lost articles.

type   The distinguishing characteristics of a breed, as called for in the breed standard.

undershot   When the front or incisor teeth of the lower jaw extend beyond the front or incisor teeth of the upper jaw.

withers   The top of the first dorsal vertebra, or the highest part of the body just behind the neck. Often referred to as the top of the shoulders. A dog's height is measured from the ground to the withers.

Resources for the Rottie

Books

Barwig, Susan and Stewart Hilliard, *Schutzhund Theory and Training Methods*, 1991, Howell Book House, New York.

Blackmore, Joan, *A Dog Owner's Guide to the Rottweiler*, 1987, Salamander Books, Ltd., London.

Brace, Andrew H. (editor), *The Ultimate Rottweiler*, 1995, Howell Book House, New York.

Fox, Dr. Michael W., *Superdog*, 1990, Howell Book House, New York.

Freeman, Muriel, *The Complete Rottweiler*, 1984, Howell Book House, New York.

Hodinar, Dr. Dagmar, *The Rottweiler, An International Study of the Breed*, 1985, Von Palisaden Publications, Paramus, New Jersey.

Johnson, Norman H., D.V.M., *The Complete Puppy and Dog Book*, 1993, Galahad Books, New York.

Michels, Linda and Catherine Thompson, *The Rottweiler*, 1998, Howell Book House, New York.

Monks of New Skete, *How to Be Your Dog's Best Friend*, 1991, Little, Brown and Company, Toronto.

Pitcairn, Richard H., D.V.M., Ph.D., and Susan Hubble Pitcairn, *Dr. Pitcairn's Complete Guide to Natural Health for Dogs and Cats*, 1982, Rodale Press, Emmaus, Pennsylvania.

Magazines

Journal of Veterinary Medical Education, Dr. Richard B. Talbot, Editor VA-MD, College of Veterinary Medicine Virginia Polytechnic Institute and State University, Blacksburg, VA 24061.

Rottweiler, 121 Weathervane Drive, Cherry Hill, NJ 08002.

Rottweiler Quarterly, 1405 Villa Real, Gilroy, CA 95020.

Videos

Let's Talk About Rottweilers, Joan R. Klem, JRK Videos.

The Rottweiler, American Kennel Club.

Dog Steps, Rachel Page Elliot, American Kennel Club.

In the Ribbons, Rottweiler, Canine Training Systems.

Competitive Agility Training, Canine Training Systems.

CD-ROMs

The Rottweiler CD, Sherluck MultiMedia, 29001 176th Avenue SE, Kent, WA 98042.

Web Sites

Alternative Veterinary Medicine
www.altvetmed.com

American Kennel Club
www.akc.org

American Rottweiler Club
www.amrottclub.org

American Veterinary Medical Association
www.avma.org

National Animal Poison Control Center
www.napcc.aspca.org

Organizations

American Kennel Club
5580 Centerview Drive
Raleigh, NC 27606-3390
(919) 233-9767

United Kennel Club
100 E. Kilgore Road
Kalamazoo, MI 49001
(616) 343-9020

American Rottweiler Club
Doreen LePage, Corresponding Secretary
960 S. Main Street
Pascoag, RI 02859

Index